Aristotle and the Eleatic One

OXFORD ARISTOTLE STUDIES

General Editor
Lindsay Judson

Aristotle and the Eleatic One

Timothy Clarke

OXFORD
UNIVERSITY PRESS

OXFORD
UNIVERSITY PRESS

Great Clarendon Street, Oxford, OX2 6DP,
United Kingdom

Oxford University Press is a department of the University of Oxford.
It furthers the University's objective of excellence in research, scholarship,
and education by publishing worldwide. Oxford is a registered trade mark of
Oxford University Press in the UK and in certain other countries

First Edition published in 2019

Published in the United States of America by Oxford University Press
198 Madison Avenue, New York, NY 10016, United States of America

British Library Cataloguing in Publication Data
Data available

Library of Congress Control Number: 2018955537

ISBN 978-0-19-871970-0

For S.H.C.

Contents

Acknowledgements

I began work on this topic in 2009, when I was a graduate student at Yale. My most important debt is to Verity Harte, my advisor, for her guidance and encouragement over many years. I am also deeply indebted to the other members of my dissertation committee: Susanne Bobzien, Alan Code, and Michael Della Rocca. I am grateful to Peter Momtchiloff at Oxford University Press for his patient support of the project, and to my two readers for the press, Lindsay Judson and Laura Castelli, for their very helpful comments. I would like to thank Richard Lawrence for his careful reading of the final manuscript and Manuela Tecuşan for her copyediting.

I benefited greatly from trying out material from the book in my Fall 2013 graduate seminar at Berkeley, as well as in talks in Austin, Berkeley, Berlin, Davis, Florence, London, Los Angeles, Munich, New York, Oxford, and Rome. Thanks to everyone who gave me feedback on those occasions. In addition, I have benefited from conversations with many friends and colleagues, including Peter Adamson, Simona Aimar, Andreas Anagnostopoulos, Lucas Angioni, Joachim Aufderheide, Jonathan Beere, Joseph Bjelde, István Bodnár, David Bronstein, David Charles, Riccardo Chiaradonna, Klaus Corcilius, Paolo Crivelli, Michel Crubellier, Ana Laura Edelhoff, Matthew Evans, Paolo Fait, Andrea Falcon, John Ferrari, Mary Louise Gill, Pavel Gregorić, Sungil Han, Brad Inwood, Sean Kelsey, Jim Lennox, Tony Long, Hendrik Lorenz, Sara Magrin, Marko Malink, David McNeill, Stephen Menn, Ben Morison, Jessica Moss, Calvin Normore, Scott O'Connor, Christian Pfeiffer, Diana Quarantotto, Christof Rapp, Jacob Rosen, Barbara Sattler, Whitney Schwab, Jan Szaif, Justin Vlasits, Stephen White, and Kenneth Winkler. Special thanks to Pieter Sjoerd Hasper for his comments on an early version of Chapter 5, and to Francesco Ademollo for his comments on versions of Chapters 2, 5, and 6. I am also grateful to Rachel Barney and Stephen Menn for sharing with me their unpublished work on Simplicius' commentary on *Physics* 1.1–2.

I would like to take this opportunity to acknowledge my continuing debts to my teachers in philosophy at Sheffield and King's College London, especially M.M. McCabe and Stephen Makin. It was Steve's brilliant lecture courses at Sheffield which first introduced me to Aristotle and the Presocratics.

Much of the final version of the book was written during a sabbatical in 2015–16, the first semester of which was supported by a Berkeley Humanities Research Fellowship. Thanks to Fiona Leigh, Véronique Munoz-Dardé, Mike Martin, and everyone in the Philosophy Department at UCL for hosting me in London in the autumn of 2015, and to Jonathan Beere and Stephen Menn for inviting me to visit the Humboldt University in the spring and summer of 2016. My stay in Berlin was supported by a fellowship from the DFG-funded Research Training Group 'Philosophy, Science, and the Sciences'. The finishing touches to the manuscript were made at LMU Munich in the summer of 2017, while I held a visiting professorship there. I am grateful to Christof Rapp and everyone at the Munich School of Ancient Philosophy for their hospitality.

Chapters 1–3 incorporate material that first appeared in my paper 'Physics I.2', published in D. Quarantotto (ed.), *Aristotle's Physics Book I: A Systematic Exploration*, Cambridge (2018), 60–81. Thanks to Cambridge University Press for permission to reproduce this material.

Abbreviations

Alexander of Aphrodisias

In Metaph.	*Commentary on Aristotle's Metaphysics*

Aristotle

Cael.	*De Caelo*
Cat.	*Categories*
EE	*Eudemian Ethics*
EN	*Nicomachean Ethics*
GA	*Generation of Animals*
GC	*De Generatione et Corruptione*
Int.	*De Interpretatione*
Metaph.	*Metaphysics*
PA	*Parts of Animals*
Phys.	*Physics*
Post. An.	*Posterior Analytics*
Pr. An.	*Prior Analytics*
Rhet.	*Rhetoric*
SE	*Sophistical Refutations*
Top.	*Topics*

Pseudo-Aristotle

MXG	*On Melissus, Xenophanes, Gorgias*

Philoponus

In GC	*Commentary on Aristotle's De Generatione et Corruptione*
In Phys.	*Commentary on Aristotle's Physics*

Plato

Parm.	*Parmenides*
Phil.	*Philebus*
Pol.	*Statesman*
Soph.	*Sophist*
Theaet.	*Theaetetus*

Plutarch

Col.	*Against Colotes*

The Presocratics

DK	Diels, H. and Kranz, W. (1951–2) *Die Fragmente der Vorsokratiker*, 6th edn, 3 vols, Berlin.[1]

Simplicius

In Cael.	*Commentary on Aristotle's De Caelo*
In Phys.	*Commentary on Aristotle's Physics*

Themistius

In Phys.	*Paraphrase of Aristotle's Physics*

---

[1] I use DK's numbering system when referring to the Presocratic fragments.

Introduction

This book is a study of Aristotle's engagement with Eleatic monism, the theory of Parmenides of Elea and his followers that reality is 'one'. Parmenides wrote a single philosophical poem, sometime in the early fifth century BCE. This poem, which now survives only in fragments, is widely acknowledged to be a pivotal work in the history of Greek philosophy. It tells the story of a young man who is taken on a journey by the daughters of the Sun. After passing through the gates of the paths of Night and Day, he is greeted by a goddess:

> O youth, companion to the immortal charioteers
> and to the mares which bear you as you arrive at our home,
> welcome, since no evil fate sent you forth to travel
> this road—for indeed it is far from the path of men—
> but Right and Justice. It is necessary for you to learn all things,
> both the unshaken heart of well-rounded truth,
> and the opinions of mortals, in which there is no true trust.[1]
>
> (B 1.24–30)

The rest of the poem divides into two parts, traditionally known as the *Alētheia* (or 'Way of Truth') and the *Doxa* (or 'Way of Opinion'). In the first part, the *Alētheia*, the goddess gives a complex a priori

---

[1] ὦ κοῦρ' ἀθανάτῃσι συνήορος ἡνιόχοισιν | ἵπποις θ', αἵ σε φέρουσιν, ἱκάνων ἡμέτερον δῶ | χαῖρ', ἐπεὶ οὔ τί σε μοῖρα κακὴ προὔπεμπε νέεσθαι | τήνδ' ὁδόν, ἦ γὰρ ἀπ' ἀνθρώπων ἐκτὸς πάτου ἐστίν, | ἀλλὰ θέμις τε δίκη τε· χρεὼ δέ σε πάντα πυθέσθαι, | ἠμὲν ἀληθείης εὐκυκλέος ἀτρεμὲς ἦτορ | ἠδὲ βροτῶν δόξας, τῆς οὐκ ἔνι πίστις ἀληθής. The text here is Coxon's (2009), except that I read εὐκυκλέος (with Simplicius) instead of εὐπειθέος at line 29. All translations are mine, unless otherwise noted.

argument for a series of remarkable conclusions about reality. These are outlined at the beginning of the long fragment B 8:

> what is[2] is ungenerated and imperishable,
> a whole of one kind, unshaken and complete,
> nor ever was it, nor will it be, since it now is, all together,
> one, continuous.[3]   (B 8.3–6)

Once the goddess has completed her 'trustworthy speech and thought about truth', she then bids the young man to 'learn mortal opinions, hearing the deceptive order [kosmos] of my words' (B 8.50–2).[4] In this second part of the poem, the Doxa, she proceeds to set out a detailed theory of the natural world, similar in its scope to the cosmological theories of Parmenides' Milesian predecessors Anaximander and Anaximenes.[5]

Already in antiquity Parmenides' poem was thought to be obscure and hard to interpret. Nevertheless, there was general agreement that he was putting forward two principal claims: that the universe is *one* and *unchanging*.[6] This theory was subsequently supported by Parmenides' fellow citizen Zeno, the author of the paradoxes of plurality and motion.[7] Later on, in the mid- to late fifth century, the Parmenidean

---

[2] Parmenides' word is ἐόν, the present participle of the verb εἶναι ('to be'). I take this to be an existential use of εἶναι ('what exists'). As we shall see, this is also how Aristotle interprets Parmenides. Following Brown (1986) and Kahn (2004), I think that we can talk of an existential use of εἶναι without committing ourselves to the claim that there is a sharp semantic distinction to be drawn between existential and copulative uses of the verb.

[3] ἀγένητον ἐὸν καὶ ἀνώλεθρόν ἐστιν, | οὖλον μουνογενές τε καὶ ἀτρεμὲς ἠδὲ τελεστόν· | οὐδέ ποτ' ἦν οὐδ' ἔσται, ἐπεὶ νῦν ἔστιν ὁμοῦ πᾶν, | ἕν, συνεχές. For arguments in favour of this text, see Tarán 1965, 88–95.

[4] ἐν τῷ σοι παύω πιστὸν λόγον ἠδὲ νόημα | ἀμφὶς ἀληθείης· δόξας δ' ἀπὸ τοῦδε βροτείας | μάνθανε κόσμον ἐμῶν ἐπέων ἀπατηλὸν ἀκούων.

[5] Not much of the second part of Parmenides' poem has survived. The relevant fragments are B 8.50–61 and B 9 through 19.

[6] See e.g. Plato, Theaet. 180d7–e4 and 183e3–5; Aristotle, Phys. 1.2, 184b26 and 1.5, 188a19–22.

[7] See Parm. 128b7–e4 for Plato's account of the purpose behind Zeno's book of plurality paradoxes. The character Zeno describes the book as 'a kind of support [βοήθειά τις] for Parmenides' theory against those who try to make fun of it' (128c6–d1). Zeno's goal, according to this passage, was to help out his older friend

position was defended once again by Melissus of Samos. These three philosophers—Parmenides, Zeno, and Melissus—are conventionally known as the 'Eleatics'.

At the beginning of the *Physics*, one of the first items on Aristotle's agenda is to examine the Eleatic theory. (He does not explicitly include Zeno as one of the proponents of this theory, perhaps because he leans towards seeing Zeno's aims as purely negative.[8]) Aristotle starts by telling us that the task of responding to the Eleatics is not in fact a task for the physicist or natural philosopher. But then he goes on to criticize their theory anyway, as a sort of prolegomenon to his philosophy of nature.[9] So *Physics* 1 contains an extensive treatment of the Eleatics, with Aristotle responding at length to their arguments for monism and against the possibility of change.

My topic in this book is Aristotle's engagement with the first aspect of the Eleatics' theory, their monism. Aristotle discusses Eleatic monism in several places in the corpus, but the main text is *Physics* 1.2–3. This section of the *Physics* is extremely opaque and has received relatively little attention from scholars, despite its historical and philosophical interest.[10] In what follows I offer a detailed reconstruction of the argument of these chapters. My aim is to explain how Aristotle understands the Eleatics' monistic position and its motivation,

by showing that Parmenides' pluralist opponents are committed to consequences 'even more ridiculous' than those suffered by Parmenides' own theory. We do not know whether Zeno himself meant to endorse Parmenides' theory, or whether he was more interested in exposing the complacency of Parmenides' opponents. On the question of how Zeno's aims were understood in antiquity, see Sedley 2017, 1–6.

[8] There is a passage in the *Sophistical Refutations* where Aristotle refers to Zeno and Parmenides as joint proponents of an argument for monism (*SE* 33, 182b26–7; cf. *SE* 10, 170b21–4). Typically, however, Aristotle does not name Zeno as one of the philosophers who claim that 'what is is one and unchanging'.

[9] By describing the critique of the Eleatics as a 'prolegomenon', I am not suggesting that it has the status of a mere digression within *Physics* 1 (contrast Osborne 2006a, 6). Aristotle's engagement with the Eleatics is integral to his overall argument, as I explain in what follows.

[10] Earlier studies include Natorp 1890, Mansion 1953, Gershenson and Greenberg 1962, and Bostock 2006. On *Phys*. 1.2, cf. Crubellier, forthcoming; on *Phys*. 1.3, cf. Castelli 2018b and Quarantotto, forthcoming.

how he attempts to refute their position, and how he thinks their arguments should be resisted.

The interpretation of Parmenides is a matter of controversy, and much of the controversy centres on the question of his monism.[11] Was he really a monist, and if so what sort of a monist was he? Did he mean to reject outright the pluralistic world that appears to the senses? One of my main claims will be that Aristotle takes Parmenides to be a particularly uncompromising sort of monist. Generally speaking, to be a monist about Fs is to think that there is only one F. There are, accordingly, many different kinds of monism, corresponding to different values of 'F'.[12] For example, one kind of monism is *material monism*: the view that there is only one basic type of matter, which composes everything (or every material thing) that exists. Another kind of monism is *substance monism*: the view that there is only one (token) substance.[13] Both of these monisms are bold, striking theses. But they are relatively tame in comparison with the theory that I think Aristotle typically attributes to Parmenides.

I shall argue that Aristotle interprets both Parmenides and Melissus as proponents of two extremely radical forms of monism:

Entity monism: There is just one (token) entity.[14]

Essence monism: Reality is all of the same essence.

---

[11] For a classic modern treatment of this question, see Barnes 1979. The debate over the nature of Parmenides' monism goes back at least to Plutarch's *Against Colotes*, in which Plutarch disputes the Epicurean Colotes' interpretation of Parmenides as an extreme monist: see *Col.* 1113e–14f.

[12] Cf. Rapp 2006, 162–6; Schaffer 2007, 178 n. 10.

[13] Aristotle ascribes both material monism and substance monism to Thales, Anaximenes, and Heraclitus, among others. They hold that there is just one basic material substratum (water, air, or fire), and they regard this substratum as a single substance, demoting everything else to the status of a mere affection ($\pi\acute{a}\theta o\varsigma$) or state ($\acute{\epsilon}\xi\iota\varsigma$) of this one substance. For this interpretation of their theory, see *Metaph. A* 3, 983b6–984a8 and *Phys.* 2.1, 193a23–6. Aristotle himself rejects substance monism, but he may be a certain kind of material monist, depending on how we decide the question of his commitment to prime matter.

[14] By 'entity' I mean anything that exists. I shall speak interchangeably of 'entities', 'beings', and sometimes just 'things'.

The universe consists of a single, solitary entity: this is the 'Eleatic One' of my title. Moreover, this one entity, which constitutes the whole of reality, is all of the same essence or nature. It follows that our experience of plurality and differentiation—of the world's containing many things, and many different kinds of thing—is completely illusory.[15] What could have led the Eleatics to propose such an incredible theory? At least in its outlines, Melissus' primary argument for monism is fairly easy to understand. Melissus' monism is based on his rejection of the possibility of generation and destruction. If nothing comes to be or passes away, then anything that exists must be both eternal and (Melissus claims) spatially unlimited. This leaves room for only one entity. He then argues that the uniqueness of this one entity entails its uniformity.[16]

How Parmenides argued for monism—if he did—is far less clear. There is no consensus on this subject among modern scholars. Aristotle clearly found an argument for monism in Parmenides' poem,[17] and he evidently thought of it as more sophisticated than Melissus'.[18] But Aristotle never attempts to explain the Parmenidean argument in any detail. His extensive criticisms seem to assume that his audience is already more or less familiar with how the argument is supposed to go. Nevertheless, I shall suggest that we can work out how Aristotle interpreted Parmenides' argument, by looking carefully at these criticisms.

A recurring theme in Aristotle's critique of the Eleatics in *Physics* 1.2–3 is their restrictive conception of what it is to *be*—their failure

---

[15] In claiming that Aristotle attributes this theory both to Melissus and to Parmenides, I am taking issue with John Palmer's suggestion that Aristotle thinks of Parmenides' monism as less extreme than Melissus'. According to Palmer (2009, 36–8; 42–5), Aristotle is inclined to see Melissus as an entity monist (in Palmer's terminology, a 'strict' monist), and Parmenides as a substance monist who allows for the existence of a plurality of non-substantial entities (a 'generous' monist). Palmer takes this as the starting point for his own interpretation of Parmenides.

[16] See B 1–6 for Melissus' argument that there is only room for one thing; and see *MXG* 1, 974a12–14 for his move from entity monism to the claim that reality is all alike.

[17] As did Plato: see *Parm.* 128a8–b1.

[18] This difference in attitude towards their respective arguments is clearest at *Phys.* 1.2, 185a8–12, where Melissus' argument is sharply criticized.

(as he sees it) to recognize that 'being is said in many ways', or as I shall paraphrase this claim, that there are many ways of being.[19] Aristotle thinks that Parmenides' monism ultimately stems from this narrow conception of being. This points to an interpretation of Parmenides' argument that is (I shall argue) both textually and philosophically appealing. So Aristotle's criticisms promise us insight into the origins of the Eleatic One.

It must be said that Aristotle has a reputation as an unreliable and historically insensitive critic of his Presocratic predecessors.[20] When it comes to Parmenides in particular, Aristotle's interpretation—or what is thought to be his interpretation—has been dismissed as obviously wrong.[21] However, surprisingly little effort has been devoted to working out what his interpretation of Parmenides actually was. I want to remedy this here. It is not part of my aim to argue that Aristotle's interpretation of Eleatic monism is correct—that would take a much longer book—but I do want to argue that, in this central case at least, his negative reputation as a critic of his predecessors is unjustified.[22] Once we take the time to understand his objections, he emerges as a perceptive reader of the Eleatic texts.

Of course, even if we were to conclude that Aristotle's interpretation of the Eleatics is mistaken, it would still be worthwhile to try to understand his criticisms of their monism. The Eleatics occupy a prominent place in the first book of the *Physics*, which suggests that Aristotle sees them as posing a significant challenge to the project of natural philosophy. In order better to understand Aristotle himself, it is important to know how he conceives of this challenge, and how he attempts to answer it.

---

[19] My use of the terminology of 'ways of being' follows that of Frede (1987, 85). Cf. also McDaniel 2017. I defend this paraphrase in Chapter 2. Others prefer to understand Aristotle as claiming that 'being' has many senses: see e.g. Bostock 1994, 45.

[20] See especially Cherniss 1935.

[21] See e.g. Tarán 1965, 291: 'Aristotle's testimony concerning Parmenides is of almost no positive value.'

[22] Cf. also Hussey 2012 for a sympathetic assessment of Aristotle's treatment of Presocratic physics.

The structure of the discussion that follows will largely be determined by the structure of *Physics* 1.2–3. To make progress with my questions about how Aristotle interpreted and responded to Eleatic monism, the best strategy will be to work through this difficult text stage by stage.[23]

Chapter 1 considers Aristotle's preface to his critique of the Eleatics (*Phys.* 1.2, 184b25–185a20). Here he denies that it is the natural philosopher's job to investigate whether reality is one and unchanging. After first situating the discussion of the Eleatics within the larger argument of *Physics* 1, I ask why he thinks that the task of examining their theory lies beyond the scope of natural philosophy, and why he undertakes this task in the *Physics* nonetheless.

In Chapter 2 I then examine Aristotle's refutation of the Eleatic doctrine that reality is one. In *Physics* 1.2 he gives a series of arguments to show that this theory is impossible. These arguments rest on two fundamental claims of Aristotelian metaphysics: that *being* and *one* are 'said in many ways'. I suggest that we can make sense of these arguments when we see them as targeting entity monism and essence monism. I ask whether Aristotle's criticisms beg the question against the Eleatics: Is it legitimate for him, in this context, to start from the claim that being (or one) is said in many ways? In the final section of the chapter I consider whether Aristotle is being fair when he interprets the Eleatics as radical monists.

In the middle of his critique of Eleatic monism Aristotle breaks off to discuss some post-Eleatic thinkers. These 'more recent' thinkers inherited certain Eleatic concerns; specifically, they worried about how the same thing could be both one and many at the same time. Chapter 3 looks at Aristotle's discussion of these thinkers and their problems of one and many. I suggest that this discussion is best seen as an excursus, but that we can nevertheless understand why Aristotle decides to include it here.

---

[23] For convenience I include a complete text and translation of *Physics* 1.2–3 in the Appendix. I use Ross's (1936) edition of the Greek text. Departures from Ross are indicated in the notes to the Appendix.

Over the next three chapters I consider Aristotle's response to the Eleatics' arguments for monism. Chapter 4 considers his reply to Melissus. Aristotle thinks of Melissus' argument as 'crude' in comparison with Parmenides', but at the same time he suggests that some similar criticisms can be made of both philosophers. This means that Aristotle's objections to Melissus can also shed some light on his understanding of Parmenides.

After his critique of Melissus, Aristotle sets out what he calls his 'solution' to Parmenides' argument for monism (*Phys.* 1.3, 186a23–8). As I argue in Chapter 5, this solution presupposes a certain interpretation of how Parmenides' argument is meant to work. It suggests that Aristotle sees the argument as depending on two key ontological assumptions, and as attempting to establish two monistic conclusions: that reality is (*a*) a single continuous object, and (*b*) all of the same essence. I explain how it is possible to find such an argument in Parmenides. My proposal about how Aristotle understands Parmenides' argument receives further support from his discussion of the Eleatics in *De Generatione et Corruptione* 1.8.

In Chapter 6 I give a detailed analysis of Aristotle's response to Parmenides' argument (186a23–b35). This section of *Physics* 1.3 presents serious exegetical difficulties, and some commentators have doubted whether it is really a unified whole.[24] On my reading, the section offers a coherent (if complex) set of objections to Parmenides' argument, focused primarily on his failure to recognize properties as entities distinct from the things that have them.

In the final part of *Physics* 1.3 Aristotle criticizes some unnamed philosophers for 'giving in' to two Eleatic arguments. In Chapter 7 I defend the view that these anonymous respondents are the fifth-century atomists, Leucippus and Democritus, and I explain why Aristotle sees them as giving in to the arguments in question. This passage is important evidence for how Eleatic monism led to the development of atomism.

---

[24] See e.g. Gershenson and Greenberg 1962; Bostock 2006, 111–15.

Turning away from the *Physics*, Chapter 8 asks whether Aristotle's interpretation of Parmenides stays the same throughout the corpus. The critique of the Eleatics in *Physics* 1.2–3 suggests that Aristotle favours what I call an 'anti-cosmological' interpretation of Parmenides' poem. According to this interpretation, the *Alētheia* presents Parmenides' official view of reality, whereas the cosmological theory of the *Doxa* is intended to describe a world of mere appearance. But does Aristotle consistently interpret Parmenides in this way? Some scholars have denied this on the basis of Aristotle's discussion of the Eleatics in *Metaphysics A* 5. This discussion has been thought to show that Aristotle reads the *Alētheia* and *Doxa* as presenting mutually compatible accounts of two different orders or aspects of reality. Accordingly, it has been suggested that Aristotle changes his mind about Parmenides, and comes to see him as endorsing a kind of pluralism. Against this, I argue that Aristotle consistently favours an anti-cosmological interpretation of Parmenides' poem, and consistently reads him as a radical monist.

1

Eleaticism and the Philosophy of Nature

1.1 Introduction

The opening book of the *Physics* is the opening book of Aristotle's natural philosophical corpus. And yet a significant portion of the book is devoted to a task that lies beyond the scope of natural philosophy—the task of responding to the Eleatics.[1] In this first chapter I want to consider Aristotle's prefatory remarks about the status of his critique of the Eleatics (*Phys.* 1.2, 184b25–185a20). Why does he think that such a critique lies beyond the scope of physical enquiry? What does this tell us about how he understands the Eleatics' theory? And why, if refuting the Eleatics is not a task for the natural philosopher, does Aristotle nonetheless decide to include an extensive treatment of their theory at the beginning of the *Physics*?

1.2 The Principles of Natural Beings

Before taking up these questions, it will be helpful to start by thinking about Aristotle's larger project in *Physics* 1. The main aim of the book is to determine 'the causes and principles of natural beings' (*Phys.* 1.7, 190b17–18).[2] 'Natural beings' are the constituents of the natural

---

[1] Aristotle spends more time on the Eleatics than he does on any of his other predecessors in *Physics* 1. By my count, his discussions of the Eleatics in *Phys.* 1.2–3 and 1.8 occupy 185 Bekker lines—almost one third of the book.

[2] αἰτίαι καὶ ἀρχαὶ τῶν φύσει ὄντων. Cf. *Phys.* 1.1, 184a10–16; 1.7, 191a3–4.

world—things such as animals and plants, the elements, and the heavenly bodies. To enquire into the causes (*aitiai*) or principles (*archai*) of such things is to enquire into the fundamental factors that explain what they are and how they come to be (for those of them that do come to be). The book opens with a famous description of the path to be followed in determining the principles in some domain. We must pass from 'what is more knowable and clearer to us' to 'what is clearer and more knowable by nature' (*Phys*. 1.1, 184a16–18). This involves starting with what is given to us in perception and proceeding, by a process of 'division', to the principles. After these methodological preliminaries, Aristotle then gives a classification of the different theories of principles:[3]

There must either be one principle or more than one. If there is one, it must either be unchanging, as Parmenides and Melissus say, or changing, as the natural philosophers say, some saying that the first principle is air, others that it is water. And if there is more than one, there must either be a limited or an unlimited number. If a limited number greater than one, there must either be two or three or four or some other number. And if there are an unlimited number, then either, as Democritus says, the genus is one and they are distinguished by shape or by species, or they are also contraries.

(*Phys*. 1.2, 184b15–22)

This initial classification does not represent Aristotle's final view of how best to catalogue the positions of his predecessors. He suggests revisions as the book goes on. For example, just a few lines later he argues that Parmenides and Melissus should not really be seen as

---

[3] This sort of classification is not unique to Aristotle. Something similar appears in Plato's *Sophist*, where the Eleatic Visitor lists various earlier theories of 'how many beings there are and what they are like' (242c4–243a1). Another related classification is given by Isocrates at *Antidosis* 268. One difference is that Aristotle is classifying theories of *principles*, whereas Plato and Isocrates are classifying theories of *beings* (τὰ ὄντα). Aristotle adverts to this difference at 184b22–5 and implies that it is merely terminological. The philosophers presented by Plato and Isocrates as enquiring into the number of 'beings' are primarily enquiring into the number of *fundamental* beings. This means that they are effectively enquiring into the number of principles. On the origins of these classifications, see Mansfeld 1986.

offering a theory of principles at all (1.2, 185a3–5). And in *Physics* 1.5 he proposes alternative ways of thinking of the theories of the material monists and of Democritus (188a19–27).

Nonetheless, the classification serves to provide the framework for the book's subsequent investigation of principles. Aristotle first argues against the two most extreme positions mentioned here: the monistic theory of the Eleatics (1.2–3), and then the Anaxagorean theory that there are an unlimited number of principles, some of which are contraries (1.4). Once these two extreme positions have been refuted, he then goes on to develop his own positive theory of the number and nature of the principles, in *Physics* 1.5–7. According to this theory, the principles of natural beings are (at least on one way of counting) *three*: the underlying substratum (or matter), the form, and the opposed privation. A natural being is a composite of substratum and form, and comes to be when the substratum changes from being characterized by the relevant privation to being characterized by the form.[4]

An important benefit of Aristotle's theory of principles is that it allows him to answer the Eleatics' influential argument against the possibility of coming to be, as he explains in *Physics* 1.8.[5] Finally, in the last chapter of the book, he differentiates his own theory of principles from the superficially similar theory of the Platonists.

1.3   The Status of the Critique of the Eleatics

Following the initial classification of theories, the first stage in this complex argument is the critique of the monistic theory of Parmenides and Melissus. Over the course of *Physics* 1.2–3 Aristotle argues that this theory is impossible (*Phys.* 1.2, 185a20–b25), and then explains

---

[4] At *Phys.* 1.7, 191a3–4, Aristotle indicates that this theory concerns specifically those natural beings that are subject to generation. For an extension of the theory to eternal natural beings, see *Metaph. Λ* 2.

[5] I discuss Aristotle's response to this argument in Clarke 2015.

why the Eleatics' arguments for their view do not succeed (*Phys.* 1.3, 186a4–b35). Aristotle's primary focus in *Physics* 1.2–3 is the Eleatics' claim that reality is *one*. He will have more to say about their claim that reality is *unchanging* in 1.8, when he addresses their argument against coming to be. (This argument had led the Eleatics to deny the possibility of change in general: see 191b31–3.) There is a good strategic reason for Aristotle to split up his treatment of the Eleatics in this way. His criticisms of their monism do not rely on his own theory of principles (as we shall see below). By contrast, it is only when that theory of principles is on the table that it is possible to answer the Eleatic argument against coming to be.[6]

Before starting his critique of the Eleatics' monism, Aristotle argues that an engagement with their theory falls outside the scope of natural philosophy:

Now, to investigate whether what is is one and unchanging is not to investigate into nature. For, just as for the geometer too there is no longer any argument to give against an opponent who destroys the principles [*sc.* of geometry], but this is instead something either for another science or for one common to all, so too for the person [investigating] principles. For there is no longer any principle if it [*sc.* what is] is only one, and one in this way; for a principle is a principle *of* some thing or things. So, to investigate whether it is one in this way is like arguing dialectically against any other thesis[7] put forward for the sake of argument (like the Heraclitean thesis, or if someone should say that what is is one human being), or like solving an eristical argument, which is just what both arguments contain, both Melissus' and Parmenides'. For they assume falsehoods, and are not deductive. Or rather, the argument of Melissus is crude and contains no difficulty—grant him one absurdity and the others follow: this is not very hard. But, for our part, let it be assumed that natural things, either all or some of them, undergo change. This is clear from induction. And at the same time nor does it belong [to us]

---

[6] For the latter point, see *Phys.* 1.8, 191a23–4 and 191b33–4.

[7] The word 'thesis' here has a technical meaning, explained at *Top.* 1.11, 104b19–20: 'a *thesis* is a paradoxical belief of someone who is well-known in philosophy' (θέσις δέ ἐστιν ὑπόληψις παράδοξος τῶν γνωρίμων τινὸς κατὰ φιλοσοφίαν). As examples, Aristotle mentions Antisthenes' claim that contradiction is impossible, Heraclitus' theory that everything is in motion, and Melissus' claim that 'what is is one'.

to solve everything, but only those things which someone falsely proves from the principles, but not others, just as it is the task of the geometer to solve the quadrature by way of segments, but not the quadrature of Antiphon. (184b25–185a17)

Aristotle's argument makes use of an analogy with geometry. Consider someone who denies one of the principles of geometry—perhaps they deny that lines exist, or that a line is a breadthless length. It does not fall to the geometer (at least, not insofar as they are a geometer) to examine this opponent's view.[8] The geometer starts from such principles; it is not their job to investigate whether or not they are true. Similarly for the philosopher of nature—or, more specifically, for the person investigating the principles of nature. Such a person takes certain things for granted, just as the geometer takes for granted the principles of geometry. One of the things a person investigating principles takes for granted is *that there are principles*. It is not their job to consider whether or not this assumption is true, or to answer an opponent who denies it.

The Eleatics, in Aristotle's view, effectively deny the existence of principles. (This means that their theory is not really a theory of principles at all, notwithstanding its inclusion in the initial classification.) The existence of a principle requires that there be some further entity, or entities, of which that principle is the principle: 'a principle is a principle *of* some thing or things'. So the existence of a principle requires that there be a minimum of two entities. And this is incompatible with the Eleatics' monism.

This argument is a crucial piece of evidence for how Aristotle understands the Eleatics' monistic position. It shows that he interprets both Parmenides and Melissus as entity monists—as claiming that

---

[8] Aristotle says that the task of answering someone who destroys the principles of geometry falls either to 'another science' or to 'one common to all'. The referent of the latter phrase is unclear. Some take him to be alluding to metaphysics, which he regards as a 'universal' science: e.g. Ross (1936, 461), who cites *Metaph. E* 1, 1026a30. Alternatively Aristotle may mean to refer to dialectic, even though this is not strictly speaking a science. As Bolton (1991, 15 n. 16) points out, the latter option is supported by *Rhet.* 1.1, 1354a1–3: 'Rhetoric is the counterpart of dialectic. For both are concerned with certain sorts of things that are, in a way, common to all to know [κοινὰ τρόπον τινὰ ἁπάντων ἐστὶ γνωρίζειν], and which belong to no definite science.'

reality as a whole ('what is') consists of only one token entity. Entity monism is the only form of monism that would rule out the existence of principles for the reason given here.[9] The fact that the Eleatics rule out the existence of principles is one reason why the task of answering them does not fall to the natural philosopher. But there is also a second reason: the Eleatics deny a second basic assumption of natural philosophy when they deny the existence of change.[10] Aristotle says that we—that is, we natural philosophers—must assume that some or all natural things undergo change (185a12–13). It is not the natural philosopher's job to try to establish the truth of this claim; we should take it as evident on the basis of induction.[11] Nor is it our job to answer the Eleatics' arguments that change does not exist.[12]

If the task of examining the Eleatic theory does not fall to the natural philosopher, then whose task is it? Aristotle's language suggests that he thinks the task belongs to the dialectician.[13] Investigating the truth of the theory is not part of natural philosophy, but 'is like arguing dialectically [dialegesthai] against any other thesis put forward for the sake of argument . . . or like solving an eristical argument' (185a5–8).[14]

---

[9] Palmer (2008, 542) acknowledges that this passage goes against his claim that Aristotle reads Parmenides as a generous monist (that is, as allowing for the existence of a plurality of non-substantial entities). His response is to deny that Aristotle is consistent: in some passages, such as this one, Aristotle confuses Parmenides' position with Melissus', whereas in other passages he distinguishes them. Palmer sees Aristotle as drawing a particularly clear distinction between Parmenides and Melissus in *Metaphysics A* 5 (2008, 542–3; 2009, 221–3). I shall address this in Chapter 8.

[10] Cf. the similar argument at *Phys.* 8.3, 253b2–6.

[11] We move by induction from the repeated perceptions of individual instances of natural change to the generalization: 'some or all natural things undergo change'.

[12] Aristotle returns to the analogy with geometry to make the latter point, saying that it is the geometer's job 'to solve the quadrature by way of segments, but not the quadrature of Antiphon' (185a16–17). The authorship and the details of the former quadrature are unclear: for discussion see Mueller 1982, 157–8 and Lloyd 1987. Antiphon's 'quadrature' of the circle is explained by Simplicius at *In Phys.* 54.20–55.11.

[13] Cf. also Irwin 1988, 67; Bolton 1991, 14–15; Falcon 2005, 28.

[14] Cf. also 185a19–20: 'it is presumably a good idea to have a little dialectical discussion [διαλεχθῆναι] about them [sc. the Eleatics]'. The verb διαλέγεσθαι does not

Another possibility, favoured by some commentators, is that the task belongs to the higher science of metaphysics.[15] This may appear to receive some support from Aristotle's brief remarks about the Eleatics in *De Caelo* 3.1, where he claims that they should not be thought to speak 'as natural philosophers' (*phusikōs*), because 'the fact that some beings are ungenerated and entirely unchanging belongs instead to a different investigation and one prior to natural philosophy' (298b19–20).[16] This comment suggests that Aristotle is prepared to treat the Eleatics as contributors to metaphysics, which is clearly the 'prior' investigation that he has in mind here.

On the other hand, the question alluded to in *De Caelo* 3.1 (whether some things are ungenerated and unchanging) is different from the question at issue in *Physics* 1.2 (whether reality as a whole is one and unchanging). The fact that the former is a question for the metaphysician does not mean that the latter is too. Moreover, the argument at 185a1–5 is completely general: it does not fall to *the person investigating principles* to answer an opponent who denies the existence of principles. There is no indication that this is true only for some investigations of principles but not for others. And metaphysics, like natural philosophy, studies principles—in the case of metaphysics, the principles of being *qua* being. So it would seem that if it is not the natural philosopher's job to answer the Eleatics, then nor is it the job of the metaphysician, for the same reason.[17]

---

always mean 'to engage in dialectic'; it can just mean 'to discuss'. But here, given the context—Aristotle is making a point about disciplinary status—it is likely to have its technical, 'dialectical' sense.

[15] See e.g. Mansion 1953, 172–3; Wicksteed and Cornford 1957, 12; Berti 1969; Judson, forthcoming.

[16] τὸ γὰρ εἶναι ἄττα τῶν ὄντων ἀγένητα καὶ ὅλως ἀκίνητα μᾶλλόν ἐστιν ἑτέρας καὶ προτέρας ἢ τῆς φυσικῆς σκέψεως.

[17] I take this to be consistent with the fact that Aristotle's subsequent critique of the Eleatics is in some sense 'metaphysical': it is 'metaphysical' insofar as it relies on various metaphysical claims, such as the claims that being and one are said in many ways. These claims fall within the scope of the enquiry into being *qua* being (cf. *Metaph. Γ* 2, 1004a28–b4 and 1005a11–18). The dialectician may appeal to metaphysical claims, just as they may appeal to claims pertaining to other fields of enquiry (natural philosophy, ethics, and so on).

1.4 Why Is There a Discussion of the Eleatics at the Beginning of the *Physics*?

Although Aristotle says little about his positive view of the status of his critique of the Eleatics, his negative claim is clear: the critique does not belong to natural philosophy. But in that case, what explains its inclusion at the start of the *Physics*?

The final lines of the preface offer a brief explanation:

However, although [the Eleatics] do not speak about nature, they nonetheless happen to state physical difficulties.[18] So it is presumably a good idea to have a little dialectical discussion about them. For the investigation does contain some philosophy. (185a17–20)

The Eleatics do not speak about nature: in rejecting the existence of plurality and change they are rejecting the existence of the natural world.[19] However, they do happen to raise 'physical difficulties' (*phusikai aporiai*). I take the term 'physical difficulties' to refer to difficulties that are *relevant* to natural philosophy, even if they are not difficulties that it belongs to the natural philosopher to solve. The difficulties in question are presumably the puzzles about plurality and change that Aristotle will go on to address in the remainder of *Physics* 1.2–3 and in 1.8. One way in which these Eleatic puzzles are

---

[18] Here I follow Ross's punctuation: οὐ μὴν ἀλλ᾽ ἐπειδὴ περὶ φύσεως μὲν οὔ, φυσικὰς δὲ ἀπορίας συμβαίνει λέγειν αὐτοῖς. Alternatively, one could place the comma after μέν, in which case Aristotle would be justifying his discussion of the Eleatics on the grounds that 'they happen to speak about nature, although they state difficulties that are not physical'. See Simplicius, *In Phys.* 70.5–32 for these two ways of construing the sentence. The latter construal is preferred by Mansion (1946, 66 n. 48), Pellegrin (1994, 126–8), and Crubellier (forthcoming). My reason for favouring the former construal is that I find it unlikely that Aristotle would now be granting that the Eleatics speak περὶ φύσεως, when just a few lines earlier he had claimed that to investigate whether what is is one and unchanging is *not* to investigate περὶ φύσεως.

[19] It is plausible that Aristotle is here taking issue with the standard titles (or descriptions) of the works of Parmenides and Melissus. (Cf. *GC* 2.6, 333b18, on Empedocles.) While Parmenides' poem is unlikely to have had a title originally, at some point it came to be known as a work *On Nature* (Περὶ φύσεως). The disjunctive title ascribed to Melissus' book by Simplicius—*On Nature, or On What Is* (Περὶ φύσεως ἢ περὶ τοῦ ὄντος)—was probably Melissus' own: see Palmer 2009, 205–6 n. 25 and Harriman 2015, 19–20.

relevant to natural philosophy is precisely that they call into question the most fundamental assumptions of this enterprise. There can be no science of nature if there are no principles, and there can be no nature if there is no change. Thus the Eleatics pose a major challenge to natural philosophy, and in Aristotle's view this challenge has yet to be properly answered.

Another, related, reason why the Eleatic puzzles are relevant to the enquiry into the principles of nature is that these puzzles greatly influenced post-Eleatic physics.[20] For example, Aristotle tells us that the atomists' theory arose out of reflection on Eleatic arguments.[21] The atomists posited atoms and void in an attempt to show how, contrary to the Eleatics, the world can be plural and changing. This means that our evaluation of atomism as a theory of the principles of nature—our stance on whether or not it is well founded—will depend in part on our own view of how best to resolve the Eleatic puzzles that motivate it.

For at least these reasons, then, the Eleatic challenge is highly relevant to natural philosophy, and in particular to the enquiry into the principles of natural beings. This accounts for Aristotle's decision to include a critique of the Eleatics in the opening book of the *Physics*, even though the critique falls beyond the scope of natural philosophy itself.

---

[20] Cf. also Castelli 2018b, 103–4.
[21] See his account of the motivation of atomism at *GC* 1.8, 324b35–325b5. I think that Aristotle also refers to the atomists' response to Eleatic arguments at the end of *Physics* 1.3; for a full defence of this controversial claim, see Chapter 7.

2

The Refutation of Eleatic Monism

2.1 Introduction

At *Physics* 1.2, 185a20–b25, Aristotle presents two sequences of criticisms of Eleatic monism. The arguments in the first sequence begin from the claim that 'being is said in many ways' (185a20–b5); those in the second sequence begin from the claim that 'one is said in many ways' (185b5–25). Aristotle's overall aim is to establish that the Eleatic theory is impossible.[1] In this chapter I examine these criticisms. How do they work, and what interpretation of Eleatic monism do they presuppose? I shall also address two potential worries for Aristotle's critique: the worry that he begs the question against his monistic opponents, and the worry that he relies on an uncharitable interpretation of their theory.

2.2 The First Sequence of Criticisms: Ways of Being

The first sequence of criticisms consists of two anti-monistic arguments. In the first of these Aristotle uses his theory of categories to construct a dilemma for the Eleatics (185a20–32). In the second he raises a related problem for Melissus' claim that what is is unlimited (185a32–b5).

---

[1] For this conclusion, see the opening sentence of *Phys.* 1.3 (186a4–6).

2.2.1 Being Is Said in Many Ways

The first argument runs as follows:

Since being is said in many ways, the most appropriate starting point [*archē*] of all is to ask in what way those who say that 'all things are one' speak [of being]—whether all things are substance, or quantities, or qualities, and again whether all things are one substance, like one human being, or one horse, or one soul, or whether all things are quality, and this is one, like white or hot or one of the other things of this sort. For all these differ a great deal, and all are impossible to maintain. For if, on the one hand, there is substance and quality and quantity, then whether these things are detached from one another or not, the things that are will be many. But if, on the other hand, all things are quality or quantity, then whether substance is or is not, this is absurd, if one should call the impossible absurd. For none of the others is separate apart from substance. For all [the others] are said of substance as a subject. (185a20–32)

According to a common reading of this passage, Aristotle starts from the claim that the word 'being' (*to on*) is ambiguous ('being is said in many ways'). There are many different senses of 'being', one for each of the different categories: substance, quantity, quality, and so on. And so there are different things that the Eleatics might mean when they say that 'what is is one' or 'all beings are one'.[2] Aristotle uses the doctrine of the categories to disambiguate the Eleatic thesis, and argues that on each of the possible disambiguations the Eleatics are committed to absurdity.[3]

This reading of the passage is tempting, but it faces a serious difficulty. If the term 'being' has different senses corresponding to the different categories, it would seem that Aristotle ought to consider the following as possible disambiguations of 'all beings are one': (A) all *substances* are one; (B) all *qualities* are one; (C) all *quantities*

[2] Aristotle formulates the Eleatic thesis in a variety of ways: 'what is [τὸ ὄν] is one' (184b26); 'the universe [τὸ πᾶν] is one' (185b7); 'all things [τὰ πάντα] are one' (185a22); 'the beings [τὰ ὄντα] are one' (185b24); 'all beings [τὰ ὄντα πάντα] are one' (185b19–20). He evidently regards these different formulations as equivalent and moves freely between them.

[3] For this interpretation, see e.g. Ross 1936, 338 and 467; Mansion 1953, 173; Gershenson and Greenberg 1962, 139–40; Palmer 2004, 49.

are one—and so on. However, he does not engage with any of these positions. His subsequent argument rests on what I shall call the 'interdependence thesis':

> Substances depend for their existence on the existence of non-substances, while non-substances depend for their existence on the existence of substances.[4]

It is hard to see how this thesis could be thought to undermine any of the monistic positions just mentioned. Take claim (A), 'all substances are one'. This presumably means either (A1) that there is just one (token) substance, or (A2) that all substances are of a single type. But both of these positions are consistent with the interdependence thesis. Even if substances cannot exist without non-substances, and vice versa, it might still be the case that there is only one token substance, or only one type of substance.

An alternative reading is therefore required—a reading which can accommodate the fact that the argument is based on the interdependence thesis. I suggest that it is a mistake to take Aristotle to be claiming that 'being' is ambiguous. As others have noted, when he says that F 'is said in many ways' (*pollachōs legetai*), it is sometimes best to interpret him as meaning, not that the word 'F' has many senses, but instead that there are many kinds of F-ness, or many ways of being F.[5] For example, when he says that *causes* (*aitia*) are said or spoken of in many ways (*Phys.* 2.3, 195a3–4), it seems best to interpret him as meaning that there are different ways of being a cause, rather than as making a point about the ambiguity of the word 'cause'. I suggest that the claim at 185a21 that 'being is said in many ways' is another case of this sort. We should take Aristotle to be distinguishing different ways of being: what it is for a substance to be

---

[4] When I say that 'X depends for its existence on the existence of Y', I mean that X cannot exist unless Y also exists.

[5] See e.g. Barnes 1995, 73–5. As Barnes points out, it is possible for two things to be F in different ways without its being the case that 'F' has different senses as applied to each of them. On the philosophical importance of distinguishing between senses of 'F' and ways of being F (or kinds of F-ness), see Matthews 1972.

is different from what it is for a quality or a quantity to be, and so on. His question, then, is about the way of being that the Eleatics want to attribute to what is. He uses the doctrine of the categories to distinguish various possible answers that they might give to this question, and then argues that each of these answers has absurd consequences. As we shall see, this reading fits much better with the fact that the argument relies on the interdependence thesis.[6]

2.2.2 The Argument's Targets

I have denied that Aristotle is using the doctrine of the categories to *disambiguate* the Eleatics' claim that 'what is is one'. But then how exactly does he understand their position? What kind, or kinds, of monism is he arguing against in this passage? When earlier he argued that the Eleatics' theory is incompatible with the existence of principles, his reason was that there cannot be any principles at all if, as the Eleatics hold, there is only one entity (185a3–5, discussed in section 1.3). We should therefore expect entity monism to be a target of the present argument. And I think it is; but it does not seem to be the only target.

After saying that we must ask 'in what way those who say that "all things are one" speak [of being]', Aristotle then raises two subquestions. First, do they hold that all things are substance, or quantities, or qualities, and so on? Second, do they hold that all things are one substance, or one quality, and so on?

---

[6] I do not mean to claim that Aristotle thinks that questions of ambiguity are irrelevant to the evaluation of the Eleatic theory. At *SE* 33, 182b26–7, he says that 'some people solve the argument of Zeno and Parmenides by saying that one and being are said in many ways' (οἱ δὲ τὸν Ζήνωνος λόγον καὶ Παρμενίδου λύουσι διὰ τὸ πολλαχῶς φάναι τὸ ἓν λέγεσθαι καὶ τὸ ὄν). Here the context makes it clear that he is talking about ambiguity: the claim is that certain people appeal to the ambiguity of the words 'one' and 'being' in order to try to answer Zeno and Parmenides' argument. Cf. also *SE* 10, 170b21–4: 'perhaps being or one signify many things, but both the answerer and the questioner, Zeno, have spoken thinking them to be one; and the argument is that all things are one'. (οἷον ἴσως τὸ ὂν ἢ τὸ ἓν πολλὰ σημαίνει, ἀλλὰ καὶ ὁ ἀποκρινόμενος καὶ ὁ ἐρωτῶν Ζήνων ἓν οἰόμενοι εἶναι εἰρήκασι, καὶ ἔστιν ὁ λόγος ὅτι ἓν πάντα. I retain the manuscripts' Ζήνων, following Sedley 2017, 7 n. 16.) Unfortunately it is hard to say anything more concrete about what the argument at issue in these *SE* passages might be, and about how an appeal to ambiguity might help to answer it. Aristotle never refers to 'the argument of Zeno and Parmenides' anywhere else.

How should we understand the first sub-question? I think that we can set aside the interpretation suggested by Ross, on which the question concerns the meaning of 'all things' (or 'all beings') as it occurs in the Eleatic claim: Does it mean 'all substances', or 'all quantities', or 'all qualities'?[7] It seems unlikely that this is Aristotle's question; as I have just noted, he does not go on to argue against the claims that 'all substances are one', 'all quantities are one', and so on. But if we do not read the question as a question about the meaning of 'all things', then how should we read it? It asks whether, according to the Eleatics, all things are substance or *quantities* (*posa*) or *qualities* (*poia*). The plurals apparently indicate that Aristotle has in his sights a version of monism that allows for the existence of a plurality of entities of a single kind. Thus the first sub-question suggests that entity monism is not his sole target. If it were, the question would make little sense. Entity monism is obviously incompatible with the existence of multiple quantities or of multiple qualities. The *second* sub-question would still of course be a relevant question (are all things one substance, or one quality...?), but the first would not.

I therefore want to suggest that Aristotle also means to argue against another kind of monism: essence monism, the view that all of reality ('what is') is of the same essence or nature. This is a view which, considered by itself, allows for the existence of a plurality of entities.[8] That Aristotle considers essence monism an authentically Eleatic doctrine is suggested by another of his criticisms later in *Physics* 1.2, where he argues, against the Eleatics, that essence monism leads to unacceptable 'Heraclitean' consequences (see 185b19–25, to be discussed in section 2.3.4). His attribution of essence monism to Parmenides is further supported by a passage in *Physics* 1.3, where he

---

[7] Ross 1936, 467.

[8] This is not to say that a *proponent* of essence monism will necessarily allow for the existence of a plurality of entities. Indeed, anyone who accepts that (1) reality consists of just a single entity (entity monism) is likely also to think that (2) reality is all of the same essence (essence monism). (If reality were not all of the same essence— if it were non-uniform—then there would be pressure to admit a plurality of entities.) In my view Aristotle attributes this conjunctive position, entity monism plus essence monism, both to Parmenides and to Melissus.

criticizes Parmenides for failing to see that he is unable to establish essence monism (186a28–32). This criticism seems to presuppose that Parmenides was *trying* to establish essence monism.[9] There is also a passage in Aristotle's critique of Melissus' argument which suggests that he attributes an equivalent position to Melissus (namely, that what is is one 'in form': see 186a19–22). So I suggest that the first sub-question is asked with essence monism in mind. If all of reality is of the same essence, then what way of being do things have? Are they substances, or quantities, or qualities (and so on)? An essence monist must choose one of these options. The universe cannot consist both of substances *and* of quantities, for instance, because then it would not be the case that all of reality is of the same essence. (If item X belongs to one category and item Y to another, then X and Y have different essences.)

The second sub-question, by contrast, is asked with entity monism in mind. If reality consists just of one token entity, what way of being does it have? Is it one substance (like a single human being), or one quality (like the property white), or a single item in one of the other non-substance categories?

My suggestion, then, is that Aristotle is arguing in the present passage against both of these varieties of monism, entity monism and essence monism. This explains the two sub-questions at 185a22–6—a detail that we could not adequately explain if he were targeting entity monism alone.

2.2.3 The Consequences of Interdependence

We now come to Aristotle's use of the interdependence thesis. As we have just seen, an essence monist is committed to saying that either

(i)   reality consists only of substances

or

(ii) reality consists only of entities of a single non-substance kind (qualities, or quantities, or relatives, and so on).

---

[9] The criticism is discussed in section 6.4.

An entity monist, on the other hand, is committed to saying that either

(iii)   reality consists only of a single substance

or

(iv)   reality consists only of a single non-substantial entity (a quantity, or a quality, or some other non-substantial item).

None of these options is possible—or, as Aristotle puts it at 185a26–7, 'all are impossible to maintain'. The reason is that they all conflict with the interdependence thesis.

Aristotle first argues that it cannot be the case either that (i) reality consists only of substances or that (iii) it consists only of a single substance.[10] At any rate, I take this to be the point of the following sentence:

For if, on the one hand, there is substance and quality and quantity, then whether these things are detached from one another or not, the things that are will be many.   (185a27–9)

It is not immediately obvious, of course, that this sentence is meant to explain why reality cannot consist only of substances or only of a single substance. After all, the claim here is that if there is substance *and* quality *and* quantity, then the things that are will be many, and not, as the Eleatics claim, only one. Nevertheless, it seems to me likely that Aristotle's intention here is to argue against claims (i) and (iii). I suggest that he is effectively relying on the first part of the interdependence thesis: substances depend for their existence on the existence of non-substances. Any substance will need to possess at least some non-substantial attributes; for example, if there is a human being, this human being must have certain features: it must have various qualities, be of a certain size, and so on. Since there can be no

---

[10] It is not that he gives two separate arguments, first an argument for why (i) is impossible, and then an argument for why (iii) is impossible. Rather, the same argument is intended to rule out both (i) and (iii) at the same time.

substances that are completely bereft of non-substantial attributes,[11] to commit oneself to the existence of a substance is thereby to commit oneself to the existence of other, non-substantial entities as well. The fact that these non-substantial entities are not 'detached' from (but rather are inherent in) the substance is irrelevant: they are additional entities all the same. It follows that reality cannot consist only of substances, or only of a single substance.[12]

According to this reading, the point being made at 185a27-9 is really this: if the Eleatics accept the existence of substance, then—because there can be no substances without non-substantial attributes—there will be substance *and* quality *and* quantity (for example). And if substance, quality, and quantity all exist, then what is will be many: reality will consist of many entities (*contra* entity monism), and of many kinds of entity (*contra* essence monism). And this will be so even if these entities are not 'detached' from one another.

This is admittedly reading quite a bit into the text at 185a27-9, but doing so seems warranted for the following reason. If Aristotle were not here arguing against the possibility that reality consists only of substances or only of a single substance, we would be given no argument against these claims. (The following lines turn to why reality cannot consist only of non-substantial attributes or of a single such attribute.) Given that they were among the options mentioned earlier on (at 185a22-4) and said to be impossible (at 185a26-7), there would then be a puzzling lacuna in Aristotle's case against the Eleatics. This seems to be a strong consideration in favour of the proposed reading of the present sentence.

---

[11] It is impossible for there to be an entity that is not *the same as itself*. Sameness is a relative property (*Metaph. Δ* 15, 1021a10). It is therefore impossible for there to be an entity that lacks all relative properties, and so impossible for there to be a substance that is totally bereft of non-substantial attributes.

[12] It is worth noting that Aristotle is sometimes taken to hold that the ontological priority of substances over non-substances consists precisely in the fact that substances *can* exist without non-substances, but not vice versa. The present argument suggests that this conception of the ontological priority of substances cannot be right. Cf. also Corkum 2008, 72-6 and Peramatzis 2011, 233-8.

He next argues that it cannot be the case either that (ii) reality consists only of entities of a single non-substantial kind or that (iv) it consists only of a single (token) non-substantial entity:

But if, on the other hand, all things are quality or quantity, then whether substance is or is not, this is absurd, if one should call the impossible absurd. For none of the others is separate apart from substance. For all [the others] are said of substance as a subject.[13]   (185a29–32)

This is the second part of the interdependence thesis: non-substances depend for their existence on the existence of substances. A quantity or a quality cannot exist on its own, without any underlying subject of which it is predicated. Thus reality cannot consist only of quantities or of a single quantity (for example). Aristotle says that the claim that all things are quantity or quality is absurd 'whether substance is or is not' (185a29–30). The idea is that if the Eleatics hold that all things are quantities or a single quantity, and yet admit the existence of substance, then they are contradicting themselves (because if substances exist, it is not the case that all things are quantities or a single quantity). If, on the other hand, they deny that substances exist, they are committed to the existence of free-floating attributes, which is absurd.

It follows that neither essence monism nor entity monism can be true. By the interdependence thesis, if the world contains anything at all, it must contain both substances and non-substantial attributes. So it cannot be the case that there is only one entity, or that all of reality is of the same essence. Whatever way of being the Eleatics want to attribute to what is, both of these varieties of monism are impossible.

2.2.4 Begging the Question

One worry that might be raised for Aristotle's argument here is that it depends on his own distinction between the different categories. This might be thought to beg the question against the Eleatics. Parmenides is sometimes taken to deny that we can intelligibly say or think

---

[13] Here 'being said of a subject' has a broader sense than at *Cat.* 2, 1a20–b9, where the *being said of* relation is distinguished from the *being in* relation. Aristotle also uses 'said of a subject' in this broader sense elsewhere, e.g. at *Phys.* 1.3, 186a34–5.

that X 'is not' Y, on the grounds that this would involve speaking or thinking of what is not. Some interpreters think that this is what leads him to his monism.[14] If we cannot intelligibly say or think that any two things are distinct from one another (that the one is not the other), then monism would seem to be the only intelligible ontological position available.

If this is how Parmenides arrives at his monism, it would certainly be question-begging for Aristotle simply to take the distinction between the various categories for granted. The distinction is legitimate only if it makes sense to say that substance 'is not' quantity, 'is not' quality, and so on. If the intelligibility of such statements is in question, the distinction cannot be presumed. Before appealing to the distinction, Aristotle would first need to explain why Parmenides is wrong to hold that we cannot intelligibly say or think that one thing 'is not' another.

In Aristotle's defence, however, there are other—arguably better— ways of understanding Parmenides' argument for monism. Importantly, there is no evidence that Aristotle himself understands the argument as relying on the supposed unintelligibility of non-identity statements. Later on, in Chapter 5, I shall suggest that he thinks of Parmenides' argument quite differently—as being based on a rejection of void.

For this reason, I think that Aristotle can be absolved of the charge of begging the question. Of course, the theory of categories is Aristotle's own innovation; the Eleatics themselves were unaware of it. But this does not mean that it is illegitimate for Aristotle to appeal to the theory in arguing against the Eleatic position. The key point is that, in Aristotle's view, neither Parmenides nor Melissus provides a principled reason for rejecting the theory.[15]

---

[14]   See e.g. Furth 1968, 128–30.

[15]   It should be noted that, taken by itself, the distinction between the different categories is perfectly consistent both with entity monism and with essence monism. Aristotle's basic claim is that anything that exists is either a substance or a quantity or a quality (and so on). On its own, this says nothing about how many entities or essences there are.

This is not to say that the theory could not be challenged. It is a substantive commitment, and someone wishing to defend the Eleatics' position could conceivably try to reject it. For example, a neo-Eleatic could try defending an anti-realist theory of properties. This would allow them to deny Aristotle's claim that non-substantial attributes are beings, which would in turn allow them to block his argument at 185a20–32. While this sort of response is conceivable, however, such a theory of properties goes a long way beyond what can plausibly be attributed to Parmenides and Melissus themselves.[16]

2.2.5 Against Melissus' Unlimited One

The other argument in the first sequence of criticisms is directed specifically against Melissus, and focuses on his claim that what is is unlimited (a claim Melissus argues for in B 2–4). Melissus takes the unlimitedness of what is to entail entity monism, the thought being that if anything that exists is unlimited in extent, there can be no room for more than one thing (B 6).[17] In response, Aristotle argues that the unlimitedness of what is actually entails entity pluralism:

And Melissus says that what is is unlimited. Therefore what is is a quantity [poson]. For the unlimited is in the [category of] quantity, and it is not possible for a substance or a quality or an affection to be unlimited, except accidentally, if they are at the same time also certain quantities. For the account of the unlimited employs quantity, but not substance or quality. If, therefore, it is both a substance and a quantity, what is is two and not one. But if it is substance alone, then it is not unlimited, nor even will it have any magnitude at all. For then it will be a quantity.   (185a32–b5)

Aristotle's initial move is to argue that Melissus' claim that what is is unlimited commits him to the claim that what is is a *quantity*. How should we understand this latter claim? The word *poson*, which I am translating as 'quantity', is ambiguous between a quantitative *property*

---

[16] In my view, and I think in Aristotle's view as well, Parmenides and Melissus do not entertain the possibility that properties are beings. This means that they are neither realists nor anti-realists about properties. (An anti-realist about properties is someone who explicitly denies that properties exist.)

[17] In Chapter 4 I provide a fuller account of Melissus' argument for monism.

(such as the property of being six feet tall) and the *bearer* of such a property (such as a person six feet tall).[18] In previous lines (185a23 and 28) the word was used to refer to the property, not the property-bearer. But the fact that a thing is unlimited obviously does not entail that it is a quantitative property. Aristotle should therefore be understood as making the point that the unlimitedness of what is entails, not that what is *is* a quantitative property, but that it *has* a quantitative property.[19] The point is that, given what it is to be unlimited, a thing cannot be unlimited without thereby being the bearer of a quantitative property.

That what is should be the bearer of a quantitative property is not absurd in itself, of course; the problem arises from the fact that Melissus also claims to be a monist. If what is is unlimited, and so the bearer of a quantitative property, then it cannot be that there is just one entity. There will be at least two entities: the quantitative property and the thing that has it, a substance. If, on the other hand, only the substance were to exist, bereft of any quantitative properties, Melissus' one being could not be unlimited. Indeed, Aristotle adds (185b4–5), if only the substance were to exist, bereft of quantitative properties, Melissus' one being would not have any size at all.[20]

It seems reasonable to think that Aristotle intends this argument against Melissus to serve as a specific instance of a more general objection, namely that the Eleatics' attribution of various properties to their one being is incompatible with their monism. We might

---

[18]   See *Cat.* 6, where ποσά is used for the bearers of quantitative properties as well as for quantitative properties themselves. The word ποιόν ('quality') is similarly ambiguous between qualitative properties (e.g. white) and the bearers of such properties (e.g. a white stick): see e.g. *Cat.* 8, 8b25 for the latter use.

[19]   The occurrence of ποσά at 185b1–2 must likewise be read as meaning 'bearers of quantitative properties'. Otherwise Aristotle would be implying that one and the same thing can be both a substance and a quantitative property.

[20]   I do not think that Aristotle here means to suggest that if Melissus *were* to deny that what is has size, he would then—at last—be occupying a defensible position. In the light of the first argument at 185a20–32, we must conclude that Aristotle thinks that it is impossible for there to be just one entity, regardless of whether this entity is spatially extended or not. Even a spatially unextended substance will need to have some attributes, such as the property of being the same as itself.

speculate that he singles out the Melissan property of unlimitedness because he likes the particular irony of the example. Melissus explicitly claims that unlimitedness entails monism, whereas in fact it entails its negation.

The Eleatics themselves apparently saw no tension between their monism, on the one hand, and their attribution of many different properties to what is, on the other. A plausible explanation of this is that they considered only the underlying bearers of properties to be beings, and not the properties themselves. Aristotle can thus be seen as highlighting (what he sees as) the Eleatics' naive and restrictive conception of being. In his view, properties are beings too. I shall come back to the significance of this point below.

2.3 The Second Sequence of Criticisms: Ways of Being One

Aristotle's second sequence of criticisms begins from the claim that one, like being, is said in many ways:

Further, since one itself is also said in many ways, just as being is, it is necessary to investigate in what way they say that the universe is *one*. And we call one either the continuous, or the indivisible, or those things of which the account of their essence is one and the same, such as *methu* and *oinos*.[21]

(185b5–9)

I argued above that the claim that 'being is said in many ways' at 185a21 should be understood as a claim about ways of being, and not about senses of the word 'being'. Similarly for the claim that 'one is said in many ways': we should take Aristotle to be distinguishing three different ways of being one, rather than three different senses of the word 'one'.[22]

---

[21] These are two words for wine.

[22] *Pace* e.g. Cherniss (1935, 63–4), Ross (1936, 338), Wicksteed and Cornford (1957, 23–5), Gershenson and Greenberg (1962, 140), Stokes (1971, 1), Horstschäfer (1998, 66), Palmer (2004, 49), Bostock (2006, 103), and Coxon (2009, 33).

To see this, consider the first item on the list: *continuous*. If Aristotle were suggesting that this is a possible sense of 'one', he would effectively be suggesting that the Eleatics' claim that 'the universe is one' might be interpreted as the claim that 'the universe is continuous'. But in that case the objection that follows would fail:

Now, if it is continuous, the One is many.[23] For the continuous is divisible to infinity. (185b9–11)

The objection is that if the one being is continuous, then it will consist of infinitely many parts. But if the Eleatics' thesis that 'the universe is one' *just is* the thesis that 'the universe is continuous', this consequence is hardly problematic. A thing's having infinitely many parts is obviously consistent with its being continuous. So if 'continuous' is intended to be a candidate for what the Eleatics *mean* by 'one', Aristotle has failed to come up with a good objection to their position.

In order to rescue the argument, we should take Aristotle to be suggesting that continuity is a *way* in which the universe might be one. Some objects are one by being continuous: what makes them one object, rather than many, is that each of their parts shares a boundary or a limit with some other part.[24] But suppose that the Eleatics are entity monists. Then we can easily understand why (in Aristotle's view) they cannot consistently say that the universe is one in this way. If the Eleatics' universe is continuous, then it is divisible into infinitely many parts, in which case there are many entities, not one. The 'way of being one' reading therefore gives Aristotle a good objection, whereas the 'sense of "one"' reading does not.

It is best, then, to take Aristotle to be distinguishing three different options about the way in which reality is one: (1) reality is one by being continuous, (2) reality is one by being indivisible, and (3) reality is one in account. This is not an exhaustive list of ways of being one; further ways are distinguished in the discussions of oneness in

---

[23] Some manuscripts instead have 'what is [τὸ ὄν] is many' at 185b10. The point would be the same either way.

[24] For this understanding of continuity, see *Phys.* 5.3, 227a10–12.

Metaphysics Δ 6 and *I* 1.[25] Rather, the three options are selected for their relevance to the discussion of the Eleatics. Each is a plausible candidate for what the Eleatics might have in mind as to how reality is one.

2.3.1 Continuity

Let us now look more closely at Aristotle's arguments against each of the three options. The first option, as we have seen, is that reality is one by being continuous. This is the way in which a lump of clay is one, for example. It is reasonable to think that Parmenides holds that reality is one in this way. He explicitly claims that what is (*eon*) is continuous at B 8.6,[26] and he argues for this claim at B 8.22–5:

> Nor is it divided,[27] since it is all alike;
> nor is it any more here, which would prevent it from holding
>   together,
> nor any less, but it is all full of being;
> thus it is all continuous, for being draws near to being.[28]

On what I take to be the most straightforward interpretation of this passage, it contains an argument that what is is a spatially continuous object. There are no gaps between regions of being ('it is all full of being'); therefore what is is a spatially continuous thing.[29] It is plausible that this is at least part of Parmenides' basis for claiming that what is is 'one' (B 8.6), given that anything that is continuous is thereby a unity.[30]

---

[25] On which see Castelli 2010 and 2018a.

[26] Assuming that the orthodox reading of the start of the line—ἕν, συνεχές ('one, continuous')—is correct.

[27] Alternatively: 'divisible'.

[28] οὐδὲ διαιρετόν ἐστιν, ἐπεὶ πᾶν ἐστιν ὁμοῖον· | οὐδέ τι τῇ μᾶλλον, τό κεν εἴργοι μιν συνέχεσθαι, | οὐδέ τι χειρότερον, πᾶν δ᾿ ἔμπλεόν ἐστιν ἐόντος· | τῷ ξυνεχὲς πᾶν ἐστιν· ἐὸν γὰρ ἐόντι πελάζει.

[29] I discuss this argument in more detail in section 5.4. Some think that Parmenides intends a temporal rather than a spatial sense of 'continuous' at B 8.22–5 (see e.g. Owen 1960, 97; Barnes 1982, 210–12). However, the spatial interpretation is strongly suggested by the use of the spatial adverb 'here' (τῇ) at line 23 and by the language of 'drawing near' (πελάζει) at line 25.

[30] Cf. also Barnes 1979, 11: 'When Parmenides juxtaposes "ἕν" ["one"] and "συνεχές" ["continuous"], it is only reasonable to suppose that the second word is intended to explicate the first'.

Aristotle's objection to the claim that what is is one by being continuous is based on the principle that 'the continuous is divisible to infinity'.[31] It may be worth clarifying the notion of divisibility here. I take it that Aristotle does not mean that continuous things are *physically* divisible to infinity, where 'physical division' refers to a process whereby formerly adjoining parts of a thing come to be separated by a spatial interval.[32] This does not seem to be what he intends, since he is making a general claim about continuous things, and on his view there are continuous things that are not subject to physical division, such as periods of time. I suggest that for something to be 'divisible' in the relevant sense it is enough if different parts of it can be distinguished from one another, regardless of whether or not they can be physically separated. The claim, then, is that for any continuous thing, C, it is possible to distinguish different parts of C, and of each of these different parts it is possible to distinguish further subparts, and so on ad infinitum.[33]

Must an Eleatic agree that it is possible to distinguish multiple parts of any continuous being? Parmenides may be thought to deny this when he says, at the beginning of the passage quoted above, 'Nor is it [sc. what is] divided [*diaireton*], since it is all alike' (B 8.22). The argument appears to be that, because what is is uniform, it is not divided (or perhaps: not divisible) into parts.[34] But to this Aristotle might reasonably reply that if something is continuous then it *must* contain parts, even if it is perfectly uniform. Something continuous (*suneches*) is literally something that 'holds together' (*sunechetai*).

---

[31] Aristotle sometimes treats this as a definition of 'continuous': see e.g. *Phys.* 6.2, 232b24–5 and *Cael.* 1.1, 268a6–7; cf. also *Phys.* 3.1, 200b16–20.

[32] I take this definition of 'physical division' from Furley 1967, 4.

[33] This allows us to respond on Aristotle's behalf to a problem raised by Bostock (2006, 104). Bostock worries that Aristotle's own doctrine of parts is that the parts of a whole exist only insofar as they are capable of being separated from that whole. Since the Eleatics will claim that the putative parts of their one entity are incapable of being separated, they therefore have Aristotelian grounds on which to resist the present objection. In response to this worry, Aristotle can say that even if the Eleatic One lacks separable parts, it is nonetheless the case that different parts of it can be distinguished from one another.

[34] Cf. Sedley 2008, 322. For an alternative interpretation, see Owen 1960, 92–3.

But it is hard to know what it could mean for a thing to 'hold together' if not that it has *parts* that 'hold together' *with one another*. And once the Eleatics have conceded this, they are in trouble. Or rather, they are in trouble if their position is that reality consists of just a single entity.

2.3.2 The Part and the Whole

Immediately after arguing that the continuity of the One would contravene the Eleatics' (entity) monism, Aristotle mentions a problem about parts and wholes:

And there is a difficulty with regard to the part and the whole, although presumably it is not [a difficulty] for the argument [*pros ton logon*], but [a difficulty] in its own right [*autēn kath' hautēn*]. That is, whether the part and the whole are one or more than one, and how they are one or more than one, and if they are more, how they are more.[35] This also applies with regard to non-continuous parts.[36] And if each [part] is one with the whole by being indivisible [with respect to the whole], then [there is the difficulty] that they [*sc.* the parts] also bear this relation to one another.   (185b11–16)

The basic problem is that of the relation between a whole and one of its parts, a pen and its nib, say: Are they one thing or two?[37] There seems to be a clear sense in which they are not *two* things. They are not, after all, two separate things; the pen includes the nib. On the other hand, there seems to be an equally clear sense in which they are not *one* thing. They are not identical with one another: if a whole were identical with each of its parts, then (by the transitivity of identity) each part would be identical with each other part, which

---

[35] A slight oddity here is that 'if they are more, how they are more' seems superfluous. Some scholars think that the text is corrupt at this point (see e.g. Natorp 1890, 10 n. 1).

[36] The point of this sentence is that this problem is not specific to continuous wholes, such as the Parmenidean One. It is a general problem and applies equally to non-continuous wholes. A *continuous* whole is a whole each of whose parts is continuous with some other of its parts. A *non-continuous* whole is a whole that lacks this property (examples would be a flock of sheep or an army).

[37] This should be distinguished from the problem 'of how something that has *many* parts can at the same time be *one*', *pace* Koslicki (2008, 125). Aristotle is not here asking whether (and how) *the whole* is one or many, but whether (and how) *the whole and the part* are one or many.

is absurd.[38] So the part and the whole are non-identical, and are thus two things, not one.

Why does Aristotle mention this problem here? The answer, presumably, is that his preceding argument (against the claim that what is is one by being continuous) rests on a certain view about the relation of a whole to one of its parts, namely that there is a sense in which the whole and the part are *two entities*. The part is not identical to the whole of which it is a part. It is therefore another item, existing in addition to the whole. This is why the many parts of the continuous One add to the total number of entities in existence, creating a problem for the Eleatic entity monist. If the part and the whole were simply identical with one another, Aristotle's criticism would not succeed. The divisibility of the continuous One into parts would not add to the total number of entities in existence, and so would not threaten entity monism.

This, I take it, is why Aristotle mentions the problem of the whole–part relation here. Now, he also says that the problem is not *pros ton logon* but is *autēn kath' hautēn*. But I doubt that he means to claim that the problem is *irrelevant* to his argument against the Eleatics, contrary to the usual view of interpreters.[39] (If so, why mention it?) More likely, I think, he is saying that the whole–part problem is not a problem *for his argument*, even though it nonetheless is a problem *in its own right*. The reason why the whole–part problem is not a problem for Aristotle's own argument is that, however it is to be resolved, it is obvious that the correct solution will *not* be to say that the relation between a whole and one of its parts is that of identity. In Aristotle's eyes, that answer is an obvious non-starter, and yet it is the

---

[38] Aristotle is effectively making this point in the last part of the passage, where he explains why the part cannot be one with the whole 'by being indivisible' with respect to the whole. I suggest that for X to be 'indivisible with respect to' Y is for X to be *indistinguishable* from Y, that is, for X and Y to have all the same properties. If X and Y are one in this way, they are identical. The claim at the end of the passage is that the part cannot be one with the whole in this way, because it would then follow (absurdly) that the many parts bear this same relation to one another.

[39] See e.g. Wicksteed and Cornford 1957, 23; Owen 1961, 96–7 n. 79; Charlton 1992, 3.

only possible answer that could threaten his foregoing argument against the Eleatics.

2.3.3 Indivisibility

What is cannot be one by being continuous, at least not if the Eleatics are to be consistent entity monists. The second option that Aristotle considers is that it is one by being indivisible. I take this to be a second way in which the Eleatic entity monist's one entity might be one. The previous criticism was that anything that is one by being continuous must be divisible into parts, and the existence of multiple parts is incompatible with entity monism. So it would seem that a better option for the Eleatic entity monist is to drop the claim that reality is one by being continuous, and to say instead that it is one simply by virtue of its being indivisible into parts.

As before, the relevant notion of divisibility here is not physical divisibility. If the Eleatics are to avoid the problem raised against the first option, it is not enough for them to say that reality is physically indivisible, because physical indivisibility is compatible with having multiple parts. Rather, to avoid the objection, they must say that reality is indivisible in the sense of being absolutely partless: a mereological atom. As I noted above, Parmenides might be read as claiming that reality is indivisible in this sense at B 8.22. Melissus also seems to have rejected the existence of parts, although this is controversial.[40]

Aristotle's objection to this second option (unlike his objection to the first) is not that it contravenes entity monism. The objection this time is that the view conflicts with other Eleatic commitments:

> But if it is one by being indivisible, then nothing will be a quantity or a quality, nor then will what is be unlimited, as Melissus says, nor limited, as Parmenides says. For the limit is indivisible, but not the limited thing. (185b16–19)

---

[40] See Simplicius, In Phys. 87.6-7 (= the second half of B 9): 'Being one, he [sc. Melissus] says, it must not have body; but if it had thickness, it would have parts, and no longer be one' (ἓν ἐόν, φησί, δεῖ αὐτὸ σῶμα μὴ ἔχειν· εἰ δὲ ἔχοι πάχος, ἔχοι ἂν μόρια καὶ οὐκέτι ἓν εἴη). The attribution of this argument to Melissus has been questioned on the grounds that he should not want to claim that his infinitely large, plenistic One lacks 'body' and 'thickness'. For discussion, see Palmer 2003.

The underlying assumption here is that a thing can be extended only if it has parts.[41] Given this assumption, an indivisible or partless Eleatic One must be unextended, like a geometrical point. It will therefore lack any quantity or size. Yet on Aristotle's interpretation both Parmenides and Melissus hold that the One is extended. So, if they want to claim that what is is indivisible in the sense of being absolutely partless, they will be forced to abandon this view.

A little strangely, Aristotle also suggests that if what is is indivisible then it will lack any qualitative properties. This is odd because it does not in general seem true that indivisible things lack qualities. Consider the first mover as described in *Metaphysics Λ* 7. It is indivisible in the sense of being partless (1073a5–7), and yet it is also supremely good (1072b29), which I take to be a quality. The probable explanation is that Aristotle is really thinking of the kinds of qualities that the Eleatics want to attribute to their One, such as, in Parmenides' case, its sphericity.[42] If the One is indivisible, then it will lack size, and if it lacks size, it will lack the sorts of qualities the Eleatics want.[43]

The claim that reality is indivisible (in the sense of being partless) is also inconsistent with Melissus' claim that it is unlimited. This is for the simple reason that a thing cannot be unlimited unless it is extended, and cannot be extended unless it has parts. Finally, Aristotle argues that the indivisibility of reality is incompatible with Parmenides' view that it is limited: 'For the limit is indivisible, but not the limited thing.' The limit L of a thing is indivisible, because

---

[41] Cf. also Charlton 1992, 58. While this assumption is plausible, it is not indisputable. On the possibility of 'extended simples', see e.g. Simons 2004.

[42] Shapes are Aristotelian qualities: see *Cat.* 8, 10a11–16. Aristotle does not explicitly say that the Parmenidean One is spherical, but it seems likely that he interprets B 8.42–4 in this way, given that he takes literally Parmenides' description of what is as a spatially finite object 'equally balanced from the middle' (μεσσόθεν ἰσοπαλές): see *Phys.* 3.6, 207a15–17, to be discussed in section 5.2. Plato too seems to take this description literally: at *Soph.* 244e2–7 the Eleatic Visitor infers from it that the One has a middle and extremities, and thus multiple parts, contrary to Parmenides' monism.

[43] Charlton (1992, 58) also adopts a version of this solution; however, he suggests that Aristotle's thought is that, '[i]f the universe is not extended, it will not have the qualities... which Parmenides wants to attribute to it, *heat and cold*' (my italics). I doubt that Aristotle thinks that the Parmenidean universe is meant to have such properties: see Chapter 8 for discussion of Aristotle's interpretation of the *Doxa*.

if *L* were divisible (and so extended) it would not really be the thing's limit; *L* would *itself* have a limit (call it *L**); and *that* would be the real limit of the thing. Something limited, by contrast, is divisible, because anything with limits necessarily has some extension. (A geometrical point does not have limits, for example.) And if a thing has extension, it is divisible into parts.

2.3.4 One in Account

The third and last option is that what is is one in account. Aristotle provides two pairs of examples to illustrate what he means by 'one in account'. First, *oinos* and *methu* are one in account: the account of the essence of *oinos* is the same as the account of the essence of *methu* (185b9). Similarly for cloak and mantle (185b20): the account of the essence of the former is the same as that of the latter. So, to say that 'what is is one in account' is to say that *everything that is* has the same account and the same essence. This is equivalent to the position I have been calling 'essence monism', the position that all of reality is of the same essence.

As with the preceding two options, this third option too has a basis in the Eleatic texts. While there are variant readings, scholars now generally agree that at B 8.4 Parmenides claims that what is is *mounogenes*. One natural way (if not the only way) of interpreting him here is as claiming that what is is 'of one kind'.[44] And a plausible restatement of this, in Aristotelian terminology, is that all of reality is of the same essence, or (equivalently) that all beings are one in account. There seems to be further evidence of the Eleatics' commitment to essence monism in their claim that what is is 'all alike' (see Parmenides B 8.22, Melissus B 7.1, and *MXG* 1, 974a12–14).

The objection to this final option runs as follows:

But if all beings are one in account, as are mantle and cloak, then it follows that they are affirming the account of Heraclitus. For to be good and bad[45]

---

[44] For this translation of μουνογενές, see e.g. Mourelatos 2008, 113–14. The other possible translation is 'unique', which is defended by McKirahan (2008, 221 n. 10).

[45] These phrases are shorthand ways of referring to *what it is to be good* (τὸ τί ἦν ἀγαθῷ εἶναι) and *what it is to be bad* (τὸ τί ἦν κακῷ εἶναι)—in other words, to the essences of good and bad.

will be the same, and to be good and not-good, so that the same thing will be good and not-good, and a human and a horse, and their account will not be about the fact that the beings are one, but about the fact that they are nothing. And to be this quality and this quantity will be the same.   (185b19–25)

On the face of it, this objection is puzzling. The objection appears to be that the claim that 'all beings are one in account' entails, for example, that the properties good and bad have the same essence. But surely this is not a consequence of that claim. Certainly, if one agrees that there *are* such properties as good and bad, the claim that 'all beings are one in account' entails that they have the same essence. But why think that the Eleatics are committed to the existence of such things?[46]

My suggestion is that Aristotle is implicitly attributing to the Eleatics the view that *it is impossible to speak or think of what is not*.[47] This view commits one to saying that, when we speak of the properties of good and bad, our terms 'good' and 'bad' each refer to something that is (because we cannot speak of what is not). Hence, if all beings are one in account, it follows that the referents of 'good' and 'bad' are one in account. Similarly, the view commits one to saying that, when we *think* of good and bad, we are thinking, in each case, of something that is (because we cannot think of what is not). Hence, if all beings are one in account, it follows that we are thinking of the same property in each case.

Aristotle's criticism of the third option now becomes rather more intelligible. If an essence monist accepts that it is impossible to speak or think of what is not, then it seems that they must agree that the essence of the property we call or think of as 'good' is the same as the essence of the property we call or think of as 'bad'. And so there is reason to think that essence monism commits the Eleatics to the

---

[46] In the objection at 185a20–32, Aristotle argued that the Eleatics are committed to the existence of at least some properties. But the present question is: Why think that they are committed to the existence of properties *such as good and bad*?

[47] Many commentators take this view to be expressed in Parmenides B 2.7–8: 'For you could not apprehend what is not, for that is impossible, | nor indicate it' (οὔτε γὰρ ἂν γνοίης τό γε μὴ ἐόν, οὐ γὰρ ἀνυστόν, | οὔτε φράσαις). Melissus seems to have accepted the view too: see Simplicius, *In Phys.* 103.15–16.

'Heraclitean' consequence that opposite properties are identical, which in turn entails that anything that has the property of being F also has the property of being not-F.[48]

This is obviously a deeply problematic result for the Eleatics— especially given how adamant they are that nothing is both F and not-F.[49] If nothing is both F and not-F, *and* anything F is also not-F, then it follows that nothing at all exists. (At least, this follows given the uncontroversial assumption that a thing cannot exist without some predicate, F, belonging to it.) I suggest that this is why Aristotle claims that, if all beings are one in account, the Eleatics' account 'will not be about the fact that the beings are one, but about the fact that they are nothing' (185b23–5). It turns out that the Eleatics are committed not to monism but to nihilism, the (by their own lights) unthinkable and unspeakable thesis that nothing exists at all.

The final point that Aristotle makes as part of the present criticism is that 'to be this quality and this quantity will be the same'. That is, it will follow from the thesis that all beings are one in account that any particular quality (such as white) has the same essence as any particular quantity (such as being six feet tall). The point here is that the Eleatic position is in fact even more extreme than the 'Heraclitean' position, since the former is not limited merely to the claim that *opposite* properties are identical. The Eleatics must say—even more radically—that *all* properties are identical, even properties that belong to different categories.

2.4 Are Aristotle's Criticisms Fair?

We have now looked at each of Aristotle's criticisms of Eleatic monism in *Physics* 1.2. I have suggested that he is targeting two

---

[48] It is worth mentioning that Aristotle elsewhere shows some hesitation about whether Heraclitus really adopted such a view. See *Metaph.* Γ 3, 1005b23–5: 'For it is impossible for anyone to believe that the same thing is and is not, *as some people think* Heraclitus says [καθάπερ τινὲς οἴονται λέγειν Ἡράκλειτον].'

[49] See especially Parmenides B 7.1: 'For never shall this prevail, that things that are not are' (οὐ γὰρ μήποτε τοῦτο δαμῇ εἶναι μὴ ἐόντα).

forms of monism in particular—entity monism and essence monism. But is it fair of him to interpret the Eleatics in this way?

When it comes to Melissus, Aristotle would seem to be on safe ground. It is uncontroversial that Melissus is an entity monist: he clearly argues that, since anything that is is unlimited in extent, there can only be room for one thing (B 6). He then proceeds to argue that this one entity is 'all alike' (B 7.1; cf. *MXG* 1, 974a12–14), which presumably entails that reality is all of the same essence. So it would seem that Melissus is rightly understood both as an entity monist and as an essence monist.

As I noted in the Introduction, the nature of Parmenides' monism is much more controversial: he is not always read as an extreme monist. Some interpreters think that the two main parts of the poem are supposed to provide complementary accounts of two different orders or aspects of reality. For example, it has been suggested that the *Alētheia* gives us Parmenides' theory of the intelligible world, and the *Doxa* his theory of the (really existing) perceptible world.[50] If this reading is correct, then even if the *Alētheia* presents a monistic theory, it is not a monistic theory of reality as a whole. Other interpreters think that Parmenides' official theory of reality is confined to the *Alētheia*, but they deny that the theory of the *Alētheia* is radically monistic.[51]

Despite the availability of these non-monistic readings, however, Aristotle's interpretation has much to recommend it. To start with, Parmenides seems to warn us against accepting the pluralistic theory of the *Doxa*. At the end of B 1, the goddess contrasts the theory of the *Alētheia*—'the unshaken heart of well-rounded truth'—with the theory of the *Doxa*, which represents 'the opinions of mortals, in which

---

[50] For this Platonic-sounding (or Platonizing?) interpretation, see Plutarch, *Col.* 1113e–14f, with discussion in Kechagia 2011, 154–7. Cf. also Simplicius, *In Phys.* 38.28–39.12. Interpretations of this kind are defended in detail in Palmer 2009, Johansen 2016, and Tor 2017, 295–303.

[51] See e.g. Barnes 1979. Barnes suggests we read Parmenides' claims about 'what is' as claims about 'anything that is'. On this interpretation, the claim that 'what is is one' is the non-monistic claim that *anything that is* is one, and not the monistic claim that *reality as a whole* is one. Cf. also Curd 1991 and 1998.

there is no true trust'. She amplifies her criticism of mortal opinions in B 6 and 7, where she tells the youth to withhold his thought from the 'backwards-turning' path of mortals, who are 'deaf and blind alike' and who 'know nothing'. And when she finally moves, towards the end of B 8, from the *Alētheia* to the *Doxa*, she warns him once again:

> With this I cease for you my trustworthy speech and thought about truth. From this point on learn mortal opinions, hearing the deceptive order of my words.[52] (B 8.50–2)

A natural interpretation of all of this is that Parmenides, in the voice of the goddess, is urging us not to accept the erroneous mortal opinions of the *Doxa* and telling us that we must trust instead in the theory of the *Alētheia*.[53]

If Parmenides' official theory of reality is the theory of the *Alētheia*, then should we say that he is a radical monist? Well, the goddess does claim that what is is 'one', that it is a continuous, undivided (or indivisible) whole, and that 'nothing else is'.[54] And she says that it is *mounogenes* and all alike. These statements can be read in different ways, but one appealingly straightforward interpretation is surely Aristotle's: we are being told that reality ('what is') consists of just one thing—continuous, indivisible, and all of the same kind or essence. There is nothing else besides this one entity.[55]

It is not unreasonable, then, to interpret both Melissus and Parmenides as endorsing entity monism and essence monism. And when their

---

[52] ἐν τῷ σοι παύω πιστὸν λόγον ἠδὲ νόημα | ἀμφὶς ἀληθείης· δόξας δ' ἀπὸ τοῦδε βροτείας | μάνθανε κόσμον ἐμῶν ἐπέων ἀπατηλὸν ἀκούων.

[53] Cf. Long 1963; Barnes 1982, 156. An alternative interpretation is that Parmenides merely means to downgrade the epistemic status of these mortal opinions, but not to reject them entirely. See e.g. Simplicius, *In Phys.* 39.10–12. This is not the place to enter into a discussion of this alternative interpretation; my present point is only that the goddess's criticisms are naturally read as indicating that the mortal opinions are false.

[54] I follow DK at 8.36–7: 'nothing else <either> is or will be | besides what is' (οὐδὲν γὰρ <ἢ> ἔστιν ἢ ἔσται | ἄλλο πάρεξ τοῦ ἐόντος). For a defence of this text, see Tarán 1965, 128–9.

[55] For this kind of reading of the *Alētheia*, cf. also Zeller 1892, 557–63; Burnet 1930, 178–82; Furley 1967, 57–8; Furth 1968, 130; Guthrie 1969, 32–6; Mackenzie 1982, 1–3; Sedley 1999, 117–23; Wedin 2014, 105–18.

theory is understood in this way, we have seen that Aristotle has powerful arguments against them. Even so, we might still wonder whether his criticisms are entirely fair. Aristotle very often translates his predecessors' theories into his own philosophical idiom. Take this classic example from the first book of the *Metaphysics*:

Of those who first philosophized, then, most thought that the principles of the material kind were the only principles of all things. For that from which all beings are, and from which they first come to be, and into which they finally perish, the substance remaining but changing in respect of its attributes, this they say is the element and principle of the things that are.[56]

(*Metaph. A* 3, 983b6–11)

Here Aristotle reformulates the theory of the early natural philosophers in terms of the concepts of matter, substance, and attribute. These are his own concepts, not theirs. He is utilizing what Rachel Barney has called his 'very expansive version of the principle of charity, which he deploys in order to state, translated into his own terms, what his predecessors were really getting at'.[57]

Given that for Aristotle this is standard exegetical practice, it may seem strange that he does not consider a similarly reformulated version of Eleatic monism. His criticisms in *Physics* 1.2 show that he regards the Eleatic One as a spatially extended bearer of properties,[58] and so it seems that he could easily have reformulated the Eleatics' theory as follows:

There is just a single substance, which is homogeneous and unchanging in respect of its attributes.

Of course, the Eleatics do not put it like this themselves, but we might be tempted to say that this is just because they lack the sophisticated

---

τῶν δὴ πρῶτον φιλοσοφησάντων οἱ πλεῖστοι τὰς ἐν ὕλης εἴδει μόνας ᾠήθησαν ἀρχὰς εἶναι πάντων· ἐξ οὗ γὰρ ἐστιν ἅπαντα τὰ ὄντα καὶ ἐξ οὗ γίγνεται πρῶτον καὶ εἰς ὃ φθείρεται τελευταῖον, τῆς μὲν οὐσίας ὑπομενούσης τοῖς δὲ πάθεσι μεταβαλλούσης, τοῦτο στοιχεῖον καὶ ταύτην ἀρχήν φασιν εἶναι τῶν ὄντων.

[57] Barney 2009, 113.   [58] Recall especially sections 2.2.5 and 2.3.3.

conceptual resources (the distinction between substance and attribute, say) by which to express their view more precisely.

There is evidence that in certain contexts Aristotle is prepared to treat the Eleatic theory as though it were a version of substance monism. At the beginning of *Metaphysics Z*, he suggests that the traditional enquiry into being should really be understood as an enquiry into substance:

Indeed, the question which was long ago and is now and always the object of enquiry, and always puzzled over—'What is being?'—is just this: 'What is substance?' For it is this [*sc.* substance] that some say is one, and others that it is more than one, some that it is limited and others that it is unlimited. Which is why, for us too, the most important, the primary, and practically the only task is to consider, concerning what is in this way [*sc.* as substance], what it is.[59] (*Metaph. Z* 1, 1028b2-7)

Parmenides and Melissus are surely in the first group of philosophers mentioned here. When they claim that 'what is' is one, what they 'really' mean is that there is just one substance.

Notice, however, that a reformulated, substance monistic version of the Eleatic theory would be immune to the various criticisms that Aristotle puts forward over the course of *Physics* 1.2. The claim that there is just one substance is consistent with there being a plurality of properties and a plurality of spatial parts, so long as these many properties and parts are not themselves counted as substances.[60] This means that an Eleatic substance monist would not be vulnerable to any of the objections given at 185a20–b19. Nor would an Eleatic substance monist be committed to the 'Heraclitean' consequences described at 185b19–25. The claim that the one *substance* is homogeneous clearly does not have the Heraclitean consequence that the essences of the *attributes* good and bad are one and the same. So the

---

[59] καὶ δὴ καὶ τὸ πάλαι τε καὶ νῦν καὶ ἀεὶ ζητούμενον καὶ ἀεὶ ἀπορούμενον, τί τὸ ὄν, τοῦτό ἐστι τίς ἡ οὐσία (τοῦτο γὰρ οἱ μὲν ἓν εἶναί φασιν οἱ δὲ πλείω ἢ ἕν, καὶ οἱ μὲν πεπερασμένα οἱ δὲ ἄπειρα), διὸ καὶ ἡμῖν καὶ μάλιστα καὶ πρῶτον καὶ μόνον ὡς εἰπεῖν περὶ τοῦ οὕτως ὄντος θεωρητέον τί ἐστιν.

[60] At *Cat.* 5, 3a29–32, Aristotle suggests that the spatial parts of a substance are also substances, but it would be open to a substance monist to challenge this view.

worry arises that by neglecting to deploy his usual principle of charity, and neglecting to consider a reformulated version of the Eleatic theory, Aristotle is failing to give the Eleatics a fair hearing.

This worry can, I think, be answered. It is true that in *Physics* 1 Aristotle does not consider a reformulated version of the Eleatic theory. But this should not be put down to a lapse of interpretative charity or to some desire to score an easy victory over his opponents. Rather, there are legitimate reasons for Aristotle to target the Eleatic theory as it is originally stated (or as he thinks it is originally stated), and not a reformulated version.

First, I suggest that Aristotle's primary aim in attacking Eleatic monism in *Physics* 1 is to defend the existence of principles against a theory which, taken literally, would eliminate them.[61] As he argues at 185a3–5, if reality were to consist of just one entity, there could be no principles at all. This helps to explain why he targets (what he takes to be) the Eleatics' stated position. It is only their stated position which threatens the existence of principles. The reformulated version is consistent with the existence of a plurality of entities, and is therefore consistent with the existence of principles.

Second, I suggest that, as well as wanting to refute a theory that rules out the existence of principles, Aristotle also means to draw our attention to the Eleatics' naive, overly restrictive conception of being, and in particular to their failure to recognize properties as beings. This is a further reason for him to focus on the original version of the Eleatic theory, which manifests this metaphysical naivety. The Eleatics were able to claim that 'what is' is one and of one kind precisely because they were overlooking the existence of properties. Aristotle highlights the Eleatics' restrictive conception of being by taking their monistic claims literally, and as they are intended—as claims about reality ('what is') as a whole. He then argues that because the Eleatics turn out to be committed to the existence of other entities besides their one being, their radical monism is impossible. The lesson here is not just

---

[61] See section 1.4.

that their stated position is impossible, but also that it is based in part on a mistake about what counts as a being.[62]

Why should Aristotle want to draw attention in this way to the Eleatics' narrow conception of being? An important reason, I think, is that he is looking ahead to the theory of principles that he will go on to develop in the latter half of *Physics* 1—the theory of substratum, form, and privation. According to this theory, natural things are ontologically complex: they are composed of entities of different ontological kinds.[63] A natural substance (such as a plant) is a composite of an underlying substratum and a form, while the precursor of such a substance (such as a seed) is a composite of an underlying substratum and a privation.[64] This theory cannot be formulated unless we recognize properties as well as property-bearers as entities within our ontology: the underlying substratum is a property-bearer; the form and the privation are properties predicated of the substratum.[65] So when Aristotle takes the Eleatics to task for overlooking the existence of properties, he is effectively preparing the way for the positive account of principles that will follow.

---

[62] Cf. *Soph.* 242b10–250e4, where the Eleatic Visitor criticizes Parmenides and other philosophers for pursuing the question of 'how many beings there are and what they are like' without first getting clear on what it is to be. I take the main point of the anti-monistic arguments at 244b6–245e5 to be to reveal Parmenides' confusion about being.

[63] I borrow the terminology of 'ontological complexity' from Koslicki 2008, 109. Cf. also Mann 2011.

[64] On the complexity of the precursor, see Morison, forthcoming.

[65] See *Phys.* 1.7, 190b28–9 for evidence that Aristotle regards the form as a κατηγορούμενον, a property predicated of the substratum.

3

Problems of One and Many

3.1 Introduction

After his arguments against the Eleatics' monistic position, Aristotle appends a short discussion of some later philosophers, 'the more recent of the early thinkers':

And the more recent of the early thinkers[1] were also troubled lest the same thing should turn out for them to be at the same time both one and many. This is why some took away the 'is', like Lycophron, while others refashioned their speech, saying not that the human 'is white', but that he 'has whitened', and not that he 'is walking', but that he 'walks', so that they would never make the one be many by adding the 'is', supposing that one or being is said in only one way. But the things that are are many, either in account (for example, to be white and to be musical are different, yet the same thing is both; therefore the one is many), or by division (as with the whole and the parts). But here [*sc.* with regard to the whole and the parts] they were already in difficulty, and they conceded that the one is many, as though it were not possible for the same thing to be both one and many—although not the opposites. For the one is both potentially and actually.   (185b25–186a3)

The first sentence of the passage ('the more recent of the early thinkers were *also* troubled...') implies that the Eleatics were themselves troubled by the possibility that the same thing might be both one and many. There are indeed some signs of this. After arguing that what is is one, Melissus went on to argue for a series of corollaries:

---

[1] Some manuscripts have the variant: 'And the more recent thinkers too were troubled, just as the early ones were...' (οἱ ὕστερον καθάπερ οἱ ἀρχαῖοι).

And being one, it is in every way alike; for if it were unlike, then, being more, it would no longer be one, but many.[2] (*MXG* 1, 974a12-14)

And neither could it perish, become larger, be rearranged, or suffer pain or grief. For if it underwent any of these, it would no longer be one.[3] (B 7.2)

Being one, he says, it must not have body; but if it had thickness, it would have parts, and no longer be one.[4] (B 9 = Simplicius, *In Phys.* 87.6-7)

If what is were not all alike, then it would be many, not one; but it has already been shown to be one; so it must be all alike. Again, if it were to change or be affected, then it would be many, not one; but it has already been shown to be one; so it must be changeless and unaffected. Finally, if it were to have parts, then it would be many, not one; but it has already been shown to be one; so it must be partless. Melissus apparently thinks that because he has shown that what is is one, it cannot have any feature that would cause it to be many. His assumption appears to be that the same thing—in this case, what is itself—cannot be both one and many at the same time.

A similar assumption may have played a role in another Eleatic argument, Zeno's small–large paradox. Zeno argues that if there are many things, then each of them must be both small and large: so small as to have no size at all, and so large as to be infinite.[5] Simplicius, our source, does not quote the 'small' half of the antinomy, but he does say

---

[2] ἓν δὲ ὂν ὅμοιον εἶναι πάντῃ· εἰ γὰρ ἀνόμοιον, πλείω ὄντα οὐκ ἂν ἔτι ἓν εἶναι, ἀλλὰ πολλά.

[3] καὶ οὔτ' ἂν ἀπόλοιτο οὔτε μεῖζον γίνοιτο οὔτε μετακοσμέοιτο οὔτε ἀλγεῖ οὔτε ἀνιᾶται· εἰ γάρ τι τούτων πάσχοι, οὐκ ἂν ἔτι ἓν εἴη. Cf. also *MXG* 1, 974a18-23: 'And since the One is like this, it is without distress or pain, is healthy and not ill; nor does it undergo rearrangement in position, alteration in form, or mixture with anything else. For in all these ways the One is compelled to become many, what is not is compelled to be born, and what is is compelled to perish. And these things are impossible' (τοιοῦτον δὲ ὂν τὸ ἓν ἀνώδυνόν τε καὶ ἀνάλγητον ὑγιές τε καὶ ἄνοσον εἶναι, οὔτε μετακοσμούμενον θέσει οὔτε ἑτεροιούμενον εἴδει οὔτε μιγνύμενον ἄλλῳ· κατὰ πάντα γὰρ ταῦτα πολλά τε τὸ ἓν γίγνεσθαι καὶ τὸ μὴ ὂν τεκνοῦσθαι καὶ τὸ ὂν φθείρεσθαι ἀναγκάζεσθαι· ταῦτα δὲ ἀδύνατα εἶναι).

[4] ἓν ἐόν, φησί, δεῖ αὐτὸ σῶμα μὴ ἔχειν· εἰ δὲ ἔχοι πάχος, ἔχοι ἂν μόρια καὶ οὐκέτι ἓν εἴη. As I noted in Chapter 2, the attribution of this last argument to Melissus is controversial.

[5] Simplicius, *In Phys.* 139.8-9; 141.6-8. This is one of the plurality paradoxes referred to at *Parm.* 127e8-128a3.

that Zeno proved that nothing has size 'from the fact that each of the many things is the same as itself and one' (*In Phys.* 139.18–19).[6] This suggests the following argument. If there are many things, then each of these many things is one thing. But anything that has size has a plurality of parts, and anything that has parts is the same as those parts, and so is many, not one. So, if there are many things, each of them is one, and if each of them is one, then none of them has any size.

If this is Zeno's 'small' argument, it relies on the idea that a whole of parts is many *and not one*; once again the crucial thought seems to be that the same thing cannot be both one and many at the same time.[7]

The 'more recent' people at issue in the excursus at 185b25–186a3 are not Eleatics, but they inherited the Eleatic concern about the same thing's being both one and many. They saw two problems in particular. The first is a problem arising from our characteristic way of ascribing properties to things (call this the 'predication' problem). The second is a problem concerning the relation between a whole and its parts (call this the 'whole–parts' problem). I shall examine each of these problems in turn, before asking about the point of the excursus.

3.2 The Predication Problem

It is common sense that individual objects—individual human beings, individual horses, and so on—each have many different attributes. The more recent thinkers' first worry is that our typical way of expressing this ordinary thought leads to contradiction. We say that Socrates is human, is white, and is musical. But this way of speaking has the supposedly paradoxical consequence that *one thing*, Socrates, *is many different things* (human, white, musical).

---

[6] ὃ δείκνυσι προδείξας ὅτι οὐδὲν ἔχει μέγεθος ἐκ τοῦ ἕκαστον τῶν πολλῶν ἑαυτῷ ταὐτὸν εἶναι καὶ ἕν.

[7] Cf. also Eudemus *apud* Simplicius, *In Phys.* 97.11–21 (partially repeated at 138.31–139.3). Eudemus traces the problems at issue at *Phys* 1.2, 185b25–186a3 back to Zeno.

To avoid this consequence, the more recent thinkers proposed some linguistic reforms. Some of them, like the sophist Lycophron, 'took away the "is"'. It seems that Lycophron proscribed the use of the word 'is' (*esti*) in sentences such as 'Socrates is white', and recommended using instead the verb-free formulation 'Socrates white'.[8] Others, whom Aristotle does not name,[9] 'refashioned their speech', replacing the copula-plus-predicate phrase 'is white' (*leukos esti*) with the single verb 'has whitened' (*leleukōtai*).[10]

These two reforms have a similar effect: they allow us to escape the conclusion that the one is many, by giving us other ways of expressing the claims that Socrates has the properties of whiteness, musicality, and so on. If we can express these claims without actually saying that Socrates '*is* white' and '*is* musical', then it seems that we can avoid the problematic result that one thing *is* many things.

In Aristotle's view, the more recent thinkers were led to these reforms because they mistakenly supposed 'that one or being is said in only one way' (185b31–2). Here he seems to be suggesting two possible diagnoses of their problem. The first is that they assumed that *one* is said in a single way. This assumption excludes the possibility that a thing is simultaneously both one (in one way) and *not* one (in another way). And so it excludes the possibility that something is

---

[8] Cf. Simplicius, *In Phys.* 91.13–14: 'Lycophron would take away the "is" from predications, saying "Socrates white".' Eudemus (*apud* Simplicius, *In Phys.* 97.21–4) suggests that Lycophron nonetheless allowed complete uses of 'is': 'Now in predications, some people, among them Lycophron, did not think one should attach the "is". Instead they would say "a human is", but did not say "a human is white".'

[9] Philoponus (*In Phys.* 49.18–19) suggests Menedemus of Eretria as an example of someone who refashioned their speech in this way, but Menedemus' dates make it impossible that Aristotle could have been thinking of him. Modern commentators have suggested Stilpo and Antisthenes as other possible candidates (see e.g. Ross 1936, 469). Stilpo was certainly interested in the predication problem, but the solution he adopted is different (see Plutarch, *Col.* 1119c–20b). In any case, as a younger contemporary of Aristotle's he is unlikely to be among the 'the more recent of the early thinkers'. As for Antisthenes, while he too may have been interested in this problem, there is no evidence that he recommended a linguistic reform of the sort that Aristotle describes here. In short, we do not know who these anonymous 'others' were.

[10] I translate λελεύκωται as 'has whitened' rather than 'has been whitened' so as to avoid using a form of 'to be'.

simultaneously both one and many. The second diagnosis is that the more recent thinkers assumed that *being* is said in a single way. The thought here seems to be that their problem arises from their assimilating all statements of the form '*X* is *F*' to statements of identity.[11] If Socrates is (identical to) human, is (identical to) white, and is (identical to) musical, then one thing is identical to many different things, which is absurd.

Aristotle himself rejects both these assumptions, and so avoids the more recent thinkers' problem without the need for their linguistic reforms. Statements of the form '*X* is *F*' are not always statements of identity; so we can say that Socrates both 'is white' and 'is musical' without committing ourselves to the absurd claim that one thing is identical to many different things. These statements do of course entail that one thing, Socrates, is also many insofar as he has many different properties (white and musical). But this is not problematic, because one and many are said in many ways. So there is no problem with Socrates' being both one and many at the same time: he is one insofar as he is a single, unified object, and many insofar as he has many properties,[12] and these ways of being one and many are not incompatible with one another.

Before we move on to consider the more recent thinkers' second problem, it is worth pointing out that the first problem bears a very close resemblance to a problem described in a well-known passage of Plato's *Sophist*:

ELEATIC VISITOR Now, let's say in exactly what way we on each occasion call this same thing by many names.

THEAETETUS What do you mean? Give me an example.

ELEATIC VISITOR We speak of a human being, I presume, applying many names to him, ascribing to him colours, shapes, sizes, vices, and virtues; in all

---

[11] Cf. Code 1976, 168.

[12] Socrates is 'many in account' ($\pi o\lambda\lambda\grave{\alpha}\ \lambda\acute{o}\gamma\omega$), where this means that he has many properties (white, musical, and so on) the definitional accounts of which are non-identical. This use of '*n* in account' should be distinguished from the related use at *Phys.* 1.2, 185b19–20.

these cases and countless others, not only do we say that he is a human, but we also say that he is good and infinitely many other things; and with regard to other things, by the same account, supposing each in this way to be one we in turn call it many and speak of it with many names.

THEAETETUS That's true.

ELEATIC VISITOR From this, I think, we've prepared a feast for the young and for the late learners among the old, because it's easy for anyone immediately to object that it is impossible for the many to be one and the one many, and presumably they delight in not letting us call a human good, but [only] the good good and the human human. I imagine, Theaetetus, that you often meet people enthusiastic for such things, sometimes rather old men, who because of their intellectual poverty are amazed at such things and think themselves to have discovered in this very thing something extremely wise.

(251a5–c6)

Much has been written about who these 'late learners' might be, and about how to understand their problem and their proposed solution to it.[13] For our purposes, it is important just to note that, while the late learners and the 'more recent' thinkers of *Physics* 1.2 appear to be concerned with the same problem, the two groups should not be identified with one another. Their solutions to the problem are very different.

Like the more recent thinkers, the late learners are worried by a problem that arises from our everyday practice of ascribing properties to things. If our claims that Socrates 'is human', 'is white', and 'is musical' are all true, then it seems that one thing (Socrates) is many things (human, white, and musical). But, unlike the more recent thinkers, the late learners do not try to come up with non-paradoxical ways of expressing these predicative claims. Rather, they respond by taking the extraordinary step of denying that one thing can have many properties (*Soph.* 252b8–c9). The problem thus leads them to embrace a radically counter-intuitive metaphysics.[14] The more

---

[13] Two helpful overviews of the interpretative options are Brown 2008, 440–3 and Crivelli 2012, 103–9.

[14] Cf. Harte 2002, 169–70. Harte emphasizes that the late learners' linguistic proscriptions are a consequence of their radical metaphysics.

recent thinkers, by contrast, want to preserve the ordinary view that individual objects each have many properties, and it is this that motivates their linguistic reforms.

3.3 The Whole–Parts Problem

The more recent thinkers were also troubled by a second problem of one and many: that wholes of parts appear to be both one and many at the same time. Take Socrates again: he appears to be both one thing (a single human being) and many different things (his head, torso, arms, and legs). So, once again, the one appears to be many, which seems impossible.[15]

Aristotle says that the more recent thinkers were unable to find a solution to this second problem, and so were here forced to accept the unwelcome (to them) result that the one is many. At first sight it might seem strange that, despite having a solution to the first problem, the more recent thinkers were at a loss when it came to the second. In particular, it might seem strange that they did not pursue their strategy of linguistic reform. Surely they could have refused to say that Socrates 'is' his many parts, and chosen to say instead that he 'consists of' his many parts? With this minor linguistic modification it seems that they could have avoided having to say that the same thing 'is' both one and many.

I suspect that the reason the more recent thinkers did not pursue this linguistic strategy is that they assumed that a whole is identical to its parts.[16] Given this assumption, wholes of parts are genuinely puzzling entities.[17] If a whole and its parts are identical, then anything that is true of the parts should also be true of the whole, and vice versa. But there are many parts (and not just one), and there is just

---

[15] For this problem, cf. Plato, *Parm.* 129c4–d6 and *Phil.* 14d4–e4.

[16] To be clear, this is an assumption about the relation between a whole and *all of its parts*, and not about the relation between a whole and *one of its parts*. (The latter relation was at issue back at 185b11–16: see section 2.3.2.)

[17] See Harte 2002, 26–32.

one whole (and not many). It is genuinely puzzling that some thing or things should have both these properties (*being many and not just one; being just one and not many*) at the same time.

If the more recent thinkers were making this identity assumption, it is not surprising that they found the second problem much harder to deal with than the first. The strategy of linguistic reform would this time be ineffective. It is not enough merely to revise how we speak. As long as the identity assumption goes unquestioned, the difficulty will remain: a whole of parts seems to be one thing that is identical to many things, and this is paradoxical.

In the final lines of the passage Aristotle hints at a way of addressing the whole-parts problem:

> But here [*sc*. with regard to the whole and the parts] they were already in difficulty, and they conceded that the one is many, as though it were not possible for the same thing to be both one and many—although not the opposites. For the one is both potentially and actually.   (185b34–186a3)

These lines are highly elliptical, but the train of thought seems to be the following. The more recent thinkers were unable to solve the whole-parts problem, and so here they conceded that the one is many. They regarded this consequence—'the one is many'—as unwelcome, because they assumed that it is impossible for the same thing to be both one and many at the same time. But in fact, Aristotle suggests, this *is* possible, so long as it is not the case that the thing in question is one and many in opposed ways. For there are different ways of being one (and, accordingly, different ways of being many): for example, *being potentially one* is different from *being actually one*.

Aristotle does not explain how the distinction between actuality and potentiality is meant to help with the whole-parts problem, but it is relatively clear how this is supposed to go. In general, a thing can be actually *F* and potentially un-*F* at the same time: a cup of tea may simultaneously be actually hot and potentially cold. Similarly with regard to one and many: a thing may simultaneously be actually one and potentially many. Socrates, for instance, is actually one insofar as he is a single human being, but he is also potentially many insofar as he has the potential to be decomposed into his various parts. Since these ways of being one and many are not opposed to one another, there is no difficulty in our saying that Socrates has both these properties at once.

Does Aristotle want to say that the distinction between actuality and potentiality is all we need to solve the whole–parts problem? This would be a bold, not to say dubious, claim. While it may perhaps be true of some wholes that they are actually one and merely potentially many, it is doubtful that this is true in general. Take an army. The whole army is actually one. But it is not the case that the parts—the many soldiers—exist in the army merely potentially; they actually exist, and are actually many.[18] Thus the army would appear to be both actually one and actually many. The distinction between actuality and potentiality will be of no help in explaining how this is possible. So, while the distinction may be used to explain how *some* wholes can be both one and many, it cannot be used to explain how *all* wholes can be both one and many.

Fortunately we need not take Aristotle to be making the bold (and dubious) claim. We can take his point to be simply that the whole–parts problem can be addressed by distinguishing different ways of being one and many. The actual–potential distinction is one example of such a distinction, but this is not to say that it will serve in all cases.

How, then, would Aristotle solve the problem in the case of the army? Presumably he would start by denying that the one army is identical to the many soldiers. (This can be seen from the fact that the soldiers can all continue to exist even when the army is disbanded: a similar point is made in *Metaph. Z* 17, 1041b12–16.) The one army is 'many', then, not insofar as it is identical to the many soldiers—a claim that would be genuinely problematic—but insofar as it is composed of the many soldiers, where composition is not identity. The army's being many in this way is compatible with its also being

---

[18] Aristotle himself accepts that some wholes contain parts that exist actually and not merely potentially: see *Metaph. Δ* 26, 1023b32–4.

one, because it is one not by its being composed of one thing, but by its being a unified whole of parts.

3.4 The Point of the Excursus

What is the point of discussing these post-Eleatic thinkers and their struggles with these problems of one and many? Certainly the discussion is prompted by Aristotle's examination of the Eleatics—the worry about being one and many at the same time is Eleatic in origin. Nevertheless, the passage does not seem to contribute directly to Aristotle's refutation of Eleatic monism. Why, then, does he include it? It seems likely that he is looking ahead again to the theory of principles that he will argue for later in the book. That theory presupposes that it is possible for something to be both one and many at the same time. The underlying substratum is one in number but many in form or account,[19] and the generated natural substance is one insofar as it is a single unified object, but also many insofar as it is a composite of the substratum and the form. By taking the opportunity to address the persistent worry that being one is incompatible with being many—a worry which arises with the Eleatics, but which continues to trouble these 'more recent' thinkers—Aristotle is thus removing a potential obstacle to his own theory of principles.

[19] See *Phys.* 1.7, 190a14–17 and 190b23–4.

4

Criticisms of Melissus' Argument

4.1 Introduction

In *Physics* 1.3 Aristotle addresses the Eleatics' arguments for monism. He starts by repeating his earlier claim that both Parmenides and Melissus reason eristically (*Phys.* 1.3, 186a6–7; cf. 1.2, 185a8–12).[1] He then proceeds to give objections first to Melissus' argument (186a10–22) and then to Parmenides' (186a22–186b35). The long and complex critique of Parmenides' argument will be the subject of Chapters 5 and 6. The present chapter considers the shorter and simpler critique of Melissus.

Aristotle has already told us, in no uncertain terms, what he thinks of Melissus' argument: it 'is crude and contains no difficulty—grant him one absurdity and the others follow: this is not very hard' (185a10–12). But what exactly does Aristotle object to? We now get some more detailed criticisms, as follows:

That Melissus argues fallaciously is clear. (i) For, in assuming that everything which has come to be has a beginning, he thinks he has also assumed that that which has *not* come to be *does not* have a beginning. (ii) Next, this is also

---

[1] When he says that the Eleatic arguments are 'eristical', I take it that he simply means that they are unsound in various ways (see the explanation given at 185a9–10: 'For they assume falsehoods, and are not deductive'; cf. Rossi 2017, 221). On eristical arguments in general, see *Top.* 1.1, 100b23–5; *SE* 2, 165b7–8. To label an argument 'eristical' is not necessarily to impugn the motives of the arguer. Contrast this with labelling a *person* 'eristical': *SE* 11, 171b25–6.

absurd, that there is a beginning of everything—of the thing and not [only] of the time, and not [only] of simple coming to be but also of alteration, as though no change takes place all at once. (iii) Next, why is it unmoving, if it is one? For just as even the part, being one—for example, this water—moves within itself, why not the universe too? (iv) Next, why could there not be alteration? (v) But nor indeed is it possible for it to be one in form, except with regard to what it is from [sc. the matter]. And even some of the natural philosophers say that it is one in this way, although not in that way. For human is different from horse in form, and the contraries [are different in form] from one another.   (186a10–22)

I have distinguished five different points here. Aristotle begins with two objections to Melissus' argument for monism, and then gives two objections to his arguments against the possibility of change. (This is despite the fact that the official topic of discussion is the Eleatic case for monism: see 186a4–6.) The function of Aristotle's fifth point is less clear, since *prima facie* it does not seem to target any of Melissus' arguments.

4.2 Overview of Melissus' Argument for Monism

In order to understand Aristotle's criticisms in this passage, we should start by thinking about the structure of Melissus' argument. Our sources suggest that Melissus' main argument for monism proceeded in four stages:[2]

Stage 1: What is is. It seems that Melissus started his treatise with an argument that there *is* such a thing as what is: 'If there is nothing, what could be said about it as though it were something?'[3] (Simplicius, *In Phys.* 103.15–16) The thought here is Parmenidean. It would be

---

[2] Cf. Harriman, forthcoming, for a detailed reconstruction of Melissus' argument. Supplementary considerations in favour of monism are given in B 8; see Makin 2005 for discussion.

[3] *Εἰ μὲν μηδὲν ἔστι, περὶ τούτου τί ἂν λέγοιτο ὡς ὄντος τινός;* Whether the sentence is genuinely Melissan has been doubted, but for arguments in favour of its authenticity see Harriman 2015, 23–5.

impossible to speak about what is if it did not exist to be spoken about. But we obviously can speak about it—we are doing so now. Therefore, it exists.

Stage 2: What is is ungenerated (and indestructible). Melissus then argued that what is cannot come into existence (and similarly cannot be destroyed). It always existed and always will exist, without changing its identity:

It always was whatever it was and always will be.[4] For if it came to be, it must have been nothing before it came to be. So, if it was nothing, in no way could anything come to be from nothing.[5]   (B 1)

Stage 3: What is is unlimited in extent. From the claim that what is is ungenerated, Melissus infers that it is unlimited. The details of this stage of the argument are difficult, but the basic idea is that since what is did not come to be (as was argued in Stage 2), it follows that it does not have a 'beginning' (*archē*) or an 'end' (*teleutē*). And since it does not have a beginning or an end, it is unlimited. In Melissus' own words:

So, since it did not come to be, it is and always was and always will be, and it has no beginning or end, but is unlimited. For if it came to be, it would have a beginning (for it would have started coming to be at some time) and an end (for it would have ceased coming to be at some time);[6] but since it did not begin or end, and always was and always will be,[7] it has neither a beginning nor an end. For it is impossible for what is not all to be always.[8]   (B 2)

---

⁴ For this construal, see Kirk et al. 1983, 393.

⁵ ἀεὶ ἦν ὅ τι ἦν καὶ ἀεὶ ἔσται· εἰ γὰρ ἐγένετο, ἀναγκαῖόν ἐστι πρὶν γενέσθαι εἶναι μηδέν· εἰ τοίνυν μηδὲν ἦν, οὐδαμὰ ἂν γένοιτο οὐδὲν ἐκ μηδενός.

⁶ Reading the better attested γινόμενον instead of DK's γενόμενον in the two parenthetical clauses.

⁷ Following Reale (1970, 372–3), I reject Kranz's supplement of καί before οὐκ ἔχει ἀρχήν.

⁸ ὅτε τοίνυν οὐκ ἐγένετο, ἔστι τε καὶ ἀεὶ ἦν καὶ ἀεὶ ἔσται καὶ ἀρχὴν οὐκ ἔχει οὐδὲ τελευτήν, ἀλλ' ἄπειρόν ἐστιν. εἰ μὲν γὰρ ἐγένετο, ἀρχὴν ἂν εἶχεν (ἤρξατο γὰρ ἄν ποτε γινόμενον) καὶ τελευτήν (ἐτελεύτησε γὰρ ἄν ποτε γινόμενον)· ὅτε δὲ μήτε ἤρξατο μήτε ἐτελεύτησεν, ἀεί τε ἦν καὶ ἀεὶ ἔσται, οὐκ ἔχει ἀρχὴν οὐδὲ τελευτήν· οὐ γὰρ ἀεὶ εἶναι ἀνυστόν, ὅ τι μὴ πᾶν ἐστι. Cf. also B 4.

The sense of 'unlimited' here is unspecified, but the word seems likely to connote being spatially extended without limit.[9] This interpretation is supported by a further fragment in which Melissus confirms that he takes what is to be spatially infinite: 'But just as it is always, so it must always be unlimited *in magnitude*' (B 3).[10]

The notions of 'beginning' (*archē*) and 'end' (*teleutē*) in B 2 are controversial. It is sometimes thought that Melissus means to refer to the temporal starting point and temporal end point of a thing's existence. Yet this fails to make sense of the reason he gives for why, if what is had come to be, it would have an end: 'it would have ceased coming to be at some time'. The fact that something has ceased *coming to be* tells us nothing about whether or not it has an 'end' in the sense of a temporal end point of its existence. Why should it not go on existing forever?

Melissus' explanation makes better sense if by 'end' he is referring to the final spatial part of a thing to have come into existence. Think about the process whereby a house comes into existence. If the house has come to be, then it must have *ceased* coming to be at some time. This in turn suggests that it has a last spatial part—a spatial part that was added last of all (perhaps: the last tile that was added to the roof). Similarly, the house must have *started* coming to be at some time. This suggests that it has a 'beginning' in the sense of a first spatial part—a spatial part that was present before all the others (such as the first foundation stone, laid at the start of the building process). Melissus' argument for unlimitedness, on this reading, is that an ungenerated entity will lack such a 'beginning' and such an 'end'—a first spatial part and a last spatial part—and will consequently be spatially infinite.

---

[9] As opposed to meaning 'temporally unlimited', as suggested by Burnet (1930, 325). For arguments in favour of the spatial interpretation, see Ross 1936, 471–2 and Kirk et al. 1983, 394.

[10] ἀλλ' ὥσπερ ἔστιν ἀεί, οὕτω καὶ τὸ μέγεθος ἄπειρον ἀεὶ χρὴ εἶναι.

Stage 4: What is is one. Finally, Melissus infers that since what is is unlimited in extent, there can only be room for one thing:

For if it were [*sc.* if it were unlimited],[11] it would be one. For if it were two, they could not be unlimited, but would have limits in relation to one another.[12]   (B 6)

4.3 A Logical Fallacy?

Aristotle says nothing in *Physics* 1.3 about Stages 1, 2, and 4 of Melissus' argument, although this should not be taken to imply that he accepts the reasoning of these stages.[13] Instead, his criticisms focus on Stage 3. The first, and best known, is a criticism of a move Melissus allegedly makes in B 2, in his argument for the conclusion that what is has no beginning:

For, in assuming that everything which has come to be has a beginning, he thinks he has also assumed that that which has *not* come to be *does not* have a beginning.   (186a11–13)

Aristotle takes Melissus to be arguing as follows:

(1) Everything that has come to be has a beginning.
(2) So, whatever has *not* come to be does *not* have a beginning. (From (1).)
(3) What is has not come to be.
(4) So, what is does not have a beginning. (From (2) and (3).)

The inference from (1) to (2) is invalid, supposedly ruining Melissus' argument for the claim that what is has no beginning, and (therefore) ruining his argument for the claim that it is unlimited in extent.[14]

---

[11] Simplicius' quotation at *In Cael.* 557.16–17 lacks the word 'unlimited', but Melissus' point is evidently that the unlimitedness of what is entails its uniqueness.

[12] εἰ γὰρ εἴη, ἓν εἴη ἄν· εἰ γὰρ δύο εἴη, οὐκ ἂν δύναιτο ἄπειρα εἶναι, ἀλλ' ἔχοι ἂν πείρατα πρὸς ἄλληλα. Cf. also B 5.

[13] He certainly rejects Melissus' argument against the possibility of generation, which is central to Stage 2.

[14] Aristotle does not explicitly object to Melissus' argument for the claim that what is has no end, but this is presumably to avoid unnecessary repetition. The same point would apply here too.

Aristotle makes essentially the same objection in the *Sophistical Refutations*, where Melissus' argument for unlimitedness appears as an example of 'the refutation that depends on the consequent':

for example, Melissus' argument that the universe is unlimited [assumes] that the universe is ungenerated (for nothing could have come to be from what is not), and that what has come to be has come to be from a beginning. If, therefore, it has not come to be, the universe does not have a beginning, so that it is unlimited. But this does not necessarily follow. For it is not the case that if everything that has come to be has a beginning, then if something has a beginning, it has come to be—just as it is not the case that if the feverish person is hot, then it is necessary for the hot person to be feverish.[15]

(*SE* 5, 167b13–20)

Does Melissus really make the fallacious move from (1) to (2)? It is true that, in B 2, Melissus claims that 'if it came to be, it would have a beginning', and then infers from the fact that it did not come to be that it has no beginning. This certainly *seems* fallacious. However, a more charitable interpretation would be that Melissus is in fact relying on the unstated premise that a thing has a beginning only if it comes to be. If by the 'beginning' of *X* Melissus means the first spatial part of *X* that came into existence, this premise is obviously true, and so he may not have felt the need to state it explicitly. In that case Aristotle's first criticism of Melissus, while understandable, would nonetheless miss the mark.[16]

4.4 Becoming without a Beginning

Aristotle's second criticism again targets Stage 3 of Melissus' deduction. The first criticism was that it is a mistake to infer from

---

[15] οἷον ὁ Μελίσσου λόγος ὅτι ἄπειρον τὸ ἅπαν, λαβὼν τὸ μὲν ἅπαν ἀγένητον (ἐκ γὰρ μὴ ὄντος οὐδὲν ἂν γενέσθαι), τὸ δὲ γενόμενον ἐξ ἀρχῆς γενέσθαι· εἰ μὴ οὖν γέγονεν, ἀρχὴν οὐκ ἔχειν τὸ πᾶν, ὥστ' ἄπειρον. οὐκ ἀνάγκη δὲ τοῦτο συμβαίνειν· οὐ γὰρ εἰ τὸ γενόμενον ἅπαν ἀρχὴν ἔχει, καὶ εἴ τι ἀρχὴν ἔχει, γέγονεν, ὥσπερ οὐδ' εἰ ὁ πυρέττων θερμός, καὶ τὸν θερμὸν ἀνάγκη πυρέττειν. Cf. also *SE* 6, 168b35–40, and 28, 181a27–30.
[16] For a further suggestion about how to exculpate Melissus, see Sedley 1999, 126–7.

(1) Everything that has come to be has a beginning,

that

(2) Whatever has *not* come to be does *not* have a beginning.

The second criticism now targets claim (1) itself. This claim, Aristotle tells us, is absurd:[17]

> Next, this is also absurd, that there is a beginning of everything [*sc.* that has come to be]—of the thing and not [only] of the time, and not [only] of simple coming to be but also of alteration, as though no change takes place all at once. (186a13–16)

As Ross points out, it seems that what Aristotle is really claiming to be absurd here is not that there is a beginning of *everything*, but rather that there is a beginning of *everything that has come to be*.[18] After all, Melissus does not accept that everything has a beginning, but he does think that, for any *X*, if *X* has come to be, *then X* has a beginning. (This is explicit at B 2: 'For if it came to be, it would have a beginning'.)

Aristotle makes two points against (1), which I paraphrase as follows:

(*a*) It is absurd to claim that, in the case of everything that has come to be, there is a beginning 'of the thing' as well as a beginning of the time.

(*b*) It is absurd to say that there is a beginning in all cases of coming to be—in cases of alteration as well as in cases of coming to be *simpliciter*.

The first point is that there are different senses of 'beginning', and while it may be true that everything that has come to be has a *temporal* beginning (a beginning 'of the time', a first moment at which it begins to exist), it is not true that there is always a beginning 'of the thing'. I take it that by 'beginning of the thing', Aristotle is

---

[17] It seems clear that Aristotle is speaking here in his own voice, *pace* Gershenson and Greenberg (1961, 7).

[18] Ross 1936, 471.

referring to a thing's *spatial* beginning, the first spatial part of it that comes to be.[19] So interpreted, his objection seems warranted. The fact that X came into existence at a certain time does not necessarily mean that there is some spatial part of X which was present before all the others, like the first foundation stone in the case of the house. Think of using your hands to mould a sphere out of a lump of clay. Suppose you pick up the lump of clay and start rolling it between your palms, stopping when it has become spherical. A clay sphere has come into existence, and it started coming into existence when you started moulding the clay. But there is no reason to think that there must be some one part of the sphere that is its spatial 'beginning', comparable to the first foundation stone. It seems perfectly reasonable to think that multiple parts of the sphere came into being at the same time.[20]

Aristotle's second point appears to be that Melissus' premise ('everything that has come to be has a beginning') is even less plausible in the case of alteration than it is in the case of coming to be *simpliciter* ('simple coming to be').[21] This is because it is obvious that there are cases of alteration where the change occurs 'all at once'.

In order to explain what Aristotle means by 'all at once' (*athroa*), commentators sometimes turn to *Physics* 8.3, 253b25–6, where he mentions freezing as an example of *athroa* alteration. However, there is disagreement as to whether he means that freezing is an *instantaneous* change, or whether he means that it is a change that *all* of the changing subject undergoes *together*. On the first interpretation, the point is that freezing happens in an instant; it is to be distinguished from a process such as making custard in saucepan, where the ingredients thicken over a period of time, gradually getting thicker

---

[19] The objection therefore implies that Aristotle favours a spatial reading of Melissus' language of 'beginning' and 'end'.

[20] This example presents a serious difficulty for Melissus' argument. Melissus wants to move from the claim that X lacks a spatial beginning and a spatial end to the claim that X is spatially unlimited. The clay sphere shows that the inference is mistaken.

[21] Roughly speaking, a thing comes to be *simpliciter* when it goes from not existing to existing. This should be distinguished from the various types of coming to be *F* (alteration, growth, diminution, locomotion). Cf. *GC* 1.3, 317a32–b5.

and thicker until finally they are the right consistency. Water does not behave like this when it freezes—it does not get thicker and thicker until finally it is ice; rather the transition from water to ice happens in an instant.[22] On the second interpretation, Aristotle means that freezing is (at least in some cases) a change that every part of a body of water undergoes simultaneously, as opposed to one part of it at a time. While both interpretations seem possible, the latter is suggested by a sentence from *De Sensu* 6:

> For it is possible for a thing to alter all at once [*athroon*], and not the one half of it first; for example, it is possible for all of the water [i.e. of some body of water] to freeze simultaneously.[23]   (447a1–3)

Going back to the criticism of Melissus, then, I take Aristotle's point to be that there are obviously cases in which a subject of alteration undergoes the change *as a whole*, as opposed to first one spatial part undergoing it, then another, then another, and so on. In other words, there are obviously cases of alteration in which there is no spatial beginning.

Why should Aristotle think that this fact is relevant to Melissus' argument for monism? This should strike us as puzzling. As I noted above, Aristotle takes Melissus to be arguing as follows:

(1) Everything that has come to be has a (spatial) beginning.
(2) So, whatever has *not* come to be does *not* have a (spatial) beginning. (From (1).)
(3) What is has not come to be.
(4) So, what is does not have a (spatial) beginning. (From (2) and (3).)

If this argument works,[24] it works even if the sense of 'coming to be' is restricted to coming to be *simpliciter*—the coming into existence

---

[22] Of course, the process of getting colder—necessary for the freezing to take place—is not instantaneous; rather, what is instantaneous is the freezing itself, the change from being water to being ice.

[23] ἐνδέχεται γὰρ ἀθρόον ἀλλοιοῦσθαι, καὶ μὴ τὸ ἥμισυ πρότερον, οἷον τὸ ὕδωρ ἅμα πᾶν πήγνυσθαι.

[24] Which of course it does not, given the fallacious inference from (1) to (2).

of a new entity. This suggests that Melissus does not need to say that (1) is also true for other kinds of coming to be, such as alteration. And if that is right, Aristotle's present objection (that in certain cases of alteration there is no spatial beginning) would seem to be beside the point.

Responding to this worry, Ross suggests that 'Melissus evidently held a view opposed to this [*sc.* to the view that alteration can take place all at once]'.[25] But there is no evidence of this in the sources. I therefore want to make an alternative proposal as to what Aristotle might have in mind. After giving his argument for monism, Melissus proceeds to deny that the universe is susceptible to any kind of change, including motion, rearrangement, and alteration. His argument against the possibility of alteration in B 7.2 relies on the following claim:

For if it alters, it is necessary that what is is not alike, but what was before perishes, and what is not comes to be.[26]

Thus Melissus takes alteration to involve coming to be and ceasing to be *simpliciter*. For example, when an apple turns from green to red, he wants us to understand this as the coming to be *simpliciter* of what previously was not (the red apple, say), and the ceasing to be *simpliciter* of what once was (the green apple, say).[27]

But this gives rise to a problem. If Melissus holds that all cases of alteration involve coming to be and ceasing to be *simpliciter, and* he concedes that there are cases of alteration in which there is no spatial beginning, then it seems that he must *also* concede that there are cases of coming to be *simpliciter* in which there is no spatial beginning. But if he concedes this, then he cannot consistently maintain premise

[25] Ross 1936, 471.

[26] εἰ γὰρ ἑτεροιοῦται, ἀνάγκη τὸ ἐὸν μὴ ὁμοῖον εἶναι, ἀλλὰ ἀπόλλυσθαι τὸ πρόσθεν ἐόν, τὸ δὲ οὐκ ἐὸν γίνεσθαι.

[27] Cf. also the following argument against rearrangement in B 7.3: 'But nor is it possible for it to be rearranged. For the arrangement that was before does not perish; nor does the arrangement that is not come to be' (ἀλλ' οὐδὲ μετακοσμηθῆναι ἀνυστόν· ὁ γὰρ κόσμος ὁ πρόσθεν ἐὼν οὐκ ἀπόλλυται οὔτε ὁ μὴ ἐὼν γίνεται). A similar point is made again at B 8.6.

(1) in his argument for the claim that what is lacks a beginning, even when that premise is understood as a claim only about coming to be *simpliciter*. If, on the other hand, he denies that alteration involves coming to be and ceasing to be *simpliciter*, this would undermine his argument that what is does not alter.

This, I suggest, is the explanation of why Aristotle makes the seemingly incongruous point about alteration. Melissus effectively faces a dilemma. Either he continues to understand alteration as involving coming to be and ceasing to be *simpliciter*, in which case he must abandon premise (1) in his argument that what is lacks a beginning. Or else he denies that alteration involves coming and ceasing to be *simpliciter*, in which case he must withdraw his argument against the possibility of alteration.

4.5 The Possibility of Motion

In the next two criticisms, in a departure from his stated topic (the criticism of the Eleatics' arguments for monism), Aristotle now directly challenges Melissus' inference from monism to the impossibility of change.

In the third criticism,[28] Aristotle objects to the idea that monism entails the impossibility of motion. At least in the surviving fragments, Melissus does not explicitly say that monism has this consequence. But it nonetheless seems plausible that he takes monism to rule out the possibility of what we might call 'internal' motion, the locomotion of parts of a thing relative to its other parts. To undergo internal motion is to undergo rearrangement, and in B 7 Melissus argues that monism excludes the possibility of rearrangement:

---

[28] Bicknell (1964, 109) suggests that the third criticism in the sequence at 186a10–22 is a criticism of Parmenides and not of Melissus. While I do think that this is one of the criticisms that Aristotle regards as *also* applying to Parmenides, it is hard to believe that it is not supposed to apply to Melissus at all, given its position in the sequence.

And neither could it perish, become larger, be rearranged, or suffer pain or grief. For if it underwent any of these, it would no longer be one.[29]   (B 7.2)

Aristotle questions the idea that the oneness of what is entails that it cannot undergo internal motion or rearrangement:

Next, why is it unmoving, if it is one? For just as even the part, being one— for example, this water—moves within itself, why not the universe too?

(186a16–18)

A single body of water may be subject to internal motion, even though it is (in Aristotle's view) one thing—a single unbroken plenum.

Aristotle makes a similar sort of objection to Melissus in the discussion of void in *Physics* 4.6–9. For Melissus, if a thing is to move from position *A* to position *B*, position *B* must be empty. But there is no such thing as void, since 'the empty [or: void] is nothing', and 'what is nothing could not be' (B 7.7).[30] Aristotle's response is that locomotion does not in fact require the existence of empty space, but can occur in a plenum by virtue of 'mutual replacement' (*antiperistasis*), as happens in the case of liquids:

But nor even [is void necessary] for change of place. For it is possible for things to make way for each other simultaneously, though there is no separate interval beyond the moving bodies. And this is clear also in the rotations of continuous things, just as in the rotations of liquids.[31]

(*Phys.* 4.7, 214a28–32)

Hence Melissus is wrong to think that if a thing is to move from position *A* to position *B*, position *B* must first be empty. It is possible for a thing to move from *A* to *B* as long as the thing now occupying *B*

---

[29] καὶ οὔτ᾽ ἂν ἀπόλοιτο οὔτε μεῖζον γίνοιτο οὔτε μετακοσμέοιτο οὔτε ἀλγεῖ οὔτε ἀνιᾶται· εἰ γάρ τι τούτων πάσχοι, οὐκ ἂν ἔτι ἓν εἴη.

[30] τὸ γὰρ κενεὸν οὐδέν ἐστιν· οὐκ ἂν οὖν εἴη τό γε μηδέν. Aristotle refers to this argument against motion at *Phys.* 4.6, 213b13–14: 'If it undergoes motion, it is necessary for there to be void, he [*sc.* Melissus] says, but the void is not among the things that are' (εἰ γὰρ κινήσεται, ἀνάγκη εἶναι, φησί, κενόν, τὸ δὲ κενὸν οὐ τῶν ὄντων). Cf. also *GC* 1.8, 325a3–5.

[31] ἀλλὰ δὴ οὐδὲ τὴν κατὰ τόπον κίνησιν· ἅμα γὰρ ἐνδέχεται ὑπεξιέναι ἀλλήλοις, οὐδενὸς ὄντος διαστήματος χωριστοῦ παρὰ τὰ σώματα τὰ κινούμενα. καὶ τοῦτο δῆλον καὶ ἐν ταῖς τῶν συνεχῶν δίναις, ὥσπερ καὶ ἐν ταῖς τῶν ὑγρῶν.

simultaneously moves to some other position, *C*, and the thing now at *C* moves to some other position, *D*, and so on, with the last thing in the sequence moving into position *A*.[32] Aristotle's claim is that all locomotion can be explained in this way, on the model of liquids, without the need for void. So, even if Melissus is correct to think that the universe is an unbroken plenum, it does not follow from this that it cannot be subject to internal motion.

4.6 The Possibility of Alteration

After challenging Melissus' inference from monism to the impossibility of motion, Aristotle next (at *Phys.* 1.3, 186a18) challenges his denial of alteration: 'Next, why could there not be alteration?' It seems plausible that, although Aristotle does not make this explicit, he is here challenging the inference *from monism* to the impossibility of alteration. In other words: 'Why could there not be alteration, *if what is is one?*' (Melissus apparently took his monism to rule out all kinds of change: see B 7.2 and *MXG* 1, 974a20.)

Aristotle does not explain why he takes Melissus' rejection of alteration to be unfounded. But once again the example of water seems relevant. We might think of a body of water going from being hot to being cold. The water loses one property and takes on another, but it seems to remain a single thing throughout the change. So if a body of water can undergo alteration without sacrificing its unity, it is unclear why the same should not be true of the entire universe.

4.7 One in Form

The final point that Aristotle makes against Melissus is that what is cannot be 'one in form':

But nor indeed is it possible for it [*sc.* what is] to be one in form, except with regard to what it is from [*sc.* the matter]. And even some of the natural

---

[32] Cf. Morison 2002, 23–4. On earlier appeals to mutual replacement, see Barnes 1982, 397–402.

philosophers say that it is one in this way, although not in that way. For human is different from horse in form, and the contraries [are different in form] from one another.   (186a19–22)

Reality cannot be one 'in form' except in the relatively weak sense of its all being composed of the same matter. This is consistent with a robust sort of pluralism, as is shown by the fact that certain natural philosophers (specifically, the material monists) take the universe to consist of a single basic matter—such as air or water—while still allowing that the world contains many different kinds of thing. For instance, they accept the existence of human beings and horses, which differ from one another in form, even though they are ultimately composed of the same basic stuff.[33]

What exactly is Aristotle up to here? A *prima facie* oddity about this final point is that it sounds more like a criticism of one aspect of Melissus' *position*—specifically, his view that the universe is uniform or 'all alike'—and less like a criticism of his *argument* for his position. As a result, we might be tempted to say that lines 186a19–22 do not in fact belong to Aristotle's critique of Melissus' argument at all. David Bostock has suggested that the lines are instead 'a kind of footnote, relating to something that was not said earlier at [*Phys.* 1.2] 185b5–9, where one might have expected a mention of things that are one "in form"'.[34]

---

[33] I take the explanatory sentence ('For human is different from horse in form...') to spell out the way in which the material monists' position is pluralistic: they hold that there are such things as human beings and horses, and these things differ in form, even though they are composed of the same matter. A different interpretation stands behind Ross's decision to put the preceding sentence (about the natural philosophers) in parentheses. On Ross's view, the explanatory sentence tells us why it is impossible for reality to be one in form. The problem is that this makes it look as though Aristotle is simply begging the question against Melissus. No one who holds that reality is one in form will be persuaded otherwise by the claim that humans and horses differ in form. They will simply deny that there *are* such things as humans and horses, or else deny that they are different in form. In the light of this it is preferable to take the explanatory sentence to explain the clause that it immediately follows.

[34] Bostock 2006, 107. Bostock also suggests that Aristotle is here 'apparently breaking off any dispute with what Melissus himself did say or might have said'. But while Melissus may not have actually said that reality is 'one in form', this is not an unreasonable characterization of part of his view. Melissus clearly affirms the

Ideally, however, it would be preferable to find an explanation of why Aristotle includes the point about oneness in form *here*, and not back in *Physics* 1.2. It is worth bearing in mind that he has just been criticizing some of Melissus' arguments against the possibility of change (186a16–18). His strategy, at least with regard to Melissus' denial of motion, was to provide an example of something that is *one* thing (as the Melissan One is one thing), but which is nonetheless capable of undergoing motion, such as a body of water. Now, this line of criticism might conceivably be challenged. It might be objected that, for Melissus, what is is one not only insofar as it is a single extended object, but also insofar as it is uniform or 'one in form'. In fact, we might say, it is the latter sort of unity that explains why the universe cannot change. If the universe were to change (for example, if it were to undergo rearrangement or alteration), it would no longer be one *in form*; the pre-change universe would differ in form from the post-change universe, and the universe would thus be non-uniform (diachronically speaking).[35]

If this is Melissus' reason for holding that the unity of the universe entails its immutability, then the fact that bodies of water (say) are apparently able to undergo various kinds of change might not seem to be much of a problem for him. We do of course think that bodies of water are able to undergo internal motion and alteration, but that is only because we are ordinarily prepared to allow that they can be diachronically non-uniform.

Aristotle's final point may be read as anticipating this potential objection. His response is that, *contra* Melissus, it is impossible for reality to be one in form.[36] Since this is impossible, Melissus cannot

---

uniformity of what is at B 7.1 ('So in this way it is eternal and unlimited and one *and all alike* [ὅμοιον πᾶν]'). Cf. *MXG* 1, 974a12–14.

[35] See B 7.2: 'For if it alters, it is necessary that what is is not alike' (εἰ γὰρ ἑτεροιοῦται, ἀνάγκη τὸ ἐὸν μὴ ὁμοῖον εἶναι).

[36] Or rather, this is impossible unless 'reality is one in form' is taken to mean that everything is ultimately composed of the same matter. (But when taken in this latter way, the claim clearly does not rule out the possibility of change, as we can see by considering the theories of the material monists.)

legitimately appeal to this kind of oneness in order to justify his claim that the universe does not change.

Aristotle does not here defend his claim that it is impossible for reality to be one in form. But this is presumably because he has already argued for this in *Physics* 1.2, where he rejected the possibility that reality is one *in account* (explicitly at 185b19–25, and—I argued—implicitly at 185a20–32). The notions of being one 'in form' and 'in account' are equivalent,[37] and so the same arguments will show that reality cannot be one in form.

4.8 Which Criticisms Also Apply to Parmenides?

The transition to the discussion of Parmenides' argument begins at 186a22: 'And the same sorts of arguments apply to Parmenides too,[38] even if certain other arguments are specific [to him].'

Which of Aristotle's objections to Melissus are also applicable to Parmenides? Presumably not the first two. These target Melissus' argument for the unlimitedness of the universe, an argument and a conclusion specific to Melissus alone. There is no evidence that Aristotle takes Parmenides to have committed a fallacy of the kind addressed in the first criticism, or to have falsely assumed that everything that has come to be has a spatial beginning. And there is nothing in the fragments to suggest that Parmenides argued in this way.

It is more likely that Aristotle has in mind the third and fourth objections: the objections to Melissus' arguments against the possibility of motion and alteration. My suggestion is that Aristotle thinks that comparable criticisms can be made of Parmenides' rejection of motion and alteration.

---

[37] Cf. *Phys.* 1.7, 190a16–17: 'For by "in form" and "in account" I mean the same thing' (τὸ γὰρ εἴδει λέγω καὶ λόγῳ ταὐτόν).

[38] The claim here is not that 'Parmenides is open to *all* these objections' (Charlton 1992, 5; italics mine). If Aristotle thought that all of his criticisms of Melissus also applied to Parmenides, it would be hard to explain why he should think that Melissus' argument is 'crude' whereas Parmenides' is not.

Parmenides is often read as putting forward two main arguments against the possibility of motion. The first is based on his prior rejection of generation and destruction:

> Further, unmoving in the limits of great bonds
> it is, unstarting and unceasing, since coming to be and perishing
> have wandered very far away, and true trust has driven them off.[39]
>
> (B 8.26–8)

Motion is impossible because (in some unspecified way) it involves generation and destruction, which have already been ruled out (at B 8.6–21). The second argument is this:

> And remaining the same in the same [place] by itself it lies
> and thus it remains steadfast there. For mighty Necessity
> holds it in the bonds of a limit, which confines it all around,
> because[40] it is not right for what is to be incomplete;
> for it is not lacking; if it were, it would lack everything.[41]
>
> (8.29–33)

These lines may be read as arguing that what is cannot undergo motion, because it is 'complete'. As David Sedley paraphrases the argument, 'filling all available space up to its boundary, [what is] has no room to move'.[42] If this is the correct reading, Parmenides' argument here prefigures Melissus' argument at B 7.7 from the non-existence of void to the impossibility of motion.

There is some evidence that Plato interpreted Parmenides' second argument in this way. At *Theaetetus* 179d2–181b7, Socrates and

---

[39] αὐτὰρ ἀκίνητον μεγάλων ἐν πείρασι δεσμῶν | ἔστιν ἄναρχον ἄπαυστον, ἐπεὶ γένεσις καὶ ὄλεθρος | τῆλε μάλ' ἐπλάγχθησαν, ἀπῶσε δὲ πίστις ἀληθής.

[40] Another possibility is that οὕνεκεν means 'therefore'. See e.g. the translation of Kirk et al. (1983, 252), who nevertheless note: ' "Because" is the more usual meaning in epic usage, and is preferred by many here.'

[41] τωὐτόν τ' ἐν τωὐτῷ τε μένον καθ' ἑαυτό τε κεῖται | χοὕτως ἔμπεδον αὖθι μένει· κρατερὴ γὰρ ἀνάγκη | πείρατος ἐν δεσμοῖσιν ἔχει, τό μιν ἀμφὶς ἐέργει, | οὕνεκεν οὐκ ἀτελεύτητον τὸ ἐὸν θέμις εἶναι· | ἔστι γὰρ οὐκ ἐπιδευές· [μὴ] ἐὸν δ' ἂν παντὸς ἐδεῖτο. I accept Bergk's excision of μή at 8.33, as do DK and most other editors.

[42] Sedley 1999, 119. For this reading cf. also Burnet 1930, 179–82; Bicknell 1967; Guthrie 1969, 34–8. For scepticism see Kirk and Stokes 1960.

Theodorus discuss a battle being fought between two opposing groups of philosophers. The first group are the Heraclitean flux theorists, who hold that the world is in constant motion. The second group are 'Melissuses and Parmenideses',[43] who according to Socrates hold that 'all things are one' and that this one thing 'stands still, itself within itself, *not having any room in which to move*' (180e3–4).[44] This characterization suggests that Plato saw the 'no room to move' argument as common to both Melissus and Parmenides.[45]

We might suppose that Aristotle likewise read Parmenides as putting forward the 'no room to move' argument. If he did, then we can understand why he should think that the kinds of criticisms he makes of Melissus can also be made of Parmenides. There seem to be other objects which, like the Parmenidean One, are 'complete' in the sense of filling all available space up to their outer limits, but which are nonetheless capable of undergoing motion and alteration. Think of a sealed jar, filled with water up to its lid. The water in the jar fills up all the available space, and yet it can still move around inside the jar, and be heated up and cooled down. So something similar to Aristotle's third and fourth criticisms of Melissus would seem to be applicable to Parmenides as well.

---

[43] The pluralizations poke fun, of course, at the monists.
[44] ὡς ἕν τε πάντα ἐστὶ καὶ ἕστηκεν αὐτὸ ἐν αὑτῷ οὐκ ἔχον χώραν ἐν ᾗ κινεῖται.
[45] Cf. Burnet 1930, 181 n. 1.

5

Parmenides' Argument for Monism

5.1 Introduction

We now come to Aristotle's critique of Parmenides' argument for monism (*Phys.* 1.3, 186a23–b35). In this chapter, my aim is to reconstruct Aristotle's interpretation of this argument, using his two main objections to the argument as my guide.

Aristotle provides a brief summary of Parmenides' argument in *Metaphysics A* 5:

For, holding that besides what is, what is not is nothing, he [*sc.* Parmenides] thinks that, of necessity, what is is one, and nothing else is—we have spoken about this more clearly in the *Physics*.[1]   (986b28–31)

This summary, which is echoed by Aristotle's followers Theophrastus and Eudemus,[2] has not always met with the approval of modern commentators. Jonathan Barnes, for instance, says that the 'Peripatetic interpretation could only occur to scholars desperate to find monism in Parmenides, and prepared to gaze myopically at half a dozen words, taken out of their context'.[3]

---

[1]   παρὰ γὰρ τὸ ὂν τὸ μὴ ὂν οὐθὲν ἀξιῶν εἶναι, ἐξ ἀνάγκης ἓν οἴεται εἶναι τὸ ὄν, καὶ ἄλλο οὐθέν (περὶ οὗ σαφεστέρως ἐν τοῖς περὶ φύσεως εἰρήκαμεν). On the context of this passage, see Chapter 8.

[2]   See Alexander *apud* Simplicius, *In Phys.* 115.11–14.

[3]   Barnes 1982, 207. For a similar assessment cf. Mourelatos 2008, 131 n. 41. The half a dozen (or so) words to which Barnes is referring are at B 8.36–7 ('nothing else <either> is or will be | besides what is'). I agree that Aristotle's 'nothing else is' is a

In my view, the summary in *Metaphysics A* 5 is just too brief to provide us with a good sense of what Aristotle's interpretation of Parmenides' argument actually was. It shows us that Aristotle takes Parmenides' monism to be a consequence of his rejection of 'what is not', but it is hard to say anything more than this. To get a better idea of Aristotle's interpretation, we need to look instead to the *Physics*—as Aristotle himself suggests.

Contrary to what the *Metaphysics* cross-reference might lead us to expect, Aristotle never explains in *Physics* 1.2–3 how he takes Parmenides' argument to work. He does, however, present a two-part 'solution' to this argument, at *Physics* 1.3, 186a23–8. On the basis of this passage, I shall suggest that Aristotle takes Parmenides' principal argument for monism to be an argument for the *continuity* and *uniformity* of what is, an argument which can plausibly be found at B 8.22–5. If this is right, it turns out that Aristotle has a much more appealing interpretation of Parmenides' argument than has previously been thought.

Before looking at Aristotle's solution, I first want to consider a preliminary question: How exactly does Aristotle conceive of the Parmenidean One? I shall argue that Aristotle takes literally the spatial language that Parmenides uses to describe this one entity.[4] This will help us in our subsequent attempt to work out how Aristotle understands Parmenides' monistic argument.

5.2 Aristotle and the Parmenidean One

Even among those interpreters who, like Aristotle, read Parmenides as a radical monist, there is disagreement about the nature of the Parmenidean One. The account in B 8 is pervaded by spatial terminology. Parmenides repeatedly describes what is as having a limit or

---

paraphrase of Parmenides' 'nothing else <either> is or will be'. But I shall be suggesting, *pace* Barnes, that Aristotle in fact locates Parmenides' principal argument for monism elsewhere.

[4] Cf. also Mansion 1953, 170.

limits, *peirata* (8.26, 31, 42, 49), and says that it is 'equally balanced from the middle in all directions' (8.44), famously comparing it to 'the bulk of a well-rounded ball' (8.43). He attributes to it the apparently spatial features of continuity and uniform consistency (8.23–5). Interpreters disagree about the extent to which this spatial language is to be taken literally. Some take it at face value, and read the goddess as telling us that what is is a spatially extended, concrete object, which has determinate boundaries and is literally shaped like a ball.[5] Other interpreters think that the spatial language is largely or wholly metaphorical. Some deny that what is literally has spatial boundaries;[6] others go even further and claim that the Parmenidean One is intended to be a non-spatial, 'abstract' entity, something like a Platonic Form.[7]

We have already seen some signs that Aristotle takes Parmenides' spatial language seriously.[8] At *Physics* 1.2, 185b16–19, he argues that the Eleatics cannot consistently claim that reality is one by being indivisible. Among other things, such a claim would conflict with Parmenides' view that the One is limited. If a thing is limited, then it is finitely extended; and if it is extended, then it has parts and so is divisible. This objection assumes that Parmenides' 'limits' are actual boundaries of some kind. If his talk of limits were just a metaphor, then it would not commit him to saying that the One is extended and thus divisible. Now Parmenides presumably does not think that these boundaries are *temporal* boundaries—after all, he thinks that the One is ungenerated and indestructible. So the alternative would seem to be that they are *spatial* boundaries.

In this section I want to consider three further passages which show that Aristotle favours a literal interpretation of Parmenides' spatial language. The first is *Physics* 1.3, 186b12–14, where Aristotle

---

[5] See e.g. Zeller 1892, 563–4; Burnet 1930, 178–82; Long 1996, 144; Sedley 1999, 117 and 121.

[6] See e.g. Owen 1960, 98–9.   [7] See e.g. Tarán 1965, 194–5.

[8] See section 2.3.3.

argues that Parmenides cannot consistently claim that what is has size or magnitude (*megethos*):

Therefore, nor even will what is have magnitude, if indeed what is [*to on*] is what essentially is [*hoper on*]. For the being of each of the two parts will be different.

The details of this argument are difficult and need not concern us right now (I shall return to them in section 6.7). The basic idea is just that Parmenides cannot consistently allow that the One has parts, and so he cannot consistently allow that it has size. This is supposed to be a problem for Parmenides, and it is hard to see how it could be a problem for him unless his One were supposed to be spatially extended.

My second passage occurs in Aristotle's discussion of the infinite in *Physics* 3. This passage confirms that he takes Parmenides' talk of limits literally:

So, that thing is unlimited of which it is always possible to take something outside, when we take it according to quantity. But that of which there is nothing outside is complete and a whole. For we define the whole in this way: that from which nothing is absent, such as a whole man or box. . . . And whole and complete are either exactly the same or akin in their nature. And nothing is complete which does not have an end, and the end is a limit. This is why Parmenides should be thought to have spoken better than Melissus; for the latter says that the unlimited is a whole, whereas the former says that the whole is limited, 'equally balanced from the middle'.[9] (*Phys.* 3.6, 207a7–17)

Nothing that is unlimited in extent can be said to be 'whole' or 'complete'. This means that Melissus is wrong to say that his unlimited One is a whole. Parmenides, on the other hand, avoids this error because he makes his One limited, and thus can accurately describe it as whole and complete (as he does at B 8.4, 32, 38, and 42). This

<hr />

[9] ἄπειρον μὲν οὖν ἐστιν οὗ κατὰ τὸ ποσὸν λαμβάνουσιν αἰεί τι λαμβάνειν ἔστιν ἔξω. οὗ δὲ μηδὲν ἔξω, τοῦτ᾽ ἔστι τέλειον καὶ ὅλον· οὕτω γὰρ ὁριζόμεθα τὸ ὅλον, οὗ μηδὲν ἄπεστιν, οἷον ἄνθρωπον ὅλον ἢ κιβώτιον. . . . ὅλον δὲ καὶ τέλειον ἢ τὸ αὐτὸ πάμπαν ἢ σύνεγγυς τὴν φύσιν. τέλειον δ᾽ οὐδὲν μὴ ἔχον τέλος· τὸ δὲ τέλος πέρας. διὸ βέλτιον οἰητέον Παρμενίδην Μελίσσου εἰρηκέναι· ὁ μὲν γὰρ τὸ ἄπειρον ὅλον φησίν, ὁ δὲ τὸ ὅλον πεπεράνθαι, "μεσσόθεν ἰσοπαλές".

contrast between Melissus and Parmenides again assumes that the latter's 'limits' are actual boundaries. And, again, if they are actual boundaries, then they are presumably spatial and not temporal boundaries. The final passage I want to consider is *De Caelo* 3.1, 298b11–24, a passage that occurs at the beginning of that treatise's enquiry into the sublunary elements:

And this thing itself is presumably the first thing we should consider: namely, whether [generation] does or does not exist. Now, our predecessors who philosophized about the truth were in disagreement, both with the accounts we ourselves are now giving and with one another. For some of them abolished generation and perishing completely. For they say that none of the things that are either comes to be or perishes, but that they only seem to us to do so. This is the view, for example, of the circle of Melissus and Parmenides, who, even if they speak excellently about other things, should not at any rate be thought to speak as natural philosophers. For the fact that some beings are ungenerated and entirely unchanging belongs instead to a different investigation and one prior to natural philosophy. But those people, because they suppose there to be nothing else beyond the substance of the sensible things, and were the first to understand that there must be some such [sc. ungenerated, unchanging] natures if there is to be any knowledge or thought at all, thus transferred the accounts of those things onto these things here.[10]

The last sentence of the passage (298b21–4) is especially important for our present purposes. Elsewhere Aristotle distinguishes between sensible and non-sensible substances. He tells us that some philosophers acknowledge only the first kind of substance, while others think that there are non-sensible substances as well. Plato, for example, posits non-sensible Forms and mathematical objects in

---

[10] αὐτὸ δὲ τοῦτο πρῶτον ἴσως θεωρητέον, πότερον ἔστιν ἢ οὐκ ἔστιν. οἱ μὲν οὖν πρότερον φιλοσοφήσαντες περὶ τῆς ἀληθείας καὶ πρὸς οὓς νῦν λέγομεν ἡμεῖς λόγους καὶ πρὸς ἀλλήλους διηνέχθησαν. οἱ μὲν γὰρ αὐτῶν ὅλως ἀνεῖλον γένεσιν καὶ φθοράν· οὐθὲν γὰρ οὔτε γίγνεσθαί φασιν οὔτε φθείρεσθαι τῶν ὄντων, ἀλλὰ μόνον δοκεῖν ἡμῖν, οἷον οἱ περὶ Μέλισσόν τε καὶ Παρμενίδην, οὕς, εἰ καὶ τἆλλα λέγουσι καλῶς, ἀλλ' οὐ φυσικῶς γε δεῖ νομίσαι λέγειν· τὸ γὰρ εἶναι ἄττα τῶν ὄντων ἀγένητα καὶ ὅλως ἀκίνητα μᾶλλόν ἐστιν ἑτέρας καὶ προτέρας ἢ τῆς φυσικῆς σκέψεως. ἐκεῖνοι δὲ διὰ τὸ μηθὲν μὲν ἄλλο παρὰ τὴν τῶν αἰσθητῶν οὐσίαν ὑπολαμβάνειν εἶναι, τοιαύτας δέ τινας νοῆσαι πρῶτοι φύσεις, εἴπερ ἔσται τις γνῶσις ἢ φρόνησις, οὕτω μετήνεγκαν ἐπὶ ταῦτα τοὺς ἐκεῖθεν λόγους.

addition to the sensible substances.[11] Aristotle himself thinks that there are non-sensible 'unmoved movers' which are responsible for the rotations of the heavenly spheres. When Aristotle says at *Cael.* 298b21–2 that the Eleatics 'suppose there to be nothing else beyond the substance of the sensible things', I take him to mean that the Eleatics recognized only the sensible kind of substance.[12] This is why they were led to 'transfer' accounts or descriptions appropriate to Platonic Forms or Aristotelian unmoved movers 'onto these things here', that is, onto sensible things. They held that if there is to be any knowledge at all, there must be immutable objects of knowledge. And so, because they recognized nothing beyond the sensible kind of substance, they were led to a conception of sensible, corporeal reality as entirely unchanging.

Aristotle is here ascribing to the Eleatics an epistemological view which he also ascribes to Plato—the view that knowledge requires immutable objects. In *Metaphysics* M 4 he suggests that this was what originally led Plato to introduce Forms. Because Plato was persuaded of the Heraclitean doctrine that the sensible world is in constant flux, he posited a realm of immutable, non-sensible Forms to serve as the objects of knowledge (1078b12–17). In *De Caelo* 3.1 Aristotle ascribes

---

[11] See *Metaph.* Z 2, 1028b19–21: 'Plato [thinks] that the Forms and the mathematicals are two substances [i.e. two kinds of substance], and a third is the substance of the sensible bodies [τὴν τῶν αἰσθητῶν σωμάτων οὐσίαν]'. I assume that 'the substance of the sensible bodies' means 'the kind of substance to which the sensible bodies belong'. Other texts confirm that Aristotle takes Plato to acknowledge the sensible kind of substance: see e.g. *Metaph.* H 1, 1042a6–11; M 9, 1086a24–9 and b7–11.

[12] Cf. the parallel phrase at *Metaph.* Z 2, 1028b21. An alternative would be to take 'the substance of the sensible things' (τὴν τῶν αἰσθητῶν οὐσίαν) to refer to some item which is distinct from the sensible things, and which is 'the substance of' these things in the way in which the form or the matter of an entity might be said to be 'the substance of' that entity (for this usage see e.g. *Metaph.* Z 3, 1028b34–6). However, this fails to make sense of Aristotle's explanation of why the Eleatics transferred accounts appropriate to non-sensible things 'onto these things here' (ἐπὶ ταῦτα). The neuter plural ταῦτα presumably refers to sensible things. So, if 'the substance of the sensible things' refers to an item, S, which is distinct from the sensible things, then the Eleatics' supposition that there is 'nothing else beyond' S would not explain why they transferred the accounts in question onto the sensible things, and not onto S itself.

the same epistemological view to the Eleatics, and suggests that it played an important role in the motivation of their own theory. This is a striking proposal about why the Eleatics were led to posit an entirely changeless reality. Here we can put to one side the question of whether or not it is true, and simply concentrate on what it tells us about Aristotle's conception of the Eleatic One. Aristotle claims that the Eleatics recognized *only the sensible kind of substance*, and that they transferred accounts appropriate to non-sensible things *onto sensible things*. This implies, I take it, that the immutable entities posited by Parmenides and Melissus are themselves sensible substances.

Given the Eleatics' hostility towards sense-perception as a way of accessing reality, the claim that the one being they each posit is 'sensible' is liable to strike us as strange.[13] However, I assume that Aristotle's claim is not that the Eleatics think we actually have perceptual access to these entities. Rather, he is making a point about the entities' ontological status, about the *sort of thing* they are. Unlike Platonic Forms and Aristotelian unmoved movers, the Eleatic One is the sort of thing that could be seen and touched, if, *per impossibile*, there were any perceivers around to see and to touch it. This suggests that Aristotle regards the Eleatic One—both in its Melissan and in its Parmenidean incarnations—as a spatially extended, concrete thing, and not as something abstract.

To conclude, there is clear evidence that Aristotle favours a literal interpretation of Parmenides' spatial language. Aristotle thinks of the Parmenidean One as a spatially extended, bounded, concrete object.

---

[13] See Tarán 1965, 283: '[Aristotle's] misrepresentation of the Eleatics is here patent.' Cf. also Simplicius, *In Cael.* 557.1–560.4. Simplicius' solution (such as it is) is to say that Aristotle here means to be discussing not the Eleatics' *real* view, but instead a superficial misunderstanding of their view. (For a different reading of Simplicius' comments, see Kerferd 1991, 4–7.)

5.3 The Solution to Parmenides' Argument

Having seen how Aristotle conceives of the Parmenidean One, we can now proceed to the passage in *Physics* 1.3 in which he gives his solution to Parmenides' argument:

> The solution [to Parmenides' argument] is partly that it is false, and partly that it does not establish its conclusion. It is false because it assumes that being is said in a single way, when in fact it is said in many ways. And it is inconclusive because if the white things were assumed to be the only things, and if the white signifies one thing, nevertheless the white things will be many and not one. For the white will not be one by continuity, nor in account. (186a23-8)

There are two main objections here. The first is that Parmenides' argument is 'false', the second that it is 'inconclusive'.[14]

5.3.1 The First Objection: Falsehood

In claiming that the argument is false, Aristotle means that it relies on a false premise,[15] which he identifies as the assumption that being (*to on*) is said in a single way (*haplōs*),[16] or, as he also puts it later, the assumption that being signifies one thing (see 186a32-3, 186b4, and 187a1-2). This is not a claim that Parmenides ever makes explicitly. The fact that Aristotle treats it as a *premise* suggests that he has in mind a reconstruction of Parmenides' argument on which the argument makes explicit appeal to this claim, even if for Parmenides himself it functioned as an implicit assumption.

---

[14] Cf. Aristotle's earlier charge that the Eleatics' arguments are 'eristical' because they 'assume falsehoods and are not deductive': *Phys.* 1.2, 185a9-10.

[15] For 'false' arguments, cf. *Pr. An.* 2.18, 66a16-24, and *Top.* 8.12, 162b3-15. The latter passage distinguishes four ways in which an argument can be 'false', of which the fourth is: 'if the conclusion is arrived at through false premises [ἐὰν διὰ ψευδῶν συμπεραίνηται]' (162b12).

[16] Aristotle uses the adverb ἁπλῶς to mean different things in different places. Sometimes it means 'without qualification' or 'in an unqualified way' (e.g. at *Phys.* 1.8, 191b14). Here, however, it means 'in a single way', as can be seen from the fact that it is opposed to πολλαχῶς, 'in many ways'. For other examples of this use of ἁπλῶς, see *Int.* 13, 23a7; *Top.* 8.3, 158b10; *PA* 2.2, 648b11; *EN* 2.7, 1108b7; *EE* 7.7, 1241a23; *Rhet.* 2.24, 1401a24.

It is far from obvious how this false premise or assumption is supposed to have played a role in Parmenides' argument. A number of suggestions have been made in the past, but they all seem to face difficulties. One suggestion is that Aristotle takes Parmenides to have confused the claim that

(i) F signifies one thing

with the claim that

(ii)   the term 'F' applies to one subject.[17]

This would explain how Parmenides gets from his false assumption ('being signifies one thing') to his monism. If there is only one subject to which the term 'being' applies, then there is only one being.

But this suggestion seems unlikely to be right. One problem is that if Parmenides had argued for monism in this way, his argument would be transparently fallacious. But we know that Aristotle sees Parmenides' argument as more sophisticated than the 'crude' argument of Melissus (185a8–12). On the present interpretation, Parmenides is guilty of a mistake which seems no less crude than any of those that Aristotle finds in Melissus (for which see Chapter 4). Another problem is that there is no evidence of such an argument in the fragments. We should hesitate to attribute to Aristotle an interpretation of Parmenides that bears no obvious relation to what we see in Parmenides' text.

A second proposal is that Aristotle takes Parmenides' argument to depend on a failure to distinguish the 'is' of predication and the 'is' of identity.[18] On this interpretation, Parmenides mistakenly treats the predication 'X is (a) being' as an identity claim.[19] This leads him to infer that there is only one being. (If 'X is (a) being' is an identity claim, then it follows that there cannot be two non-identical things each of which 'is (a) being'.) So interpreted, Parmenides' argument

---

[17] Cf. Natorp 1890, 153–4.   [18] See Maier 1900, 282 n. 1.

[19] Ancient Greek has no indefinite article, so this mistake is perhaps somewhat easier to make in Greek than it is in English.

may be said to depend on the assumption that 'being is said in a single way', insofar as it conflates two distinct senses of 'is'.

This second proposal faces the same sorts of problems as the first. On this second interpretation too, Parmenides' argument for monism is obviously fallacious, and surely no more sophisticated than Melissus'. And there are no indications in the fragments that Parmenides arrived at his monism by this dubious route.

A third suggestion is that Aristotle takes Parmenides' argument to be based on the supposed unintelligibility of statements of non-identity. According to this interpretation, Parmenides starts by denying that we can intelligibly speak or think of what is not.[20] From this he infers that we cannot intelligibly say or think that one thing *is not* another thing. And from this he concludes we cannot intelligibly say or think that there is more than one thing (because this would require us to say or think that there is some X and some Y such that X is not Y).[21] If this is how Parmenides arrives at his monism, then his argument may again be said to rely on a failure to appreciate that there are different senses or uses of 'is', this time the 'is' of identity and the existential 'is'. Parmenides' claim that we cannot intelligibly speak or think of what is not may have some plausibility when 'what is not' is taken to refer to *what does not exist*. But it is far less plausible when 'what is not' is taken to refer to *what is non-identical with something else*. And so, once we recognize that there are these different uses of 'is' (and of 'is not'), we can see that Parmenides' argument fails.

Once again, however, it seems doubtful that Aristotle understood the argument in this way. A central premise of the argument, on this interpretation, is that we cannot intelligibly speak or think of what is not. But in Aristotle's view this premise is false,[22] and so we would

---

[20] Cf. B 2.7–8. In section 2.3.4 I suggested that Aristotle makes use of this Parmenidean idea in constructing his argument against the Eleatic claim that what is is one in account.

[21] Annas (1976, 201) suggests that Aristotle interprets Parmenides' argument in this sort of way. Cf. also Mourelatos 2008, 131 n. 41.

[22] He holds that we can intelligibly speak and think of non-beings such as goat-stags and centaurs, for example: see *Int.* 1, 16a16–17; *Post. An.* 2.1, 89b31–3; cf. Alexander, *In Metaph.* 82.5–6.

expect him to mention it if he thought that it was playing an import-ant role in Parmenides' argument. But he does not do so. A further problem is that, as before, it is hard to find evidence of such an argument for monism in the fragments.

If we reject these previous suggestions, then how else might we under-stand Aristotle's charge of falsity? What else might he have in mind when he claims that Parmenides falsely assumes that being is said in a single way? In what follows I want to put forward a different suggestion. First, however, we will need to take a look at Aristotle's second objection.

5.3.2 The Second Objection: Inconclusiveness

The second objection is that Parmenides' argument is 'inconclusive' (*asumperantos*). Even if the argument's premises were granted, its conclusion (or conclusions) would not follow. In other words, the argument is invalid. To explain the charge of inconclusiveness, Aristotle introduces an analogy at 186a26–8, which I shall call 'the whiteness analogy'. The basic idea is that we make assumptions about the property *white* that are parallel to Parmenides' own assumptions about the property *being*. We see that these parallel assumptions about white do not entail monism about white things; that is, they do not entail that 'the white' (*to leukon*) is one and not many.[23] And so we can infer that, likewise, Parmenides' own assumptions about being fail to establish monism about beings: they fail to establish that *what is* is one and not many.[24]

The whiteness analogy gives us some important insights into Aristotle's understanding of Parmenides' argument. To begin with, it shows that Aristotle takes the argument to depend on two key ontological assumptions. Notice that he mentions two parallel assumptions about whiteness. The first is: 'if the white things were

---

[23] The expression 'the white' (τὸ λευκόν), as used at 186a28, refers to the totality of things that are white.

[24] It is significant that Aristotle chooses white as his analogue property for being; not just any property would have served his purposes here. As we shall see in the next chapter, his objection requires that the analogue property be an accident of its bearers, and white is one of his standard examples of an accident.

assumed to be the only things' (186a26). I take it that here we are meant to assume not merely that white things are the only things that *currently* exist, but rather the stronger, modalized claim:

(1W)   Necessarily, a thing is (exists) only if it is white.[25]

This assumption is evidently meant to be the analogue of a Parmenidean assumption about being:

(1B)   Necessarily, a thing is (exists) only if it is a being.

The latter claim, of course, is trivially true. The second parallel assumption about whiteness is that:

(2W)   White (*to leukon*) signifies one thing.

This is the analogue of the false Parmenidean assumption mentioned earlier (at 186a24–5):

(2B)   Being is said in a single way.[26]

So it seems that Aristotle takes Parmenides' argument to depend crucially on these two assumptions about being, (1B) and (2B).

The whiteness analogy also gives us an important clue as to how Aristotle understands Parmenides' intended conclusions. Here is how Aristotle justifies his claim that (1W) and (2W) fail to establish monism about whiteness:

For the white will not be one by continuity, nor in account.   (186a28)

That is: even if (1W) and (2W) are true, the white will be one neither by continuity nor in account. (For the time being I leave aside Aristotle's reasons for claiming that (1W) and (2W) fail to establish

---

[25] I do not think that we are here being asked to suppose that being white is somehow part of what it is to exist, or—even more strongly—that 'to exist is to be pale', *pace* Charlton (1992, 59). Rather, we are simply being asked to suppose that, necessarily, white things are the only things that exist.

[26] Since (2W) and (2B) are meant to be analogous, I think we can infer that Aristotle intends '*F* is said in a single way' and '*F* signifies one thing' to be equivalent. Cf. Angioni 2009, 98. For a different interpretation, see Castelli 2018b, 86.

these monistic claims. I shall come back to this in Chapter 6, where I discuss Aristotle's criticisms of Parmenides' argument at greater length.) We are meant to infer that Parmenides' own assumptions about being, (1B) and (2B), do not entail either (*a*) that what is is one by continuity, or (*b*) that it is one in account. Recall that these were two of the claims distinguished at *Physics* 1.2, 185b5–25 (see section 2.3). The claim that what is is one by continuity is the claim that reality consists of a single continuous object. And the claim that what is is one in account is the claim that all of reality is of the same essence.

Why should the failure of (1B) and (2B) to establish these two monistic claims show that Parmenides' argument is inconclusive? A natural answer is that Parmenides' argument was intended to establish these two claims. If Parmenides' argument was intended to establish these claims, and if his assumptions fail to establish them, then this would indeed imply that his argument is inconclusive. By contrast, if Parmenides' argument were *not* intended to establish these claims, but aimed, instead, to establish that what is is one in some other way,[27] then a failure to establish (*a*) and (*b*) would *not* imply that his argument is inconclusive.

So, the whiteness analogy shows that Aristotle takes Parmenides' argument to depend on two key assumptions about being, (1B) and (2B). And it suggests that he interprets Parmenides as deriving two monistic conclusions from these assumptions: (*a*) that what is is one by continuity, and (*b*) that it is one in account. In the next two sections I want to explain how such an argument can plausibly be attributed to Parmenides.

5.4 An Argument for Continuity

If we are hoping to find a passage in Parmenides' poem in which he argues that what is is continuous and one in account, the obvious place to look is B 8.22–5:

---

[27] Remember that there are various other ways of being one, besides being one by continuity and one in account: see *Metaph. Δ* 6 and *I* 1.

Nor is it [*sc.* what is] divided, since it is all alike;
nor is it any more here, which would prevent it from holding together,
nor any less, but it is all full of being;
thus it is all continuous, for being draws near to being.[28]

Here Parmenides explicitly argues for the continuity of what is, and may also be read as arguing for the claim that what is is all of the same essence ('all alike').[29] Let us start by looking at Parmenides' argument for continuity. He directly infers the continuity of what is from the claim that what is is 'all full of being' (8.24). I want to proceed by asking two questions about this argument. First, what entitles him to the latter claim, and, second, why does he think that this entails that what is is 'all continuous'?

5.4.1 The Pervasiveness of Being

The claim that what is is 'all full of being' is most plausibly understood as the claim that the universe is completely pervaded by being, without any regions of non-being. I shall refer to the claim, thus understood, as 'the pervasiveness thesis'. Support for this reading of the claim comes from the second half of line 25: 'for being draws near to being'. The point seems to be that reality contains no absences of being, no gaps between regions of being.[30]

Parmenides' rejection of absences of being may be explained as follows. Try to think of an absence of being: a gap between two

---

[28] οὐδὲ διαιρετόν ἐστιν, ἐπεὶ πᾶν ἐστιν ὁμοῖον· | οὐδέ τι τῇ μᾶλλον, τό κεν εἴργοι μιν συνέχεσθαι, | οὐδέ τι χειρότερον, πᾶν δ᾽ ἔμπλεόν ἐστιν ἐόντος· | τῷ ξυνεχὲς πᾶν ἐστιν· ἐὸν γὰρ ἐόντι πελάζει.

[29] Notice that the passage may also be read as containing an argument for indivisibility: 'Nor is it divided [or: divisible], since it is all alike'. This means that in B 8.22–5 Parmenides can be seen as arguing for each of the three ways of being one distinguished at *Phys.* 1.2, 185b5–9: one by continuity, one by being indivisible, and one in account. Interestingly, Aristotle does not mention indivisibility at 186a23–8. Perhaps this is because he takes the failure of this part of Parmenides' argument to be obvious. If reality is extended, as Parmenides thinks, then it could not possibly be indivisible in the sense of lacking parts.

[30] I assume that 'being draws near to being' is a figurative way of saying that each region of what is is directly adjacent to some other region of what is.

beings, say. Any gap between beings would have to be a non-being. (If it were not a non-being, it would be a being, in which case it would not be a *gap* between beings.) However, Parmenides has already claimed, earlier in the poem, that non-beings cannot be: 'For never shall this prevail, that things that are not are' (B 7.1). So there cannot *be* gaps between beings. This suggests that the universe must be completely pervaded by being, or 'all full of being', without any absences of being or regions of non-being.

The claim that 'non-beings cannot be' may itself be regarded as a consequence of (1B), the trivial truth that, necessarily, a thing is (or exists) only if it is a being. Nothing can simultaneously be both *F* and non-*F*. So, if (as is undeniable) a thing *is* only if it is a being, and if nothing can be both a being and a non-being at the same time, then it follows that non-beings cannot be. Thus it is plausible that Parmenides' claim that what is is 'all full of being' is ultimately based on (1B).

5.4.2 From Pervasiveness to Continuity

My second question is why Parmenides should think that the pervasiveness thesis entails that what is is 'all continuous'. One attractive suggestion is that he takes the pervasiveness thesis to entail that the universe is a corporeal plenum.[31] If the universe is a corporeal plenum—full of body, containing no regions of empty space or void—then it is tempting to think that it would have to be a solid, continuous mass.[32]

Suppose that this is the right explanation of how Parmenides gets from his claim that what is is 'all full of being' to his claim that it is 'all continuous'. Why might he think that the pervasiveness thesis entails that the universe is a corporeal plenum? A natural explanation is that he fails to consider the possibility that void is itself something that is. This would explain why he thinks that the pervasiveness

---

[31] See especially Burnet 1930, 181; cf. Popper 1958–9, 13–14; Guthrie 1969, 32–4. The suggestion, of course, is that this is implicit in Parmenides; he does not explicitly say that the universe is a corporeal plenum, or that there are no regions of void.

[32] To be clear, my claim is not that this inference is justified, but rather that we can see why it would have been found tempting.

thesis—the thesis that the universe is full of being, with no regions of non-being—entails that the universe is a corporeal plenum, with no regions of void. But then the question is: Why might Parmenides fail to consider the possibility that void is something that is? I want to suggest that this is where (2B) comes in. Someone who assumes that being is said in a single way, or that there is just one way of being, will be unlikely to consider the possibility that in addition to body—which obviously exists—void exists too.[33] Thus we can explain Parmenides' move from 'all full of being' to 'all continuous' if we suppose that he is taking (2B) for granted. According to this interpretation, it is because of Parmenides' narrow conception of being that he fails to countenance the possibility that void is a being, and this in turn explains why he moves from the pervasiveness thesis to the claim that the universe is a single continuous object.

In support of this reading of Parmenides' argument, it is worth emphasizing the *prima facie* strangeness of the idea that, alongside bodily stuffs and bodily objects, empty spaces are themselves things that exist. It is much more intuitive to think of what exists as what occupies or fills space. This fits with how we commonly describe (purportedly) empty regions, by saying that 'there is nothing there'.[34] And so it does not seem unreasonable to think that Parmenides could have been assimilating emptiness and nothingness, and presupposing that any empty region (that is, any region of void) would be a region of nothingness or non-being.[35]

---

[33] I take it that Aristotle would agree that, if there were such a thing as void—in his characterization, 'place deprived of body' (*Phys.* 4.7, 214a16–17)—it would have a different way of being from bodies themselves, which are substances.

[34] Cf. *Phys.* 4.7, 213b31–4: 'Now void is thought to be place in which there is nothing. The reason for this is that people think that being is body, and that every body is in a place, and a place in which there is no body at all is void, so that where there is no body, there is nothing there' (δοκεῖ δὴ τὸ κενὸν τόπος εἶναι ἐν ᾧ μηδέν ἐστι. τούτου δ᾽ αἴτιον ὅτι τὸ ὂν σῶμα οἴονται εἶναι, πᾶν δὲ σῶμα ἐν τόπῳ, κενὸν δὲ ἐν ᾧ τόπῳ μηδέν ἐστι σῶμα, ὥστ᾽ εἴ που μὴ ἔστι σῶμα, οὐδὲν εἶναι ἐνταῦθα). Cf. also Melissus B 7.7: 'the void is nothing' (τὸ γὰρ κενεὸν οὐδέν ἐστιν).

[35] Cf. Zeller 1892, 564: 'For him [*sc.* Parmenides], the real is the full ... i.e. what fills space' ('Das Wirkliche ist ihm das Volle ... d. h. das Raumerfüllende'). Cf. also Kahn

5.5 An Argument for Uniformity

So far we have been thinking about how (1B) and (2B) may be seen as underpinning Parmenides' argument for the continuity of what is. I suggested that Parmenides B 8.22–5 may also be read as containing an argument for the claim that reality is all of the same essence. At 8.22 Parmenides says that what is is 'all alike'. Here he seems to be returning to his earlier claim that what is is *mounogenes* (8.4),[36] which is plausibly understood as the claim that what is is uniform or of one kind. In Chapter 2 I suggested that this is likely to be the basis for Aristotle's attribution of essence monism ('what is is one in account') to Parmenides.

The argument of B 8 down to line 22 is largely devoted to showing that generation and destruction are impossible, which tells us nothing about whether what is is uniform. So it is likely that Parmenides' reasons for claiming that what is is 'all alike' are to be found in the lines that immediately follow this claim, and not in those that precede it.[37] At 8.23–5 we find him arguing not only for the continuity of what is, but also for the apparently connected claim that 'nor is it any more here ... nor any less'. This seems to be a rejection of degrees of density and rarity. There is no more being in one region than there is in another. Rather, the universe is of an even consistency: being is uniformly distributed throughout its extent.[38]

This is a good candidate for being what justifies the claim that what is is 'all alike'. To see why, it is helpful to bear in mind Parmenides' philosophical context. According to his material monist predecessors, the variation we see in the cosmos is ultimately attributable to differences in the density and rarity of a single underlying body (air, or water, or whatever it might be). This is how Aristotle describes the material monists' theory at the beginning of *Physics* 1.4:

1966, 260. Kahn speaks of a 'fundamental corporealism' that was a 'persistent trend in Presocratic philosophy'.

[36] Cf. Mourelatos 2008, 113. [37] Cf. Sedley 2008, 330 n. 45.

[38] Cf. Cornford 1939, 39; Guthrie 1969, 33; Hankinson 2002, 73.

some [of the natural philosophers], having made what is [to on] one body (that which underlies)—either one of the three [sc. water, air, fire] or something else which is denser than fire but finer than air—then generate the other things, making a plurality of things by means of density and rarity.³⁹ (187a12–16)

And similarly in *Metaphysics A* 4:

those who make the underlying substance one generate the other things by means of its [sc. the one substance's] affections, positing the rare and the dense as principles of [the substance's] attributes.⁴⁰ (985b10–12)

Theophrastus associates the theory with Anaximenes in particular:

And [Anaximenes says that air] differs among the substances by its rarity and density. And when rarefied it becomes fire, and when condensed wind, then cloud, and when condensed still more it becomes water, then earth, then stones, and everything else comes from these.⁴¹

(Simplicius, *In Phys.* 24.28–31; cf. 149.28–32)

According to this theory, our cosmos consists of a variety of different stuffs: fire, air, wind, cloud, water, earth, and stone. These stuffs are themselves to be understood as different states of a single underlying body, which Anaximenes identifies as air. Depending on how dense or rare this body is, it has different forms. In its rarest state it is fire; in its densest state it is stone. We are told that 'everything else comes from these'. Presumably this means that all other things are mixtures or compounds of the aforementioned stuffs.

Supposing that something like this theory of differentiation is correct, it follows that, without any differences in density and rarity, the universe would be entirely homogeneous. And so it seems plausible that Parmenides' reason for claiming that what is is 'all alike' (B 8.22) is that, in his view, and contrary to his material monist

---

³⁹ οἱ μὲν γὰρ ἓν ποιήσαντες τὸ ὂν σῶμα τὸ ὑποκείμενον, ἢ τῶν τριῶν τι ἢ ἄλλο ὅ ἐστι πυρὸς μὲν πυκνότερον ἀέρος δὲ λεπτότερον, τἆλλα γεννῶσι πυκνότητι καὶ μανότητι πολλὰ ποιοῦντες. I keep the manuscripts' ὂν at 187a13, following Cerami 2018, 108–9.

⁴⁰ οἱ ἓν ποιοῦντες τὴν ὑποκειμένην οὐσίαν τἆλλα τοῖς πάθεσιν αὐτῆς γεννῶσι, τὸ μανὸν καὶ τὸ πυκνὸν ἀρχὰς τιθέμενοι τῶν παθημάτων.

⁴¹ διαφέρειν δὲ μανότητι καὶ πυκνότητι κατὰ τὰς οὐσίας. καὶ ἀραιούμενον μὲν πῦρ γίνεσθαι, πυκνούμενον δὲ ἄνεμον, εἶτα νέφος, ἔτι δὲ μᾶλλον ὕδωρ, εἶτα γῆν, εἶτα λίθους, τὰ δὲ ἄλλα ἐκ τούτων.

predecessors, it is impossible for there to be differences in density and rarity: 'nor is it any more here... nor any less' (B 8.23–4).[42]

If this is Parmenides' argument for uniformity, then here again his argument may be understood as depending crucially on (1B) and (2B). We have already seen how these assumptions may lead to the view that the universe is a corporeal plenum. And if the universe is a corporeal plenum, then it is tempting to think that not only must it be continuous, it must also be of an even consistency.[43] It is not easy to see how a plenistic universe could exhibit different degrees of density and rarity. Intuitively, for the universe to be *denser* in one region, R_1, than in another equally sized region, R_2, is for R_1 to contain *more body* than R_2. But this seems possible only if R_1 contains *less void* than R_2. So, if there are no regions of void, it seems that there can be no differences in density and rarity.[44] And if there are no differences in density and rarity, then—assuming that the material monists' theory of differentiation is correct—it seems to follow that reality will be entirely uniform. On this interpretation, the uniformity of Parmenidean reality is, like its continuity, a consequence of Parmenides' rejection of regions of void, a rejection that is plausibly based on (1B) and (2B).

5.6 Aristotle's Interpretation of Parmenides' Argument

Earlier I suggested that Aristotle's whiteness analogy indicates that he takes Parmenides' argument to depend on two key assumptions about being, (1B) and (2B). I also suggested that it is likely that

---

[42] For the suggestion that Parmenides takes uniformity to follow from the impossibility of differences in density and rarity, cf. also Guthrie 1969, 33 and Graham 2006, 164.

[43] Parmenides clearly intends a close connection between his claim that what is is continuous and his claim that 'nor is it any more here... nor any less'. In the second half of 8.23 he says that such differences would prevent what is from 'holding together' (συνέχεσθαι), that is, from being continuous. The thought, I suggest, is that if reality were to be denser in one place and rarer in another, then it would have to contain gaps—regions of non-being—which would in turn compromise its continuity.

[44] This argument is also made by Melissus (B 7.8), although not in the context of an argument for uniformity. The converse argument—that the existence of density and rarity proves the existence of void—is reported at *Phys.* 4.9, 216b22–3.

Aristotle interprets this argument as issuing in two monistic conclusions: that what is is (a) a single, spatially continuous object ('what is is one by continuity'), and (b) all of the same essence ('what is is one in account'). We have now seen that it is indeed possible to find an argument that fits this description in Parmenides.

My proposal, accordingly, is that Aristotle reads B 8.22–5 as containing Parmenides' principal argument for monism.[45] The starting point for this argument is (1B), the uncontroversial assumption that, necessarily, a thing is (exists) only if it is a being. This entails that non-beings cannot be (B 7.1), and thus that the universe is 'all full of being' (8.24), with no regions of non-being. Parmenides regards regions of void as regions of non-being, as a result of his failure to consider the possibility that void might itself be something that is. This failure is due to (2B), his assumption that being is said in a single way. Given that Parmenides effectively takes himself to have ruled out the existence of regions of void, he infers that what is is a single, spatially continuous object ('it is all continuous'), which exhibits no differences in density and rarity, and so is all of the same essence ('it is all alike').

An obvious point in favour of this proposal is that it makes excellent sense of Aristotle's solution to Parmenides' argument. When interpreted in the way I have been describing, Parmenides' argument depends on the two key assumptions about being that are suggested by Aristotle's two objections at 186a23–8. And the argument, thus construed, is intended to establish the two conclusions

---

[45] I say 'principal' argument because I do not want to exclude the possibility that Aristotle finds other, supplementary monistic arguments in Parmenides. At *Phys.* 1.8, 191a31–3, Aristotle suggests that the Eleatics inferred monism from the impossibility of generation: 'And what is more, exaggerating what next follows from this, they deny that the many are, and say that only what is itself is' (καὶ οὕτω δὴ τὸ ἐφεξῆς συμβαῖνον αὔξοντες οὐδ᾽ εἶναι πολλά φασιν ἀλλὰ μόνον αὐτὸ τὸ ὄν). This could be a reference to Melissus B 1–6, but I suspect that Aristotle also has in mind a Parmenidean argument: since generation is impossible, a pluralistic cosmos can never emerge from the original one being, *contra* the Milesians (cf. Cornford 1939, 38–9). Such an argument might perhaps be found at Parmenides B 8.12–13: 'Nor ever from what is not will the strength of trust allow | anything to come to be besides it' (οὐδέ ποτ᾽ ἐκ μὴ ἐόντος ἐφήσει πίστιος ἰσχύς | γίγνεσθαί τι παρ᾽ αὐτό). Cf. also *Metaph.* Δ 10, 1075b14–16.

that in Aristotle's view do not follow: that what is is continuous and all of the same essence.

The proposal also fits with Aristotle's spatial interpretation of the Parmenidean One (see section 5.2). The upshot of Parmenides' argument, on the present interpretation, is that the universe consists of a single, spatially continuous, uniform body. This is just what we should expect, given Aristotle's conception of the Parmenidean One as a spatially extended, concrete, 'sensible' object.

Moreover, the present proposal allows us to appreciate why Aristotle takes Parmenides' monistic argument more seriously than Melissus'.[46] On this interpretation, Parmenides' argument is driven by an idea that has a certain plausibility—namely, that it is a necessary condition of the world's being pluralistic and differentiated that there be *absences of being*, regions of the world of which it is true to say 'there is nothing there'. This idea may ultimately be wrong, but it is easy enough to appreciate its intuitive appeal. As an analogy, think of a page of printed black type (perhaps the page you are reading now). The page contains a plurality of characters, of a variety of different kinds. What allows it to exhibit this plurality is the fact that there are *absences of ink*, regions of the page where there is no ink. Without these absences, there would be no individual letters; the page would consist of nothing but a solid black block. The idea driving Parmenides' argument is that, in a similar way, absences of being are a precondition of a pluralistic, differentiated universe. If such absences cannot be, it follows that the universe must be one—a solid, homogeneous mass.

We should also recall Aristotle's comment at the end of his critique of Melissus that 'the same sorts of arguments' can be made against Parmenides (186a22–3). My suggestion in section 4.8 was that we can make sense of this comment on the hypothesis that Aristotle attributes the 'no room to move' argument to Parmenides. This is the argument that motion is impossible because the One fills up all

---

[46] There are of course some affinities between Parmenides' argument, so interpreted, and what we find in Melissus. Melissus explicitly denies that void exists (B 7.7), and then goes on to reject degrees of density and rarity (7.8). A crucial difference, however, is that these considerations do not figure in Melissus' argument for monism.

available space—an argument that Aristotle takes to be refuted by the motion of liquids. If Aristotle interprets Parmenides as arguing against motion in this way, then this aligns with the present suggestion about how he understands Parmenides' argument for monism. Both arguments are based on the idea that the universe is a corporeal plenum, containing no regions of void or empty space.

5.7 Further Support: De Generatione et Corruptione 1.8

An additional piece of support for my proposal comes from a passage in *De Generatione et Corruptione* 1.8, where Aristotle describes the Eleatic arguments that led Leucippus to formulate the atomic theory:

For it seemed to some of the ancients that what is is of necessity one and unchanging. (i) For the void is not a being, and [what is] could not be moved if there is no separate void; (ii) and nor again could there be many things, if there is nothing to keep things apart. (iii) And if someone thinks that the universe is not continuous, but is in a divided state and in contact, this is no different from saying that there are many things (and not one), and a void.[47] For if [the universe] is divided[48] everywhere, then nothing is one, so that nor indeed are there many things, but the whole [universe] is void. But if it is divided here but not here, this looks like a piece of fiction. For up to what point and for what reason is part of the whole this way and full, and another part in a divided state? Further, it is similarly necessary for there to be no motion. So, on the basis of these arguments, passing over perception and disregarding it on the ground that one ought to follow reason, they say that the universe is one and unchanging, and—some say—unlimited (for the limit would be a limit against the void). So some people declared themselves in this way and for these reasons about the truth.[49]   (325a2–17)

---

[47] My construal of this sentence follows Philoponus, *In GC* 157.9–16.

[48] Here I translate διαιρετόν as 'divided' and not 'divisible'. The point of the argument is to show that the universe is not (actually) divided up into many distinct things, *contra* the opponent mentioned in the previous sentence. Cf. Betegh 2006, 275–6.

[49] ἐνίοις γὰρ τῶν ἀρχαίων ἔδοξε τὸ ὂν ἐξ ἀνάγκης ἓν εἶναι καὶ ἀκίνητον· τὸ μὲν γὰρ κενὸν οὐκ ὄν, κινηθῆναι δ' οὐκ ἂν δύνασθαι μὴ ὄντος κενοῦ κεχωρισμένου, οὐδ' αὖ πολλὰ εἶναι μὴ ὄντος τοῦ διείργοντος· τοῦτο δὲ μηδὲν διαφέρειν, εἴ τις οἴεται μὴ συνεχὲς εἶναι τὸ πᾶν ἀλλ' ἅπτεσθαι διῃρημένον, τοῦ φάναι πολλὰ καὶ μὴ ἓν εἶναι καὶ κενόν. εἰ μὲν γὰρ πάντῃ διαιρετόν, οὐθὲν εἶναι ἕν, ὥστε οὐδὲ πολλά, ἀλλὰ κενὸν τὸ ὅλον· εἰ δὲ τῇ μὲν τῇ δὲ

The first argument here (325a3–5) is the 'no room to move' argument. The existence of void is necessary for motion: if things are to be able to move, there must be empty space for them to move into. Since there is no void ('the void is not a being'), it follows that the universe is entirely motionless. The second argument (325a5–6) is an argument for monism. The existence of void is a precondition not only of motion but also of plurality: for the universe to contain many things, there must be regions of void to separate one thing from another. Since there are no regions of void, there can only be one thing. The third argument (325a6–13) is designed to respond to a pluralist objection to the second argument. The objection is that a voidless universe need not be a single continuous object; it could instead consist of many distinct objects in contact with one another. This pluralist objection is alleged to be incoherent, on the grounds that (i) it is impossible for the universe to be divided everywhere, and (ii) there is no principled reason for the universe to be divided at some points but not at others.

We shall examine the third Eleatic argument in more detail in the next chapter (section 6.3). For now it is important just to highlight what it shows us about the second argument. The third argument responds to a pluralist opponent who denies that the second argument is successful. In particular, this opponent denies that the second argument establishes that the universe is *continuous*—which shows that the conclusion (or at least *a* conclusion) of the second argument is supposed to be that the universe is one by continuity. The second Eleatic argument of *De Generatione et Corruptione* 1.8 therefore looks very much like the monistic argument that I am suggesting Aristotle ascribes to Parmenides. The passage confirms that Aristotle thinks

μή, πεπλασμένῳ τινὶ τοῦτ᾽ ἐοικέναι· μέχρι πόσου γὰρ καὶ διὰ τί τὸ μὲν οὕτως ἔχει τοῦ ὅλου καὶ πλῆρές ἐστι, τὸ δὲ διῃρημένον; ἔτι ὁμοίως ἀναγκαῖον μὴ εἶναι κίνησιν. ἐκ μὲν οὖν τούτων τῶν λόγων, ὑπερβαίνοντες τὴν αἴσθησιν καὶ παριδόντες αὐτὴν ὡς τῷ λόγῳ δέον ἀκολουθεῖν, ἓν καὶ ἀκίνητον τὸ πᾶν εἶναί φασι καὶ ἄπειρον ἔνιοι· τὸ γὰρ πέρας περαίνειν ἂν πρὸς τὸ κενόν. οἱ μὲν οὖν οὕτως καὶ διὰ ταύτας τὰς αἰτίας ἀπεφήναντο περὶ τῆς ἀληθείας.

that there is an Eleatic argument for monism which derives the continuity of what is from the fact that there are no regions of void. Of course, Aristotle does not identify the individual authors of the Eleatic arguments he reports at 325a2–17. Perhaps he regards the second argument as the work not of Parmenides but of one of the other Eleatics instead? This is possible, but it seems unlikely. As we have seen, an argument of this kind may plausibly be found at Parmenides B 8.22–5, whereas there is no evidence that such an argument was given by Zeno or by Melissus.[50] So I suggest that this passage corroborates my proposal about Aristotle's interpretation of Parmenides' argument.

It is sometimes said that in *De Generatione et Corruptione* 1.8 Aristotle is primarily interested in describing *Melissus'* version of the Eleatic theory.[51] If this were true, the passage would have little to tell us about how Aristotle understands Parmenides. However, the idea that Aristotle is primarily concerned here with Melissus, while quite common, does not seem to me to be warranted. Although the first argument (the 'no room to move' argument) can certainly be found in Melissus, there is reason to think that Aristotle also attributes it to Parmenides.[52] There is no evidence that Melissus put

---

[50] Melissus explicitly denies the existence of void, but there is no evidence that he argued from the non-existence of void to the monistic claim that the universe is continuous. The 'unlimited' half of Zeno's limited–unlimited antinomy (B 3) is plausibly understood as relying on the idea that A is distinct from B only if there is something separating A from B. But there is no sign that Zeno argued for monism on the grounds that there is no void to function as a separator. For the suggestion that Parmenides B 8.22–5 is likely to be the source of the second Eleatic argument mentioned at GC 1.8, 325a2–17, cf. also Furley 1967, 80 and Taylor 1999, 184. I should emphasize that it is no problem for this suggestion that Parmenides makes no explicit mention of void. The point is not that Parmenides *says* that void is not a being, but rather that his argument for continuity may plausibly be interpreted as assuming this. The Aristotelian formulation in the present passage simply makes the assumption explicit.

[51] See e.g. Kirk et al. 1983, 408–9; Graham 1999, 179 n. 24; Rashed 2005, 138 n. 2; Palmer 2009, 48–9; Brémond 2017, 43–4.

[52] If Aristotle does not attribute the 'no room to move' argument to Parmenides, then we need an alternative explanation of why he says that the same kinds of criticisms he makes of Melissus can also be made of Parmenides. I am not sure what else could explain this.

forward anything like the second argument: as I suggested, this looks to be a formulation of Parmenides' argument for continuity at B 8.22–5. Nor is there anything to suggest that Melissus was the author of the third Eleatic argument; once again we find nothing resembling this argument in our sources for Melissus.[53]

It is true that, later in the passage (325a15–16), Aristotle briefly refers to a specifically Melissan position—that the one unchanging being is unlimited. But there Aristotle also makes it clear that *not all* of the philosophers under discussion took this view.

Finally, Aristotle describes these philosophers' methodological stance in terms that strongly recall Parmenides B 7. They are said to 'pass over perception', and 'disregard it on the ground that one ought to follow reason' (325a13–14). This echoes the demand of Parmenides' goddess that we ignore the deliverances of the senses, and judge instead her strife-encompassed refutation 'by reason' (B 7.3–6).

So in fact there is little basis for thinking that Aristotle is primarily interested in describing Melissan views and Melissan arguments in *De Generatione et Corruptione* 1.8. He seems rather to be describing the arguments of several Eleatic philosophers, including Parmenides.[54]

---

[53] Kirk et al. (1983, 409 n. 4) suggest that Aristotle's source for 325a12–13 ('Further, it is similarly necessary for there to be no motion') is Melissus B 10: 'For if what is has been divided...then it moves; but if it moves it would not be' (εἰ γὰρ διῄρηται, φησί, τὸ ἐόν, κινεῖται· κινούμενον δὲ οὐκ ἂν εἴη). But I take the point at 325a12–13 to be that even if the universe were divided up into a plurality of distinct, contiguous entities, it would still be the case that motion is impossible (because there is no void). Melissus' point in B 10 is different: reality cannot have been divided, because undergoing a process of division involves being moved, which is impossible. The argument at 325a12–13 is most plausibly understood as an argument *for* immovability, whereas the argument of Melissus B 10 is an argument *from* immovability.

[54] This has implications for our understanding of the relation between the Eleatics and the atomists. For instance, it casts doubt on the claim that 'in Aristotle's eyes it is particularly Melissus' version of Eleatic doctrine which influenced Leucippus' (Kirk et al. 1983, 409 n. 4). On the other hand, the passage does seem to be evidence that Aristotle takes Melissus to have been *among* the Eleatics to whom Leucippus was responding. The latter point is relevant to the disputed question of whether Leucippus was responding to Melissus or the other way around. I shall return to the issue of the Eleatics' influence on atomism in Chapter 7.

5.8 The Appeal of Aristotle's Interpretation

In this chapter I have proposed that Aristotle takes Parmenides' main argument for monism to be the argument at B 8.22–5 for the continuity and uniformity of what is. This makes sense of Aristotle's 'solution' at 186a23–8, fits well with his conception of the Parmenidean One as a spatially extended, concrete entity, and allows us to understand why he takes Parmenides' argument seriously. In the last section, I argued that the proposal is further supported by Aristotle's discussion of Eleatic arguments in *De Generatione et Corruptione* 1.8. If my proposal is right, Aristotle has an appealing interpretation of Parmenides' argument. He is often taken to attribute to Parmenides an argument that bears little if any relation to anything that we find in the fragments.[55] On my view, by contrast, Aristotle takes Parmenides' principal argument for monism to be an argument that we know Parmenides actually gave: the argument of B 8.22–5. Moreover, Aristotle's reading of these lines is an attractive one.

I said at the end of Chapter 2 that Aristotle's radical monistic interpretation of Parmenides has much to recommend it. Now, *if* Parmenides is a radical monist, then it is highly plausible that his main argument for monism is to be found at B 8.22–5. This passage can be read as arguing for the continuity, uniformity, and indivisibility of what is. As Aristotle recognizes (*Phys.* 1.2, 185b5–9), each of these is a way of being one.

We have seen that Aristotle takes Parmenides' argument to be driven by two basic ontological assumptions: (1B), the trivial assumption that something exists only if it is a being, and (2B), the non-trivial assumption that being is said in a single way. This provides answers to several crucial interpretative questions about B 8.22–5:

Why does Parmenides claim that what is is 'all full of being'?
Answer: Because he accepts (1B), which entails that regions of non-being cannot be.

---

[55] Recall the proposals reviewed in section 5.3.1.

Why does he think that this means that what is is 'all continuous'?
Answer: Parmenides' acceptance of (2B) leads him to assimilate regions of void to regions of non-being. From this he infers that the universe is a corporeal plenum and thus a single continuous whole.

What is his basis for claiming that what is is 'all alike'?
Answer: Parmenides' rejection of void also leads him to reject the possibility of differences in density and rarity. From this he concludes that the universe is entirely uniform.

My claim is not that B 8.22–5 can only be read in this way. Other answers to these questions are possible. Even so, Aristotle's interpretation seems worthy of serious consideration. Whether or not we ultimately agree with him, it cannot be dismissed as a shortsighted misreading of Parmenides' text.

6

Resisting Parmenides' Argument

6.1 Introduction

Now that we have looked at how Aristotle interprets Parmenides' argument, we are in a better position to understand his criticisms of it. We have already seen that he puts forward two main objections: first, that the argument is based on a false assumption—that being is said in a single way—and second, that it is inconclusive. It is inconclusive because even if we were to grant Parmenides his basic ontological assumptions, his monistic conclusions would not follow: it would not follow either that reality is one by continuity or that it is one in account.

In this chapter I want to examine these objections more closely. Aristotle does not expand on his claim that Parmenides' argument relies on the false assumption that being is said in a single way. Nor does he say very much to explain why Parmenides fails to establish that reality is one by continuity. By contrast, he spends a lot of time explaining why Parmenides is unable to establish that reality is one in account. In fact, most of his discussion of Parmenides' argument is a defence of this latter point (186a28–b35). Accordingly, the latter point will be my main topic here.

6.2 Parmenides' Conception of Being

Aristotle's first objection is that Parmenides' argument depends on the false assumption that being is said in a single way, or that there is just one way of being. As I explained in the previous chapter, I read

Aristotle as taking issue with one of the assumptions that (he thinks) lead Parmenides to the view that the universe is a corporeal plenum, and hence to the view that it is continuous and uniform. Unlike Aristotle himself (in *Physics* 4.6–9), Parmenides does not give explicit arguments against the existence of void. Instead, he equates regions of void with regions of what is not, as a result of his restrictive conception of being.

In Aristotle's view, the assumption that there is just one way of being is mistaken: there are other ways of being besides that of bodies. This means that we cannot straightforwardly infer from the fact that there can be no regions of non-being ('it is all full of being') that there can be no regions without body. Of course, Aristotle himself agrees with Parmenides that the universe is a corporeal plenum; what he is challenging is the way in which Parmenides gets to this view, via a restrictive conception of being.

6.3 Why Parmenides Fails to Establish Continuity

Aristotle's second objection is that even if Parmenides' key assumptions about being were granted, his monistic argument would nevertheless fail. Parmenides' conclusions—that reality is one by continuity and one in account—do not follow from

(1B)   Necessarily, a thing is (exists) only if it is a being,

and

(2B)   Being is said in a single way.

As we have seen, Aristotle makes this objection by way of the whiteness analogy:

And it is inconclusive because if the white things were assumed to be the only things, and if the white signifies one thing, nevertheless the white things will be many and not one. For the white will not be one by continuity, nor in account.   (186a25–8)

The claim that 'the white will not be one by continuity' does not receive any further defence, but we can understand Aristotle's point as follows. Assume the parallel assumptions about whiteness:

(1W)   Necessarily, a thing exists only if it is white,

and

(2W)   White signifies one thing.

It follows from these assumptions that the universe is completely pervaded by whiteness; there are no regions that are not white. However, this does not mean that there is just a single, continuous white object. It is consistent with these assumptions that there are many distinct white things.

To explain why this is, we need to distinguish between *continuity* and *mere contiguity*, a distinction which Aristotle draws in *Physics* 5.3. As Aristotle formulates the distinction, two things are continuous just in case they have some limit or boundary in common, such as my wrist and my hand. Two things are merely contiguous just in case they touch one another, but do not have a limit or boundary in common, such as my hand and my glove. Less technically (and more loosely), we might say that two things are continuous just in case they are joined together, whereas two things are merely contiguous just in case they are in contact but not joined together.[1]

We can grant that if there is nothing that is not white, then each white object will be *contiguous* or *in contact* with some other white object (or objects). (Non-white gaps could not exist, by (1W).) However, there can be a plurality of contiguous white objects which are not continuous: think of a heap of salt crystals. And therefore (1W) and (2W) do not establish that there is just one continuous white object.

(It is worth noting that Aristotle's assertion that the white *will not* be one by continuity (186a28) is perhaps something of an overstatement. It seems that (1W) and (2W) are consistent with the claim that there is a single continuous white object, even if they do not establish

---

[1] For further discussion see Pfeiffer 2018, 158–60.

this claim. So it seems that it would be more accurate to say, not that the white 'will not' be one by continuity, but that it 'need not' be one by continuity.)

Since (1W) and (2W) do not establish that the white is one by continuity, we can infer that Parmenides' own assumptions, (1B) and (2B), do not establish that what is is one by continuity. Aristotle's objection, I take it, is that a corporeal plenum could consist of many contiguous but non-continuous bodies, just as a completely white world could consist of many contiguous but non-continuous white things. Therefore the Parmenidean assumptions do not establish that what is is a single continuous object.

Is this a good objection to Parmenides' argument? Interestingly, in the summary of Eleatic arguments in *De Generatione et Corruptione* 1.8, Aristotle mentions an Eleatic reply to exactly this kind of objection:

And [it seemed to some of the ancients that] if someone thinks that the universe is not continuous, but is in a divided state and in contact, this is no different from saying that there are many things (and not one), and a void.[2] For if [the universe] is divided everywhere, then nothing is one, so that nor indeed are there many things, but the whole [universe] is void. But if it is divided here but not here, this looks like a piece of fiction. For up to what point and for what reason is part of the whole this way and full, and another part in a divided state? Further, it is similarly necessary for there to be no motion.[3]   (325a6–13)

This Eleatic argument is designed to justify the inference from the claim that there are no regions of void to the claim that the universe is one by continuity. It replies to a pluralist opponent who, like Aristotle, holds that a corporeal plenum need not be continuous.

If the voidless universe is divided up into many contiguous objects, then at what points are the divisions to be found? There are two basic options. Either the universe is divided everywhere, or it is divided at

---

[2] I assume that 'is no different' means 'is similarly impossible'. There are clearly some differences between the views.

[3] The Greek is given in section 5.7, in n. 49.

some points but not at others. According to the second option, there are certain regions of the universe that consist of undivided, continuous wholes. According to the first option, there are no such regions; every region of the universe, no matter how small, consists of multiple items that are in contact with one another.

The Eleatic proponent of the argument seeks to show that both options are untenable.[4] Suppose that the first option is correct, and that the universe is divided at every point. On this view, any extended 'object' would in fact be many objects in contact with one another. Anything that is genuinely *one* object (and not a plurality) would have to be without size. But lacking size is tantamount to not existing,[5] and so it seems to follow that 'nothing is one'. If, however, nothing is one, then nor can there be many things. This is because every member of a plurality is one thing; a plurality is a plurality of units. Finally, if there is nothing that is one, and there is no plurality, then it would seem that the universe cannot contain anything at all. It must be completely empty ('the whole [universe] is void').[6]

The other option is that the universe is divided at some points but not at others. The objection is that this seems arbitrary ('like a piece of

---

[4] It is not clear who first came up with this argument, although it has plausibly been associated with Zeno, on the basis of some recognizably Zenonian elements.

[5] For this view, see Zeno B 2, and cf. Aristotle, *Metaph.* B 4, 1001b8–11: 'For that which neither when added makes [a thing] bigger nor when subtracted makes it smaller, this he [*sc.* Zeno] denies is among the beings, evidently supposing that being is magnitude, and if magnitude, then corporeal' (ὃ γὰρ μήτε προστιθέμενον μήτε ἀφαιρούμενον ποιεῖ μεῖζον μηδὲ ἔλαττον, οὔ φησιν εἶναι τοῦτο τῶν ὄντων, ὡς δηλονότι ὄντος μεγέθους τοῦ ὄντος· καὶ εἰ μέγεθος, σωματικόν).

[6] My reconstruction of this horn of the dilemma differs from that suggested by Betegh (2006, 275–6). On Betegh's reading, the argument relies on the implicit premise that 'void is the condition of divisibility'—in other words, that the condition of something's being divided into multiple objects is the presence of void at the division points. From this it follows that if the universe is divided everywhere, there is void everywhere, in which case the whole universe is void. My worry is that, so interpreted, the argument would not be dialectically effective against the Eleatics' present opponent. The opponent is someone who concedes that there is no void, but who claims that the world may nonetheless consist of many contiguous objects. This opponent effectively denies that void is the condition of divisibility, and so an argument which takes this claim for granted (without seeking to motivate it) would be unable to get them to change their mind.

fiction'). If there is no void, then what explains why *this* region of the universe consists of an undivided, continuous object, whereas *that* region consists of multiple objects that are in contact?[7]

It seems that the only philosophically respectable thing to say is that the universe is not divided anywhere. But in that case it is 'all continuous' after all. Thus the original Parmenidean inference—from the absence of void to the continuity of the universe—is vindicated.

I suggested that Aristotle rejects the Parmenidean inference. But then how does he think he can escape the above dilemma? In order to understand this, we need to think about the second horn of the dilemma a little more. In particular we need to think about why the Eleatic proponent of the argument holds that, without void, it would be arbitrary to say that the universe is divided at some points but not at others.

Suppose that you have two identical solid steel hemispheres, and that you place them together so that they form a sphere, with no layer of void between them. The sphere constituted by these two touching hemispheres is (let us suppose) a corporeal plenum: it contains no regions of void. But there seems to be a perfectly good, non-arbitrary answer to the question, 'Where is this plenum divided?' It is divided where the two hemispheres meet, and nowhere else. This suggests that it is not always arbitrary to say that a corporeal plenum is divided at some points but not at others.

So why does the Eleatic proponent of the argument think that it would be arbitrary to say that a plenistic *universe* is divided at some points but not at others? The reason, I suggest, is that the Eleatic is assuming that motion is impossible in a world without void.[8] This

---

[7] A puzzling feature of the second horn is the reference to fullness at 325a11: 'For up to what point and for what reason is part of the whole this way [*sc.* undivided] *and full* [καὶ πλῆρές ἐστι], and another part in a divided state?' An implication of this seems to be that in the opponent's view a divided region of the universe is *not* full. But this is not the opponent's position: they hold that divided regions of the universe are just as full as undivided regions. It is not clear to me how to deal with this problem.

[8] This is the Eleatic argument reported by Aristotle at *GC* 1.8, 325a3–5. It is reiterated at 325a12–13: 'Further, it is similarly necessary for there to be no motion.' The claim here is that even if the opponent were right that the universe is divided into

entails that, unlike our two touching hemispheres, no two adjoining parts of a plenistic universe can ever come to be separated by a spatial interval. We are happy to say that the plenum consisting of the two hemispheres is divided here but not here, but this is only because we recognize that the hemispheres can be physically separated (pulled apart) from one another. Consider instead a spherical plenum whose parts *cannot* be physically separated from one another. Does *this* plenum consist of two touching hemispheres? Or does it consist of four touching half-hemispheres? Or a thousand very fine touching slices? There would seem to be no basis for preferring one of these answers to the others.

We can now understand why Aristotle will not be troubled by the second horn of the dilemma. This part of the argument owes its force to the Eleatic assumption that the different parts of a plenistic universe cannot be physically separated from their neighbours. But Aristotle rejects this assumption.[9] As a result, he has no reason to be worried by the present dilemma.[10] He can embrace the second option, on which the universe is divided at some points but not at others, but deny that this is arbitrary. Such a view would indeed be arbitrary if the various parts of the universe were physically inseparable from one another, but the Eleatics do not have good arguments for this claim.

6.4 Accidental Predication and Essential Difference

We have been considering Aristotle's first reason for claiming that Parmenides' argument is inconclusive: Parmenides' assumptions do not establish that what is is one by continuity. The second reason is that these assumptions do not establish that what is is one in account.

---

a plurality of touching objects, it would still be the case that motion is impossible in a world without void.

[9] Cf. *Phys.* 4.7, 214a28–32, quoted in section 4.5.
[10] Unlike the atomists, who accept the assumption.

Aristotle elaborates this point at length, at 186a28–b35. The structure of this stretch of the chapter is far from obvious, but I want to suggest that it can be divided into the following main sections:

1) First we get an explanation of why, even if (1W) and (2W) are true, the white will be many in account. This is supposed to show that Parmenides' own assumptions about being do not establish that what is is one in account (186a28–32).

2) Aristotle then explains what Parmenides would need to do to avoid the foregoing objection: he would need to make some extra assumptions (186a32–b1).

3) Even if Parmenides were to make these extra assumptions, his attempt to establish essence monism would still face serious problems. I suggest that Aristotle raises three additional problems: the first at 186b1–12, the second at b12–14, and the third at b14–35.

Let us begin with Aristotle's explanation of why the white will be many in account:

For to be white and to be the thing that has received [it] will be different—and there will not be anything separate beyond the white; for it is not by being separate but in being that the white and that to which it belongs are different. But Parmenides did not yet see this.   (186a28–32)

6.4.1 The Property and Its Recipient

The white will be many in account because 'to be white and to be the thing that has received [it] will be different' (186a28–9). The thing that has 'received' white is the subject or the bearer of the property white, whatever this might be—a swan, for example, or a sheep.[11] I take Aristotle to be claiming that the essence of white (the property) is different from the essence of any subject to which this property belongs. In other words: *what it is to be white* is different from *what it*

---

[11] For the terminology of 'receiving', cf. *Cat.* 8, 9a32–b9, where Aristotle discusses affective qualities, such as sweetness and whiteness, and the things that 'receive' these qualities, such as honey and bodies.

is to be a swan, from *what it is to be a sheep*, from *what it is to be a sugar cube*, and so on.[12] This follows from the fact that white is an accidental property (or an 'accident') of its subjects. An accidental property is a non-essential property: a property which is neither the same as nor part of the essence of the things it belongs to.[13] Where *F* is an accident of *X*, *F* and *X* differ from one another in account.[14]

Since the property white, as an accident, differs in account from its bearers (swans, sheep, sugar cubes), Aristotle infers that—even if (1W) and (2W) are both true—the white will be many in account. I assume that this is because he is counting both the property and the recipient(s) as things that are 'white'. Because the property white and any recipient of this property will differ from one another in account, it follows that the white—the totality of things that are white—will be many in account.[15]

Notice that, on this reading, the white would be many in account even if all the bearers of the property happened to share exactly the same essence. Even if the universe consisted solely of white salt

---

[12] The phrase 'to be white' (τὸ εἶναι λευκῷ) refers to what it is to be white, that is, to the essence of white. Cf. the parallel phrases at *Phys.* 1.2, 185b19–25 ('to be good', 'to be bad', etc.).

[13] Aristotle uses the term 'accident' (συμβεβηκός) in different ways. I use the term in its broad sense (see e.g. *Post. An.* 1.22, 83b17–20). This should be distinguished from the narrow sense of the term (see e.g. *Top.* 1.5, 102b4–14), in which it refers specifically to those properties that are 'separable' from their bearers (as e.g. the property of being seated is separable from Socrates, in that he can continue to exist after standing up). For discussion of the different senses of 'accident', see Tierney 2001.

[14] This can be shown by the following argument: (1) Suppose that a property, *F*, *does not* differ in account from its subject, *X*. (In other words, suppose that *F* and *X* are one in account.) (2) Then the account of the essence of *F*, and thus the account of *F* itself, is the same as the account of the essence of *X*. (3) But if the account of *F* is the same as the account of the essence of *X*, we can infer that *F just is* the essence of *X*. (4) And in that case *F* is not an accidental (non-essential) property of *X*.

[15] Alternatively, we might take Aristotle to be arguing as follows: 'Since the property white differs in account from any recipient of this property, we cannot infer from the fact that two objects *X* and *Y* are both white that *X* and *Y* are one in account. Therefore it does not follow from (1W) and (2W) that all white objects are one in account.' Although this is a possible reading of the argument, it seems to me to correspond less closely to the text. The text suggests that 'the white will not be one in account' is a direct consequence of the fact that the property and its recipient differ in account.

crystals, for example, the white would still be many in account, simply by virtue of the fact that the property white differs in account from the salt crystals: what it is to be white is different from what it is to be a salt crystal.

Has Aristotle given us a good reason to conclude that, even if (1W) and (2W) are both true, the white will be many in account? As I noted, his argument relies on the thought that both the property and the recipient(s) are 'white'. Once we allow this, however, it might seem that we are committed to saying that the term 'white' has different senses: it means one thing as applied to the property, and another thing as applied to the recipients.[16] But this seems to conflict with (2W), the claim that the white signifies one thing. A possible worry, then, is that the claim that the white will be many in account follows only if (2W) is false. But in that case Aristotle has failed to show what he wanted to show, namely, that the white will be many in account even if (1W) and (2W) are both true.

In response to this worry, I suggest that what Aristotle really intends by the claim that 'white signifies one thing' is that *there is just a single definition of white.*[17] This is consistent with the claim that the term 'white' can be used in two different ways, to refer either to the property or to its recipients. And so, while it is true that Aristotle's argument requires us to say that both the property and the recipient(s) are 'white', this does not conflict with (2W), where this is understood as the claim that there is just a single definition of white.

Another possible worry is that Aristotle's argument presupposes that white is an accident of white objects, which may be thought to conflict with (1W), the assumption that, necessarily, a thing exists only if it is white. If it is *necessary* for things to be white, then it might be objected that white is an essential property of its bearers, not an accident.[18] Again, however, this worry can be answered. Aristotle

---

[16] As Bostock (2006, 108) points out, Aristotle may be thought to suggest this view himself at *Metaph.* Z 6, 1031b22–8, where he says that τὸ λευκόν has two significations (διττὸν σημαίνειν). It signifies both the attribute white and the white object.

[17] Cf. *Metaph.* Γ 4, 1006a31–4.   [18] Cf. Bostock 2006, 108.

thinks that some accidents are necessary accidents: properties that a thing must have if it is to exist, but which do not constitute part of the thing's essence.[19] Supposing that there can be necessary accidents, (1W) is not in tension with the plausible assumption that white is an accident of its bearers. Moreover, the idea of necessary accidents is philosophically attractive.[20] Consider the property of being non-identical with the number two. This is presumably a property that you have necessarily. But it does not seem to be part of your essence— it does not seem to be any part of what you are.

6.4.2 Difference in Being versus Separation

So far I have been focusing on Aristotle's initial claim that 'to be white and to be the thing that has received [it] will be different' (186a28–9), and explaining why this distinction entails that the white will be many in account. After making this distinction, Aristotle immediately goes on to add: 'and there will not be anything separate beyond the white; for it is not by being separate but in being that the white and that to which it [sc. white] belongs are different' (186a29–31).[21] When we say that what it is to be F is different from what it is to be G, we are not hereby saying (or implying) that F things and G things are two 'separate' or independently existing kinds of thing.[22] This means that Aristotle's distinction—between what it is to be white and what it is to be the thing that has received it—does not commit us to the existence of some separate class of entities beyond what is white.

---

[19] Cf. Charles 2000, 18.   [20] For a modern defence, see Fine 1994.

[21] When Aristotle speaks of 'the white' (τὸ λευκόν) in these lines (at 186a30 and 31), I take him to mean 'that which is white'.

[22] In this context I take 'separateness' to denote the capacity for independent existence: F things are separate (χωριστά) from G things in this sense just in case F things can exist without G things. (Cf. Fine 1984.) That said, I do not think that this is always the right way to understand Aristotle's language of separation. For example, at *Phys.* 1.2, 185a31 he claims that substances are the only separate entities (cf. *Metaph. Z* 1, 1028a33–4), and yet he does not think that substances can exist in the absence of non-substantial attributes (see section 2.2.3). For some proposals as to what Aristotle means by claiming that substances are separate, see e.g. Gill 1989, 36–7 and Peramatzis 2011, 229–48.

The distinction is therefore compatible with (1W), the claim that, necessarily, a thing exists only if it is white.

6.4.3 Is Being an Accident?

Now return to the Parmenidean claim that *what is* is one in account, and to the question of whether or not that claim is justified by the Parmenidean assumptions (1B) and (2B). If what is is one in account, then everything that is has the same essence. Aristotle evidently takes the whiteness analogy to show that (1B) and (2B) do not establish this conclusion. But how exactly does the analogy show this?

Parmenides holds that something—namely, the One—is. I suggest that Aristotle takes this to commit Parmenides to the existence of a property: being.[23] And because Parmenides is committed to the existence *both* of the One *and* of the property, being, his claim that 'what is is one in account' commits him to saying that the One and being have the same essence. This means that Parmenides cannot allow that being is an accident of the One. If being were an accident, then being and the One would differ in account, just as white differs in account from a sugar cube (that is: what it is to be white is different from what it is to be a sugar cube). And if being and the One differ in account, then what is will be many in account: there will be entities that differ in account from one another.

What Aristotle has argued at 186a28–31 is that even if the parallel assumptions (1W) and (2W) are both true, it is nonetheless the case that white is an accident of its bearers, and so different from them in account. As a consequence, we can infer that Parmenides' own assumptions, (1B) and (2B), do not exclude the possibility that *being* is an accident of *its* bearers.[24] Aristotle is here relying on the

---

[23] Note that Parmenides can be committed to the existence of such a property even if he fails to acknowledge the existence of properties (see section 2.4), and even if he explicitly insists there are no other entities besides the One.

[24] Of course, given (2B), it follows that the property being has the same *way of being* as its bearers. But this will not help Parmenides avoid the present objection. In general, the fact that two things share the same way of being does not mean that the first cannot be an accident of the second.

following highly plausible thought: if some set of propositions pertaining to whiteness fails to establish that white is not an accident of its bearers, then a set of analogous propositions pertaining to being fails to establish that being is not an accident of *its* bearers. And in that case Parmenides is not entitled to conclude, on the basis of (1B) and (2B), that what is is one in account.

It is important to appreciate that Aristotle's argument here does not rely on the controversial supposition that being is an accidental property of its bearers, as white is. His point is rather that Parmenides' assumptions fail to exclude this possibility. And precisely because they fail to exclude this possibility, they fail to establish Parmenides' desired conclusion.

6.4.4 Parmenides' Oversight

There is one last sentence in this section for us to consider: 'But Parmenides did not yet see this' (186a31–2). Aristotle is suggesting, I think, that Parmenides did not see that *F* and *G* can differ in account *even when F* things and *G* things are not two independently existing kinds of thing.

Why suppose that Parmenides overlooked this? Well, *contra* our ordinary pluralistic conception of the world, Parmenides denies that there are multiple independently existing kinds of thing—humans and horses, sticks and stones, and so on. Instead, he conceives of the universe as a single homogeneous mass. This is what he means by saying that reality is *mounogenes*, or (to put this in Aristotelian terms) 'one in account'. He seems not to appreciate that even if the universe *were* a single homogeneous mass, it might still be the case that reality is many in account. For example, the property being could differ in account from what has it, without there being multiple independently existing kinds of thing. Go back to the world consisting only of white salt crystals. What it is to be white is different from what it is to be a salt crystal. But it is not the case that (in this world) there are two independently existing kinds of thing: *white things* and *salt crystals*. Parmenides 'did not yet see this', and accordingly he failed to appreciate the problem that Aristotle is raising for him in these lines.

6.5   Parmenides Needs Some Extra Assumptions

Aristotle has been explaining why essence monism does not follow from the assumptions (1B) and (2B). His argument is that it is consistent with these assumptions that being is an accident, in which case what is would be many in account. In the next section, Aristotle argues that Parmenides will need some extra assumptions if he is to avoid the preceding objection:

> It is necessary, then, [for him] to assume not only that being signifies one thing of whatever it is predicated of, but also that [it signifies] *essentially being* [*hoper on*] and *essentially one* [*hoper hen*]. For the accident is said of an underlying subject in such a way that the thing to which being is accidental will not be; for it is different from being. So, there will be a non-being.   (186a32–b1)

The first sentence of this section identifies the extra assumptions that are needed if Parmenides is to avoid the objection. This is a crucially important sentence for our overall understanding of Aristotle's criticism of Parmenides' argument, but there is considerable disagreement about its interpretation. The disagreement concerns the interpretation of the expressions I have translated 'essentially being' (*hoper on*) and 'essentially one' (*hoper hen*). So we should start by trying to get clear on what these expressions mean.

6.5.1   The Language of Essential Predication

Aristotle uses sentences of the form '*X* is *hoper F*' to indicate a certain special kind of predication, a special way in which a property, *F*, belongs to a subject, *X*. The word *hoper* is a relative pronoun (*ho*) conjoined with an emphatic particle (*per*). It corresponds to the italicized phrases in the following English sentences:

> 'That is *precisely what* they warned us about.'
> 'That is *the very thing that* I was looking for.'

As a relative pronoun, *hoper* begins a relative clause. In Aristotle's technical usage, the verb of this relative clause, 'is', is generally left implicit. So a literal translation of '*X* is *hoper F*' would be

'X is the very thing that is F'

or

'X is the very thing that F is',

depending on whether one takes 'F' to be the complement or the subject of the implied 'is'.[25]

By themselves, however, these literal translations tell us little about what the terminology means. To understand this, our guide must be how Aristotle actually uses the terminology. His typical usage suggests that X is *hoper F* just in case F is an essential property of X, or (equivalently) just in case F is predicated of X 'in the "what it is"'.[26] Hence my less literal, more informative (and more succinct) translation: 'X is essentially F'.[27]

Consider, for example, the following passage from *Topics* 4.1. (Aristotle is here going through a series of tests by which the questioner in a dialectical debate may determine that their interlocutor has incorrectly specified a thing's genus.)

> Next, see whether it [*sc.* the proposed genus] is predicated not in the 'what it is', but instead as an accident, just as white is predicated of snow, or self-moved of soul. For snow is not *hoper* white, and therefore white is not the genus of snow, nor is the soul *hoper* moved.[28] (120b21–4)

The general rule is that one may infer from the fact that F is not an essential but an accidental property of X that F is not the genus of X. Aristotle gives two examples using the *hoper* terminology: (1) snow is not *hoper* white; therefore, white is not the genus of snow; (2) the soul is not *hoper* moved; therefore, moved (or self-moved) is not the genus

---

[25] Translators disagree on whether to take 'F' as the complement or the subject. I shall not try to decide between these options here.

[26] For this interpretation of the terminology, cf. also Kung 1977, 362; Code 1986, 430; Malink 2013, 166.

[27] Cf. Joachim's translation of *GC* 2.2, 330a26–7, in Ross 1930.

[28] εἶτα εἰ μὴ ἐν τῷ τί ἐστι κατηγορεῖται ἀλλ' ὡς συμβεβηκός, καθάπερ τὸ λευκὸν τῆς χιόνος, ἢ ψυχῆς τὸ κινούμενον ὑφ' αὑτοῦ· οὔτε γὰρ ἡ χιὼν ὅπερ λευκόν, διόπερ οὐ γένος τὸ λευκὸν τῆς χιόνος, οὔθ' ἡ ψυχὴ ὅπερ κινούμενον.

of soul. Given that these examples are meant to illustrate the general rule, it seems reasonable to conclude that 'snow is not *hoper* white' means that 'snow is not essentially white', and that 'soul is not *hoper* moved' means that 'soul is not essentially moved'.

Again, consider this sentence from *Metaphysics* Γ 4:

For the white is accidental to the human being, because it [*sc.* the human being] is white but not *hoper* white.[29]   (1007a32–3)

The sentence provides a simple explanation of why white is an accidental property of a human being. If 'the human being is not *hoper* white' means 'the human being is not essentially white', then this explanation is easy to understand. Any property of X that is not an essential property is an accidental property. So, if the human being is white, but not essentially white, the only other option is that 'white is accidental to the human being'.

Assuming that this is the correct interpretation of Aristotle's terminology, we can say that Socrates (for example) is '*hoper* human', and also '*hoper* animal': he is essentially human and essentially an animal.[30] And although he may be musical, he is not '*hoper* musical': musical is not an essential but merely an accidental property of Socrates.

6.5.2 Being as an Essential Property

Bearing this in mind, we can now return to 186a32–4:

It is necessary, then, [for Parmenides] to assume not only that being signifies one thing of whatever it is predicated of, but also that [it signifies] *hoper on* and *hoper hen*.

If 'X is *hoper* F' means that X is essentially F, then 'X is *hoper on*' means that X is essentially a being (essentially an *on*). This suggests the following interpretation of 'being [*to on*] signifies *hoper on*':

---

[29] τὸ γὰρ λευκὸν τῷ ἀνθρώπῳ συμβέβηκεν ὅτι ἔστι μὲν λευκὸς ἀλλ' οὐχ ὅπερ λευκόν.
[30] Note that differentiae too are essential properties (properties predicated in the 'what it is'): cf. *Top.* 7.3, 153a15–22; 7.5, 154a23–32. So, supposing that biped is a differentia of the species human, Socrates is also 'ὅπερ biped', essentially a biped.

(A)   Anything that is a being is essentially a being.[31]

On this interpretation, Aristotle is effectively telling us that to avoid the foregoing objection, Parmenides must assume, in addition to (1B) and (2B), that being is an essential property of the things it belongs to. (I discuss Aristotle's second claim—that Parmenides must also assume that being signifies *hoper hen*—in section 6.5.3.)

Given Aristotle's use of the *hoper* terminology elsewhere, this seems to be the most plausible interpretation of 'being signifies *hoper on*'. It also makes good sense of the development of Aristotle's argument. He has just been arguing that it does not follow from Parmenides' basic ontological assumptions, (1B) and (2B), that what is is one in account. This is because, for all those assumptions tell us, being might be an accident of its bearers, in which case what is will be many in account. The natural next thought would be that Parmenides therefore needs to make a further assumption: that being is not an accidental but an *essential* property of its bearers. On the present interpretation, this is exactly what Aristotle now says.[32]

Consider also the next sentence: 'For the accident is said of an underlying subject in such a way that the thing to which being is accidental will not be' (186a34–5). Here I take Aristotle to be giving a supplementary argument for his claim that Parmenides must assume that being signifies *hoper on*. The argument, which we shall consider in more detail below, is that Parmenides is committed to denying that being is an accident of its bearers. For this to be a good argument for the claim that Parmenides must assume that being signifies *hoper on*, we need an interpretation of 'being signifies *hoper on*' on which this

---

[31] Cf. also Spangler 1979, 97; Horstschäfer 1998, 102.

[32] The present interpretation thus provides a satisfying explanation of the connection between 186a32–4 and the preceding lines. Accordingly, we can reject the proposal of Gershenson and Greenberg (1962) that *Physics* 1.2–3 consists of two independently written, self-contained critiques of the Eleatics, the first running from 184b25 to 186a32, the second running from 186a32 to the end of 1.3. On Gershenson and Greenberg's proposal, there is a sharp break at 186a32 between these two supposedly independent critiques. On the reading I am offering, by contrast, we have a single continuous line of reasoning.

follows from the claim that being is not an accident of its bearers. The present interpretation gives us this. If being is not an accident of its bearers, then anything that is a being is essentially a being. And this is what 'being signifies *hoper on*' means, if it is interpreted as I am suggesting.

Nevertheless, it is surprisingly rarely that scholars have understood the claim in this way. Various other interpretations have been proposed. For instance, some take 'being signifies *hoper on*' to mean:

(B)   Anything that is a being is numerically identical with the property being.[33]

However, this is not what the *hoper* terminology typically means. For example, the claim that 'justice is *hoper* good' (*Pr. An.* 1.38, 49a18; *Top.* 3.1, 116a25) does not mean that justice is numerically identical with the property goodness. Moreover, this interpretation fails to make sense of the justification given at 186a34–5: (B) does not follow from the claim that being is not an accident of its bearers.

Another suggestion is that 'being signifies *hoper on*' means:

(C)   Anything that is a being has being as its essence.

In other words, if something is a being, then being is its sole essential property.[34] But I think that this suggestion faces similar difficulties. As before, this is not what the *hoper* terminology usually means: the claim that 'justice is *hoper* good' does not mean that goodness is the sole essential property of justice. Nor is this suggestion able to make sense of the justification at 186a34–5: (C) does not follow from the claim that being is not an accident of its bearers. (To see this, consider the property of being an animal. This is not an accident of any of the particular animals, but nor is it their sole essential property. There is more to the essence of a horse or a sheep than simply being an animal.)

---

[33] See Wicksteed and Cornford 1957, 31–3; Bostock 2006, 109–10.
[34] See e.g. Ross 1936, 474–5; Mansion 1953, 177 n. 41; Angioni 2009, 102; Castelli 2018b, 93.

A final option worth mentioning is an interpretation favoured by several of the ancient commentators. On their view, the claim that 'being signifies *hoper on*' means:

(D)   Anything that is a being is a being *in the strict sense*—in other words, a substance.[35]

Despite its pedigree, this interpretation too seems unlikely. If the basic point is that Parmenides must assume that any being is a substance, it is difficult to understand why Aristotle does not simply use his usual word for substance, *ousia*. It is puzzling that he instead decides to use the expression *hoper on*, an expression that he never uses to designate substance anywhere else.

6.5.3 Oneness as an Essential Property

We have been considering the claim that 'being signifies *hoper on*', and I have suggested that this means that anything that is a being is essentially a being. What about the second extra assumption that Aristotle mentions? Parmenides must also assume that 'being signifies *hoper hen*'. In other words, he must also assume that anything that is a being is essentially one (*hoper hen*).

Why must Parmenides assume this? The reason, presumably, is that he must identify the properties of being and oneness. If these were different properties, then he would be committed to saying that what is is many in account: the properties of being and oneness would differ in account from one another.[36] Further, if being

---

[35] See Simplicius, *In Phys.* 122.27–9: τὸ ὅπερ ὄν 'signifies for him [*sc.* Aristotle] what strictly is and is most of all a being [τὸ κυρίως ὄν καὶ μάλιστα ὄν], which he thinks is substance [οὐσία], because it subsists in itself and is the cause of the being of other things'. Simplicius later indicates that this was also Alexander's interpretation (131.12–16). Cf. also Philoponus, *In Phys.* 68.17–18 (τὸ ὅπερ ὄν is 'what strictly is, that is to say, substance') and Themistius, *In Phys.* 9.26–9, 10.8–10, and 10.14.

[36] We might compare the beginning of the Second Deduction of the *Parmenides* (142b1–143a3), where the character Parmenides argues that if being and one signify different things, it follows that the one being will have multiple parts (the 'parts' *oneness* and *being*), and will therefore be many and not one.

and oneness are the very same property, and if being is an essential property of its bearers, then it follows (trivially) that oneness is an essential property of its bearers. So Parmenides must assume not only that anything that is a being is essentially a being (*hoper on*), but also that anything that is a being is essentially one (*hoper hen*).

Aristotle says nothing more about this second extra assumption. By contrast, the claim that Parmenides needs the first extra assumption receives explicit defence in what follows, and plays an important role throughout the remainder of the chapter. We should therefore see the claim that Parmenides needs the second extra assumption as incidental to Aristotle's main point.

6.5.4 A Supplementary Argument

Aristotle now (at 186a34–b1) goes on to explain why Parmenides needs to assume that 'being signifies essentially being [*hoper on*]'. Of course, we are already in a position to see why this is. The assumptions (1B) and (2B) do not rule out the possibility that being is an accident of its bearers, but this is a possibility that Parmenides must rule out if he is to be justified in concluding that what is is one in account. So we can already appreciate why Parmenides needs this extra assumption if he is to avoid Aristotle's objection. This suggests that we should regard the argument that Aristotle now offers as a supplementary argument, an argument intended to confirm what we are already in a position to see.

The supplementary argument is this:

> For the accident is said of an underlying subject in such a way that the thing to which being is accidental will not be; for it is different from being. So, there will be a non-being.   (186a34–b1)

This is a puzzling argument. One puzzle is that, on a natural interpretation of the first sentence, Aristotle appears to be suggesting that if a property, F, is accidental to an underlying subject, X, then X will not be F; hence, if the property being is accidental to X, X will not be a being. But that is a bizarre piece of reasoning: if F is an accidental property of X, then clearly X *will* be F. Another puzzle is that it is difficult to understand how the subordinate explanation ('for it [*sc.* the thing to which being is accidental] is different from being') is supposed to help matters.

To see the second puzzle more clearly, consider what Aristotle is saying in the subordinate explanation. I take it that the word 'different' (*heteron*) is shorthand for 'different in account'. It seems unlikely that Aristotle has non-identity in mind here. It is true of course that an accidental property will typically be non-identical with its bearers. But this is equally true of essential properties: the property human is non-identical with Socrates and with Plato. (It had better be; otherwise Socrates and Plato would be the very same person.) Yet Aristotle's argument is specifically aimed at showing why being cannot be an *accidental* property of its bearers. That means that we need an interpretation of the argument according to which 'X is different from being' follows from 'being is an accidental property of X', but does not follow merely from 'being is a property of X'. If we take 'different' as shorthand for 'different in account', we get such an interpretation. If F is an accidental property of X, then it follows that X is different in account from F. But this does not follow merely from the fact that F is a property of X; not all properties differ in account from their bearers.[37] So this suggests that by 'different' Aristotle here means 'different in account'. However, even if we can make sense of why it should follow from the fact that being is an accidental property of X that X is different (in account) from being, it is not immediately clear why it should follow from *this* that X will not be a being. After all, white is an accidental property of snow—and thus different in account from snow. But this obviously does not mean that snow is not white; on the contrary, it means that snow *is* white.

---

[37] For example, the property human is one in account with its bearers, the many particular human beings. The account of the essence of the property is the same as the account of the essence of what has the property.

Both puzzles can be resolved, I think, if we take Aristotle's argument to be presupposing that what is is one in account. The argument, as I suggest we read it, is designed to show that, *given that* Parmenides wants to claim that what is is one in account, he cannot consistently allow that being is an accidental property. Let me explain how this works.

Suppose that being is an accident of a subject, *X*. Any accident necessarily differs in account from what has it; so it follows that being (the property) and *X* differ in account. But, given that Parmenides wants to defend essence monism, he cannot allow that there are multiple beings that differ in account. So he will have to deny *either* that being exists *or* that *X* exists.

Now, it seems that Parmenides cannot reasonably deny that the property being exists: if there is no such thing as being, then there will be nothing at all. (The basic thought here is that the existence of *F* things entails the existence of *F*-ness, so if there is no such thing as *F*-ness, then there are no such things as *F*s.) And so the only other option open to Parmenides is to deny that *X* is a being, and to say instead that it is a *non*-being. This is why Aristotle says that 'the accident is said of an underlying subject in such a way that the thing to which being is accidental will *not* be; for it is different from being.'

This places Parmenides in the absurd situation of saying that there is something to which being both *does* and *does not* belong. On the one hand, *X* exists, because (as we are assuming) being is an accidental property of *X*. But the only way in which being can be an accidental property of *X*, consistently with the claim that what is is one in account, is if *X* is a non-being. So: 'there will *be* a *non-being*' (186b1). This is exactly the sort of absurdity that Parmenides wants to avoid: 'For never shall this prevail, that things that are not are' (B 7.1).

The upshot of Aristotle's supplementary argument is that Parmenides cannot allow that being is an accidental property. If he wants to claim that what is is one in account, he must say that anything that is a being is essentially a being.

6.6 First Additional Problem: Other Accidental Properties

Aristotle's initial objection was that Parmenides' assumptions (1B) and (2B) leave open the possibility that being is an accident, and so fail to establish that what is is one in account (186a28–32). To avoid this objection, Parmenides must assume, in addition, that anything that is a being is essentially a being (186a32–b1). Next Aristotle argues that even if Parmenides were to avoid the initial objection in this way, his argument for essence monism would nonetheless face additional problems (186b1–35). I suggest that Aristotle raises three additional problems. The first of these is elaborated at 186b1–12:

Now, what essentially is [to hoper on] will not be something that belongs to something different. For it will be impossible for it to be a being, unless being signifies many things in such a way that each is something. But being is assumed to signify one thing. So, if what essentially is is accidental to nothing, but <the other things>[38] are accidental to that [sc. to what essentially is], then why does what essentially is signify what is rather than what is not? For if what essentially is is also white,[39] and to be white is not essentially a being—for nor can being be accidental to it, for nothing is a being which is not essentially a being—then the white will be a non-being. And [it will be a non-being] not insofar as it is not something, but insofar as it is not at all. So, what essentially is is a non-being. For it is true to say that it is white, and this signified a non-being. So, the white too signifies what essentially is. But then being signifies more than one thing.

In this rather disorienting passage, Aristotle argues that not only must Parmenides deny that being is an accidental property of what is, he

---

[38] The text here is corrupt. Ross supplies τὰ ἄλλα at 186b5 (giving ἀλλὰ <τὰ ἄλλα> ἐκείνῳ). It seems clear that some such supplement is required if the sentence is to make sense; moreover in the following lines Aristotle does indeed raise a problem for the supposition that 'other things' are accidental to what essentially is, and the words τὰ ἄλλα could easily have dropped out by haplography. Cf. also Simplicius' paraphrase at In Phys. 125.17–19: 'For if what strictly is, which we call ὅπερ ὄν, is accidental to nothing else, but *something else* is accidental to that [ἀλλ' ἐκείνῳ ἄλλο τι συμβέβηκεν]'.

[39] This is following Ross, who deletes the manuscripts' ταὐτό at 186b6: εἰ γὰρ ἔσται τὸ ὅπερ ὄν [ταὐτὸ] καὶ λευκόν. Again, cf. Simplicius' paraphrase at In Phys. 125.21–2: 'So, if what essentially is is also white [εἰ οὖν τὸ ὅπερ ὄν καὶ λευκόν ἐστι]'.

must deny that what is (or what essentially is) has any accidental properties at all.[40]

Aristotle's argument unfolds in two main stages. The first stage (186b1–4) is a preliminary stage, in which he argues that what essentially is cannot be a property of anything that is different in account from it. The second stage of the argument (186b4–12) is a complicated *reductio ad absurdum*. Here Aristotle argues that if what essentially is were to have accidental properties, Parmenides would be committed to an absurdity: he would be forced to admit that what essentially is *is not*.

We can understand the first stage of the argument as follows. If *A* is an instance of what essentially is, then *A* cannot belong to anything else, *B*, that is different in account from it.[41] This is because it would be impossible for this other thing, *B*, to be a being.[42] If *A* and *B* differ from one another in account, and if both are beings, then what is will be many in account, contrary to essence monism. Thus, *B* would have to be a non-being, which conflicts with the Parmenidean principle that non-beings cannot be. Therefore, what essentially is cannot belong to anything that differs in account from it.

The only way to avoid concluding that *B* is a non-being would be to abandon the assumption that being signifies one thing (see 186b2–3: 'unless being signifies many things'). Suppose that there are two ways or kinds of being, so that *A* and *B* are both beings—in other words, 'each *is* something'—but they are beings in different ways. Suppose also that the claim that 'what is is one in account' is restricted to things that are beings in the first of these two ways. Then *A* and *B* could both be beings, without this falsifying the claim that 'what is is one in account'. This response is not open to Parmenides, however,

---

[40] Having already established that Parmenides must assume that any being is essentially a being, Aristotle now proceeds to talk of 'what essentially is' (τὸ ὅπερ ὄν) instead of 'what is' (τὸ ὄν).

[41] I take this to be the sense of the claim that what essentially is 'will not be something that belongs to something different [ἄλλῳ]' (186b1–2).

[42] I assume that the antecedent of 'it' (αὐτό) at 186b2 is the 'something different' (ἄλλῳ) of the previous line. For this construal, see also Ross 1936, 474 and Bostock 2006, 109 n. 12, among others.

unless he gives up one of the key assumptions motivating his monism (see 186b3–4: 'But being is assumed to signify one thing').

In the second stage of the argument (186b4–12), Aristotle uses the result of this first stage to argue that Parmenides must deny that what is (or what essentially is) has any accidental properties. If what essentially is has accidental properties, then it follows that what essentially is is a non-being.[43] The argument here focuses on an arbitrary accidental property, white. If

(1) white is an accident of what essentially is ('if what essentially is is also white'),

and

(2) the essence of white is not essentially a being ('and to be white is not essentially a being'),

then, because

(3) being cannot be accidental to the essence of white ('for nor can being be accidental to it'),

it follows that

(4) the white is a non-being.

And from this it follows that

(5) what essentially is is a non-being.

This is a complex piece of reasoning, so it will be best to go through it slowly. Claim (1) is our assumption for *reductio*: we are to suppose that what essentially is has the accidental property of being white.

Claim (2) is a claim about the essence of the property white: the essence of white is not an instance of what essentially is. This is jointly

---

[43] For this conclusion, see 186b10: 'So, what essentially is is a non-being [οὐκ ὄν]'. Cf. 186b5–6: 'why does what essentially is signify what is rather than what is not?' Here the word 'signify' (σημαίνει) indicates something like kind or class membership: X signifies K (or a K) just in case X belongs to the general kind or class K. On this use of 'signify', cf. also Sharma 2005, 142 n. 29.

entailed by (1) together with the result of the first stage of the argument. Given that what essentially is cannot belong to anything that differs in account from it (186b1–2), no accidental property can be an instance of what essentially is.[44] (Accidental properties always differ in account from their bearers.) So, if—as we are assuming, with (1)—white is an accidental property, we can infer that white is not an instance of what essentially is. Aristotle takes the property white to be identical with the essence of white,[45] and so it follows that the essence of white is not essentially a being.

Claim (3) then denies that being is an accidental property of the essence of white. As we have seen, if Parmenides is to avoid the objection back at 186a28–32, he must assume that 'nothing is a being that is not essentially a being' (186b8).

Together, (2) and (3) entail that there is no such thing as the essence of white. This in turn entails (4), that the white is a non-being. Aristotle clarifies (4) by noting that he means not

(4a) the white *is not X* (for some value of *X*),

but

(4b) the white *is not at all*.

This is a distinction between two senses in which something might be said to be a 'non-being' or 'something that is not'. A human 'is not' in the sense that, although it exists, there are many things that it is not: a horse, a dog, and so on. A centaur 'is not' in the sense that it is not 'at all'; there is no such thing. So (4) is not the anodyne claim that the white is not *X*, for some value of *X*, but rather the much stronger claim that the white does not exist.

What does Aristotle mean here by 'the white' (*to leukon*)? He might be saying that *the property white* does not exist, or he might be saying that *that which is white* does not exist. Both of these claims

---

[44] Or to put this another way: if *X* is essentially a being, then *X* is not an accidental property of anything. Cf. 186b4–5: 'if what essentially is is accidental to nothing'.

[45] See *Metaph. Z* 6, 1031b25–8.

conceivably follow from (2) and (3), but in view of how the argument proceeds, I think that the latter reading is preferable. On this reading, the idea is that if there is no such thing as the essence of white—no such thing as what it is to be white—then 'that which is white' does not exist. In other words, there are no white things.

The final step is the move to (5), the absurd result that what essentially is is a non-being. Aristotle explains this inference by saying that 'it is true to say that it [*sc.* what essentially is] is white, and this [*sc.* white] signified a non-being' (186b10–11). By our assumption for *reductio*, (1), what essentially is is white. But we have just established that nothing is white. Therefore: what essentially is does not exist.

This is Aristotle's explanation of why Parmenides cannot consistently allow that what is has any accidental properties. The argument is very elaborate—more so than might seem necessary. There is a simple explanation available for why, as an essence monist, Parmenides cannot allow for the existence of accidental properties. It is a point we have already encountered: any accident necessarily differs in account from its bearers, and so to allow that what is has accidental properties is to allow that what is is many, not one, in account. Nevertheless, I think that we can make sense of why Aristotle does not pursue this simple line of attack. I suggest that he is not *just* trying to show that Parmenides cannot consistently claim that what is has accidental properties; rather, he wants to bring out a maximally embarrassing result of this claim. The claim commits Parmenides to the result that what is (or what essentially is) *is not*, in violation of his principle that 'never shall this prevail, that things that are not are' (B 7.1).[46] Seeing that this is Aristotle's goal is crucial for making sense of this passage. It allows us to understand why he proceeds in what can seem a strangely convoluted way, when a simpler argument would seem to have served his purposes just as well.

---

[46] Notice that Aristotle pursued a similar strategy in the argument at 186a34–b1 (discussed in section 6.5.4); there he argued that if Parmenides were to allow that being is an accident, he would be committed to the existence of what is not.

The last lines of the passage consider a possible response to the preceding *reductio*:

So, the white too signifies what essentially is. But then being signifies more than one thing.   (186b11–12)

To avoid the absurdity that what essentially is is a non-being, we might try claiming that the property white is itself something that essentially is.[47] If this were so, we could deny (2) and block the *reductio*. The present lines tell us that we cannot make this response unless we also abandon the crucial Parmenidean assumption that being signifies one thing. This takes us back to a point that Aristotle has already made in the first, preliminary stage of the argument (186b1–4). If white is essentially a being, then there will be an instance of what essentially is (namely, white) that belongs to something that differs in account from it (namely, the recipient of white). As was argued at 186b1–4, this is possible only if being signifies multiple things—something that Parmenides cannot consistently allow.

6.7 Second Additional Problem: Spatial Extension

At 186b12–14 Aristotle raises a second additional problem for Parmenides, a consequence of the first. If Parmenides wants to claim that what is is one in account, he must also deny that it is spatially extended:

Therefore, nor even will what is have magnitude, if indeed what is [*to on*] is what essentially is [*hoper on*]. For the being of each of the two parts will be different.[48]

I take these lines to argue that a spatially extended Parmenidean One is incompatible with essence monism. (The present argument thus in

---

[47] This time I take 'the white' to refer to the property and not to what has it.
[48] These lines are excised, without good reason, by Wicksteed and Cornford (1957, 34).

a way parallels the argument given against Melissus at *Phys.* 1.2, 185a32–b5. The details are different, however.)

It is noteworthy that Aristotle is not here treating spatial extension as an accidental property of the One. If he were, there would be no need for this further argument: the claim that what is lacks size would follow immediately from the general claim that it cannot have any accidental properties. This suggests that Aristotle is inclined to see spatial extension as an essential property of the One. This is understandable if, as I have suggested, he regards the Parmenidean One as a corporeal object. It is natural to think that if something is a body, then it is essentially spatially extended.

The argument of 186b12–14 is telegraphic. The main thought is that Parmenides is committed (against his wishes) to saying that what is lacks size, on the grounds that, if it *were* to have size, each of its parts would have to have a different essence—a claim that is in conflict with the claim that what is is one in account. The central interpretative difficulty lies in understanding why Aristotle thinks that Parmenides must say that the different parts of what is would each have to have a different essence. It is true that the various parts of a spatially extended thing *can* have different essences (as the essence of a brick in the wall of a house differs from the essence of a tile on the roof; what it is to be a brick is different from what it is to be a tile). But it seems obvious that the different parts of a spatially extended thing *need not* have different essences. Think of a wall built entirely of bricks (and no cement): the essence of each part of the wall (each brick) is the same. So it is not immediately clear why Aristotle implies that Parmenides would have to say that the One has parts which differ from one another in account.

One way to resolve this difficulty would be to rethink what Aristotle means here by 'parts'. We might take him to be referring not to the *spatial* parts of what is, but instead to what we might call its *property* parts.[49] The 'property parts' of an object are the various properties that (as it were) 'constitute' that object, as for example Socrates may

---

[49] For the terminology of 'property parts', see Harte 2002, 70.

be thought to be 'constituted' by the properties of being a human, being a philosopher, being snub-nosed, and so on.

If this is what Aristotle means by 'parts', the argument at 186b12–14 may be understood as follows. If the One has size, then it consists of (at least) the following two property parts: the property of being an underlying subject and the property of having size. These two property parts differ from one another in account. And so, if Parmenides wants to claim that what is is one in account, he cannot allow that the One has these two property parts, and so cannot allow that it has size.[50]

To its credit, this interpretation gives us an effective anti-Parmenidean argument. Nevertheless, taking 'parts' to mean 'property parts' is something of a stretch. It would be surprising for Aristotle to be using the word in this non-standard way without giving us any warning that he is doing so. I therefore want to propose an alternative interpretation that will allow us to keep the more natural, spatial sense of 'parts'.

Aristotle holds that something has size only if it has a plurality of spatial parts.[51] It is plausible, moreover, that if two things, X and Y, are to be numerically distinct from one another, they must differ with respect to some or other of their properties. That is to say, there cannot be two numerically distinct things all of whose properties are exactly the same. (This is the principle we now know as the identity of indiscernibles.) So, if the Parmenidean One is to have size, then it must have at least two numerically distinct spatial parts—call them 'P_1' and 'P_2'—and these two spatial parts must differ with respect to some or other of their properties.

The argument of the preceding passage (186b1–12) established that Parmenides cannot consistently allow that what essentially is has any accidental properties. Further, Parmenides must assume that any being is essentially a being (186a32–4). So if the spatial parts of

---

[50] A somewhat similar interpretation of the argument is suggested by Alexander: see Simplicius, *In Phys.* 127.1–4. Cf. also Castelli 2018b, 97.

[51] Cf. section 2.3.3.

the One—P_1 and P_2—are beings, then each of them is essentially a being. And thus, by the preceding argument, neither spatial part can have any accidental properties.

Properties are either accidental or essential. So, if P_1 and P_2 are to be numerically distinct from one another, and neither has any accidental properties, the only other possibility is that they differ with respect to their essential properties. In other words, they must have different essences.

However, Parmenides wants to claim that what is is one in account. Therefore he cannot allow that there are two beings of different essences. As a result, he cannot allow that what is has a plurality of numerically distinct spatial parts, and he must accordingly deny that what is has size.

This, I suggest, is the line of reasoning that we find at 186b12–14, albeit in a considerably truncated form. Given the conclusion of the foregoing argument (that what essentially is cannot have accidental properties), it follows that—since any being is essentially a being (186b13: 'if indeed what is is what essentially is')—the only way in which two spatial parts can be distinguished from one another is if they have different essences (186b13–14: 'For the being of each of the two parts will be different'). Since this is in conflict with essence monism, it follows that what is cannot have two distinct spatial parts. And therefore what is cannot be spatially extended (186b12–13: 'nor even will what is have magnitude').

The advantage of this interpretation is that it allows us to read 'parts' as referring to spatial parts, as is most natural, while at the same time providing a satisfying explanation of why Aristotle suggests that the different (spatial) parts of what is must each have a different essence.

6.8 Third Additional Problem: Other Essential Properties

Some commentators think that by this point in *Physics* 1.3 Aristotle has completed his critique of Parmenides' argument for monism, and that in the next passage (186b14–35) he moves on to a different topic.[52] I read the passage differently: I think that he now raises a third additional problem for Parmenides' argument. I shall defend this interpretation below, but first I start with a translation of the whole passage:[53]

> But it is obvious that what essentially is [*to hoper on*] is divided into essentially some other kind of being [*hoper on ti allo*], also in respect of the account. For example, if human is essentially some kind of being [*hoper on ti*], then animal must be essentially some kind of being, and biped too. For if they [*sc.* animal and biped] are not [each of them] essentially some kind of being [*hoper on ti*], they will be accidents. So [they will be accidents] either of human or of some other underlying subject. But this is impossible. For, first, the accident is said to be this: either what is able to belong and not to belong, or that in whose account the thing to which it is accidental belongs. For example, being seated [is an accident] insofar as it is separate, while the account of nose (to which we say the snub is accidental) belongs in the snub. Further, the account of the whole does not belong in the account of those things that are in the definitional account, or from which it is composed. For example, the account of human [does not belong] in biped, and the account of white human [does not belong] in white. Therefore, if these things are so, and biped is accidental to human, either it is necessary for it to be separable, so that the human might not be a biped, or the account of human is in the account of biped. But this is impossible. For that [*sc.* biped] is in the account of that [*sc.* human]. But if biped and animal are accidental to something else [*sc.* besides human], and each is not essentially something [*hoper ti*], then human would also be among the accidents of something else. But let that which is essentially something [*to hoper ti*] be accidental to nothing, and let the thing that is composed of both [of two things] also be said of the thing of which both [of these two things] are said. Then is the universe composed of indivisibles?[54]

6.8.1 The Language of Essential Predication, Again

Earlier in this chapter we considered Aristotle's expression *hoper on* (section 6.5.2). I proposed that '*X* is *hoper on*' means '*X* is essentially a

---

[52] See Ross 1936, 476–9; Bostock 2006, 111–15. Ross takes these lines to put forward a general objection to the Eleatics. Bostock suggests that Aristotle now develops a 'logical analogue' to a Zenonian regress argument.

[53] I depart from Ross's text at several points here. See the Appendix for details.

[54] Ross punctuates this final sentence as a question, and I agree; but another possibility would be that it is an assertion: 'So, the universe is composed of indivisibles.'

being'. This interpretation fits well with Aristotle's use of the *hoper* terminology elsewhere, and makes good sense of the argument of 186a32–b1, where the talk of being *hoper on* begins. In the present passage Aristotle uses a distinct but related expression, *hoper on ti*. As before, we should start from the way in which he uses this sort of terminology elsewhere. Typically, sentences of the form

'*X* is *hoper Y ti*'

mean

'*X* is essentially *some kind of Y*'.

For instance, courage is essentially a virtue (*hoper aretē*), but is also essentially *some kind* of virtue (*hoper aretē tis*).[55] In keeping with this usage, I translate the expression *hoper on ti* as 'essentially some kind of being'.[56]

6.8.2 The Argument from Definitional Divisibility

The first sentence of the passage (186b14–15) is hard to interpret, and it will be best to come back to it after we have considered the rest. The rest of the passage presents an argument that I shall call the 'argument from definitional divisibility'. This argument is intended to establish that:

if human being is essentially some kind of being [*hoper on ti*], then animal must be essentially some kind of being [*hoper on ti*], and biped too.

(186b15–16)

Aristotle's argument for this conclusion has the following basic structure:

(1) If animal and biped were not (each of them) essentially some kind of being, they would be accidents (186b17).

---

[55] Cf. *EN* 6.4, 1140a6–8: 'the craft of building [ἡ οἰκοδομική] is ... essentially some kind of rational productive state [ὅπερ ἕξις τις μετὰ λόγου ποιητική]'.

[56] Note that on my construal the τι occurs within the ὅπερ clause. Contrast Charlton's translation (1992, 6–7): 'something [τι] which is precisely what is [ὅπερ ὄν]'.

(2) But, supposing that human is essentially some kind of being, animal and biped cannot be accidents (186b17–35).

(3) So, if human is essentially some kind of being, then animal and biped are also (each of them) essentially some kind of being (186b15–16).

We should first consider the meaning of (1); this will help us get clearer about exactly what the argument is meant to show. The claim in (1) is that if a property is not 'essentially some kind of being' (*hoper on ti*), then it is an accident. How are we to make sense of this?

I suggest that in this passage Aristotle is using '*F* is essentially some kind of being' to mean that *F* is an essential property of each of the things it belongs to. So, if *F* is not 'essentially some kind of being', it will be an accident (at least of some of its bearers). This makes sense of the claim at 186b17: 'For if they [*sc*. animal and biped] are not [each of them] essentially some kind of being, they will be accidents'.

This usage may be explained as follows. We might say that a property is an essential property of each of its bearers just in case it is the property of being *essentially something* (*hoper ti*). For example: the property human is the property of being essentially human; the property horse is the property of being essentially a horse, and so on. Similarly, we might say that a property is an essential property of each of its bearers just in case it is the property of being *essentially some kind of being* (*hoper on ti*). Accordingly, I suggest that Aristotle here uses '*F* is *hoper on ti*'—'*F* is (the property of being) essentially some kind of being'—to indicate that *F* is an essential property of each of its bearers.

If this is correct, the argument from definitional divisibility is effectively an argument for the claim that if human is an essential property of each of its bearers, then biped and animal must be essential properties of each of their bearers too.

The crucial premise in the argument is claim (2): given the supposition that human is 'essentially some kind of being', it follows that animal and biped cannot be accidents. This claim is defended at length at 186b17–35.

Aristotle starts from the thought that all accidents are accidents *of* something. He considers two options: either (A) animal and biped are accidents of human, or (B) they are accidents of some other underlying subject (186b17–18). He argues that neither of these options is acceptable, and infers that animal and biped cannot be accidents at all.

Against Option A. First, at 186b18–31, we get an explanation of why animal and biped cannot be accidents of human. The explanation is based on a division of types of accident:

For, first, the accident is said to be this: either (1) what is able to belong and not to belong, or (2) that in whose account the thing to which it is accidental belongs.   (186b18–20)

Type-1 accidents are properties that are 'able to belong and not to belong' to their bearers. Aristotle's example is the property of being seated.[57] This is a 'separable' (*chōriston*) accident, a property that it is possible for its subjects to lose. Type-2 accidents are properties that are defined partly in terms of their subjects. Such accidents are *'per se'* accidents.[58] Aristotle's example is the property of being snub. Snubness is an accident of nose, and the account of what it is to be snub makes reference to nose: for a thing to be snub is for it to be a nose of a certain shape, or as Aristotle puts it elsewhere, 'snubness is concavity *in a nose*' (*Metaph. Z* 5, 1030b31–2). Other Aristotelian examples of type-2 accidents are the properties of being even and being odd, which are *per se* accidents of number (the accounts of what it is to be even and odd make reference to number), and the properties of being male and being female, which are *per se* accidents of animal (the accounts of what it is to be male and female make reference to animal).

---

[57] Cf. the discussion of accidents at *Top.* 1.5, 102b4–14, where the example of being seated is also used.

[58] An accident, *F*, is an accident of this second type just in case its subject ('the thing to which it is accidental') belongs in the account of *F*. Such accidents belong to their subjects 'in themselves' or *per se* (*καθ' αὑτά*) in the second sense distinguished in *Post. An.* 1.4 (see 73a37–b3; cf. also *Metaph. Z* 5, 1030b16–26).

Aristotle assumes that there are no other types of accident besides these. On this assumption, he argues that animal and biped cannot be accidents of human. To start with, it is impossible for a human to lack these properties, given that a human is defined as a biped animal.[59] It follows that animal and biped cannot be type-1 accidents of human.

Nor can they be type-2 accidents of human. Aristotle assumes, plausibly, that if F is defined in terms of G, then G will not be defined in terms of F (see 186b23–6). So, given that human is defined in terms of animal and biped, it follows that neither animal nor biped can be defined in terms of human. As a result, they cannot be type-2 accidents of human either.

Against Option B. Aristotle now considers the possibility that animal and biped are accidents of some other subject besides human. This is ruled out on the grounds that if biped and animal were accidents of something else, X, then human would itself be an accident of X (186b31–3). But we are assuming that human is an essential property (not an accident) of each of the things it belongs to; therefore biped and animal cannot be accidents of X. Aristotle mentions two principles on which the argument here rests:

But let that which is essentially something [*to hoper ti*] be accidental to nothing, and let the thing that is composed of both [of two things] also be said of the thing of which both [of these two things] are said.   (186b33–5)

The first principle is that 'that which is essentially something' (*to hoper ti*) is accidental to nothing. I suggest that Aristotle is using the expression 'essentially something' (*hoper ti*) interchangeably with the expression 'essentially some kind of being' (*hoper on ti*). Thus the

---

[59] Of course, it in fact *is* possible for a human not to be a biped (as Aristotle appreciates: *Top.* 5.5, 134a11). But this is no objection to the present argument. Aristotle is here assuming his standard 'mock' definition of human (biped animal). If this is the correct definition, then it follows that there can be no humans that are not biped animals. The fact that there can be humans that are not biped animals shows that the mock definition is incorrect—but this is unimportant for the purposes of the argument. The important point is that if human is defined in terms of some genus G and some differentia D, then anything that is a human must be both G and D; in which case G and D cannot be separable accidents of human.

claim that a property is 'essentially something' is (like the claim that it is 'essentially some kind of being') equivalent to the claim that it is an essential property of each of its bearers. If this is the right interpretation of the terminology, the first principle is clearly correct: properties that are essential to each of their bearers are accidental to nothing.

The second principle is that if two properties, A and B, jointly constitute some third property, C (such that C is 'composed of' A and B), then C will be said of anything of which both A and B are said.[60] From this we can infer that if animal and biped are both said of a subject, X, then human is also said of X, given that human is 'composed of' or jointly constituted by the properties animal and biped.

We can now see more clearly how the argument is supposed to work. Aristotle is supposing that human is an essential property of each of its bearers, and his question is whether animal and biped can be accidents of some other subject, X. He assumes, for *reductio*, that animal and biped are accidents of X. By the second principle mentioned at 186b33–5, it follows from this assumption that human is a property of X. Moreover, we can infer that human is an *accidental* property of X. The reasoning here is not spelled out, but the thought is presumably this: if X were essentially a human, then X would be essentially a biped animal; and if it were essentially a biped animal, then it would be essentially a biped and essentially an animal. So, given that X is neither essentially a biped nor essentially an animal, it follows that it is not essentially a human. And so if human is a property of X, it can only be an accidental property of X.

The claim that human is accidental to X conflicts with the supposition that human is an essential property of each of its bearers. This is because, by the first principle mentioned at 186b33–5, anything that is essential to each of its bearers is accidental to nothing. We can therefore conclude that, if human is an essential property of each of its bearers, animal and biped cannot both be accidents of some other subject.

---

[60] Here, as at *Phys.* 1.2, 185a32, 'said of' has its broad sense, equivalent to 'predicated of'.

To summarize, the argument from definitional divisibility starts from the assumption that the property human is constituted by the two component properties animal and biped. (This is why I call it the 'argument *from definitional divisibility*': an assumption of the argument is that the property human is 'divided' into the two component properties that are specified in its definition.) On the interpretation I have offered, Aristotle argues that if human is an essential property of each of its bearers, then its definitional components cannot be accidents either (A) of human or (B) of some other subject. He takes this to show that animal and biped cannot be accidents. Thus, if human is an essential property of each of its bearers, then animal and biped are essential properties of each of their bearers too.

Is the argument convincing? One difficulty is that Aristotle seems to have overlooked a third possible option, besides Options A and B.[61] While he successfully shows that animal and biped cannot both be accidents of the *same* subject, it seems possible that they could each be accidents of *different* subjects. For this reason it is doubtful that the argument establishes that if human is an essential property of each of its bearers, then animal and biped cannot be accidents at all.

6.8.3 Anti-Parmenidean Implications

What is the function of the argument from definitional divisibility? As I said above, I think we ought to see it as a continuation of Aristotle's critique of Parmenides. At 186b12–14, Aristotle argued that Parmenides cannot consistently allow that the One has size, because this would commit him to the existence of things that differ in respect of their essences. Now, in the present passage, he can be read as arguing that even if Parmenides were to deny that the One has size, he would still be committed to the existence of multiple essential properties.

The argument from definitional divisibility considers a specimen essential property, human. But this is just an example, and the argument is meant to generalize. Assuming that the argument

---

[61] This problem is also noted by Bostock (2006, 112).

works, it shows that, for any property, F, if F is an essential property of each its bearers, then the definitional components of F are essential properties of each of their bearers too. The argument thus has the following anti-Parmenidean consequence. Parmenides' essence monism is the claim that all of reality has the same essence. Call this essence 'E'. It follows that E is an essential property of what is. But then—by the argument from definitional divisibility—the definitional components of E will be essential properties of what is as well. So even if Parmenides denies that what is has size (186b12–14), he would still be committed to the existence of more than one essential property. And if there are multiple essential properties, then essence monism is false, given that these essential properties will differ in account from one another.

At the end of the previous section I suggested that the argument from definitional divisibility is unconvincing. But despite this I think that Aristotle's broader anti-Parmenidean point still stands. If an essence is divisible into multiple definitional components, then any bearer of that essence will have multiple essential properties.[62] This is all Aristotle needs in order to put pressure on Parmenides.

Now there is a way in which Parmenides might try to escape Aristotle's objection. He might try to insist that, unlike the property human, essence E is indivisible and so lacks any definitional components. If this were so, he would be able to maintain his essence monism. I suggest that Aristotle is referring to this possible escape route in the question at the end of the passage (186b35): 'Then is the universe composed of indivisibles?' I suggest that the term 'indivisibles' (*adiaireta*) here refers to entities which are indivisible in respect of their essence—in other words, to entities whose essences lack definitional components.[63] The final question, then, comes to this:

---

[62] For example: if human is defined in terms of animal and biped, then anything that is essentially a human will be essentially an animal and essentially a biped. This is true even if there are subjects to which animal and biped are accidental.

[63] This is preferable to taking 'indivisibles' to refer to physically or spatially indivisible bodies. Positing such entities would not help Parmenides avoid the present objection.

'Does reality consist solely of entities with indivisible essences?' This is what Parmenides must say, if he wants to claim that reality is one in account.

It might seem odd that Aristotle should mention this escape route without saying anything to close it off. After all, the idea of an indivisible essence is not incoherent, and if the universe were 'composed of indivisibles' in this way, it would seem that Parmenides could avoid Aristotle's objection. But I suspect that Aristotle's intended point is not that the universe *could not* consist solely of entities with indivisible essences, but rather that Parmenides has given us no reason to think that it *does* consist of such entities. We should keep in mind that the main goal of *Physics* 1.3 is to explain why the Eleatics' radical monistic conclusions are unjustified, and not to explain why they are incoherent. So we can take Aristotle's point at 186b35 to be that, unless reality consists solely of 'indivisibles', Parmenides is committed to the existence of multiple essential properties, which conflicts with essence monism. Since Parmenides gives us no reason to think that reality does consist solely of such entities, it follows that his essence monism is unjustified.

6.8.4 Types of Division

We can now go back to the difficult first sentence of the passage:

But it is obvious that what essentially is [*to hoper on*] is divided into essentially some other kind of being [*hoper on ti allo*], also in respect of the account.[64]   (186b14–15)

Besides the interpretation of the *hoper* phrases, the main problem with this sentence is knowing what to do with the phrase I have translated 'also in respect of the account'. Modern translators typically take this phrase with the word 'obvious' (*phaneron*),[65] but

---

[64] ὅτι δὲ διαιρεῖται τὸ ὅπερ ὂν εἰς ὅπερ ὄν τι ἄλλο καὶ τῷ λόγῳ φανερόν.

[65] On this construal, τῷ λόγῳ tells us *by virtue of what* the content of the ὅτι clause is obvious. Bostock (2006, 113) adopts this construal, and suggests two alternative translations, differing as to the sense of λόγῳ: 'is also clear from argument', 'is clear even from [consideration of] a definition'.

I prefer to follow Alexander, who takes it with the verb 'is divided' (*diaireitai*).[66] On this latter construal, the phrase specifies a (further) respect in which what essentially is is divided, namely, in respect of its account or definition. For a thing to be 'divided' in this way is for its essence to be analysable into the multiple properties specified in its definition. We might say that a human is divided 'in respect of its account' into the properties of being a biped and being an animal.

If this construal is right, the sentence tells us that what essentially is is divided—in respect of its account—into (the property of being) essentially *some other kind* of being. In other words, being is not the only essential property of what essentially is. What essentially is also has some other essential property, F, where F is a distinct kind of being (*on ti allo*)—a kind of being that is distinct from being itself.

The argument from definitional divisibility makes this 'obvious' because it shows (or purports to show) that, by virtue of having some essence, E, what essentially is has a plurality of essential properties. As a result, the argument shows that, regardless of the specific nature of E, what essentially is has other essential properties besides being.

Finally, we can make sense of the word 'also' (*kai*) at 186b15 as follows. In effect, Aristotle's point back at 186b12–14 was that if Parmenides wants to claim that reality is spatially extended, then he must say that it divides, spatially, into a plurality of non-uniform parts. Now Aristotle moves to a different kind of division—not spatial division but definitional division—and argues that what essentially is is *also* divided in this further way.

6.9 Summary of Aristotle's Critique

Aristotle's treatment of Parmenides' argument at *Physics* 1.3, 186a23–b35 is a remarkably difficult stretch of text. Despite its difficulty, however, the passage can be seen as presenting a unified set of criticisms of Parmenides' argument for monism.

---

[66] See Simplicius, *In Phys.* 127.21–5.

It will be helpful now to summarize the central points of Aristotle's critique. As we saw already in the previous chapter, he puts forward two main objections to Parmenides' argument, both of which are stated in the 'solution' passage at 186a23–8. First, the argument depends on (2B), the false assumption that being is said in a single way. Second, the argument is inconclusive: Parmenides' assumptions (1B) and (2B) do not establish his monistic conclusions. These assumptions are consistent with the existence of a plurality of non-continuous objects, and they do not entail that reality is one in account.

Aristotle spends most of his time explaining the inconclusiveness of Parmenides' argument for the latter claim. His explanation makes use of the whiteness analogy: the analogous assumptions about whiteness do not entail that the white is one in account. This is because white is an accident of the things it belongs to, which entails that the essence of white (the property) will differ from the essence of any recipient of the property (186a28–32). We can infer that Parmenides' own assumptions about being fail to exclude the possibility that being is an accident of its bearers, and so fail to exclude the possibility that what is is many in account. Parmenides took himself to have shown that reality is *mounogenes*—all of the same essence, or one in account. But he overlooked the possibility that the property of being might differ in account from the One.

Parmenides therefore needs to assume, in addition, that being is an essential property of what has it (186a32–b1). But even if he makes this extra assumption, there are further problems for his attempt to establish essence monism. The first is that he cannot allow for the existence of any accidental properties at all (186b1–12). Here Aristotle argues that if Parmenides were to allow that the One has accidental properties, then he would be committed to the absurd result that what is *is not*.

The second additional problem (186b12–14) follows on from the first. If Parmenides denies that the One has any accidental properties, then his attempt to establish essence monism will require him to abandon his view that the One is spatially extended. In the absence of accidental properties, any two spatial parts of the One would have to differ from one another in respect of their essences, in which case reality would be many in account.

The third additional problem (186b14–35) is that even if Parmenides were to deny that the One is spatially extended, he would still be committed to a plurality of essential properties, and thus to essence pluralism. Aristotle's objection here is based on the argument from definitional divisibility. This is an argument for the conclusion that if F is an essential property of each of its bearers, then the definitional components of F are essential properties of each of their bearers too. Parmenides wants to claim that all of reality has the same essence. But then the argument from definitional divisibility implies that he is committed to further essential properties: the definitional components of this essence. To avoid this problem, Parmenides would need to find a way of showing that this essence is indivisible.

It is worth asking why Aristotle concentrates so heavily on the inconclusiveness of Parmenides' argument for essence monism. Why spend so much time explaining this, and so little time explaining why Parmenides fails to establish that the universe is one by continuity? My suggestion is that Aristotle concentrates on the former task because it gives him another opportunity to draw attention to Parmenides' metaphysical naivety. At 186a28–b35 Aristotle raises a series of problems that stem from Parmenides' neglect of the existence of properties.[67] So, in addition to showing why Parmenides' argument is inconclusive, these criticisms serve the ulterior purpose of further highlighting his restrictive conception of being—a conception of being that must be rejected if we are to be able to formulate Aristotle's triadic theory of principles.[68] Once again, Aristotle is using his critique of Eleatic monism to prepare the way for his own theory.

---

[67] Because Parmenides overlooks the existence of properties, he does not see that he needs to rule out the possibility that being is an accident (186a28–32). Nor does he see that he is committed to denying that the One has any other accidental properties (186b1–12), and thus to denying that it is spatially extended (186b12–14). Nor, finally, does he see that he must show that the One is indivisible in respect of its essence (186b14–35).

[68] See section 2.4.

7

On Giving in to the Eleatics

7.1 Introduction

In the final section of *Physics* 1.3, Aristotle considers and rejects an earlier attempt to respond to Eleatic arguments for monism. This section completes his treatment of Eleatic monism in *Physics* 1:

> But some people gave in to both arguments: to the argument that all things will be one, if being signifies one thing, [by saying] that what is not is; and to the argument from the dichotomy, by positing atomic magnitudes. But it is also obvious that it is not true that if being signifies one thing, and if it is impossible for the contradictory to hold at the same time, then there will be nothing that is not. For nothing prevents what is not from being—not from being, without qualification, but from being what is not *something*. But then it is absurd to claim that all things will be one, if there is nothing else besides what is itself. For who understands what is itself unless as what is essentially some kind of being [*to hoper on ti*]? But if this is so, then nevertheless nothing prevents the things that are from being many, as has been said.
>
> (187a1–10)

The passage raises several interpretative questions. First, there is the question of the identity of the unnamed respondents. Who was it that gave in too easily to the Eleatic arguments? Some commentators think that Aristotle is referring here to the atomists, while others think that he is talking about Plato and his followers. Is there a good reason to prefer one of these options to the other? Second, there is the question of the puzzling reference to '*both* arguments'. It seems clear that the first argument is Parmenides' argument for monism, which Aristotle interprets as relying on the assumption that being signifies one thing.[1] But the identity of the second argument, 'the argument from the dichotomy', is something of a mystery. What is this argument, and why did it lead to the introduction of atomic magnitudes? Third, once we have determined the identities of the anonymous respondents and of the arguments to which they were responding, there is the question of why Aristotle thinks that these responses amount to *giving in* to the Eleatics.

7.2 The Anonymous Respondents

I want to start by defending the view that Aristotle is referring in this section to the atomists, Leucippus and Democritus.[2] There is clearly something to be said in favour of this. Atomism is the theory that the universe consists of two basic kinds of entity, atoms and void. Aristotle calls atoms 'atomic magnitudes',[3] and 'what is not' (*to mē on*) is one of the atomists' expressions for void.[4] We also know from *De Generatione et Corruptione* 1.8 that Aristotle takes atomism to have been developed in response to Eleatic arguments. So when at the end of *Physics* 1.3 Aristotle refers to those who respond to Eleatic arguments by appealing to 'atomic magnitudes' and 'what is not', it is natural to assume that he has the atomists in mind.

Still, before we can be confident that this is right, we need to consider the alternative. On the alternative view, it was Plato who responded to Parmenides' argument for monism by introducing 'what is not', and it was Plato's follower, Xenocrates, who gave in to the argument 'from the dichotomy', with his theory of indivisible lines.[5]

---

[1] See Chapter 5. I do not think that the first argument can be Melissus' argument, *pace* Palmer (2009, 48). Aristotle has repeatedly emphasized that Parmenides' argument for monism depends on the assumption that being signifies one thing (see 186a24–5, a26–7, a32–3, b3–4, b12), whereas he never characterizes Melissus' argument in these terms.

[2] Cf. Ross 1936, 479–81; Furley 1967, 82; Makin 1993, 51. While this is not an uncommon view, it has not previously been defended in detail.

[3] See e.g. *GC* 1.2, 317a1.

[4] See e.g. *Metaph. A* 4, 985b4–9; *Phys.* 1.5, 188a22–3.

[5] This view goes back at least to Alexander: see Simplicius, *In Phys.* 134.14–138.18. See also Philoponus, *In Phys.* 83.28–84.26, and Themistius, *In Phys.* 12.1–18. It is also

7.2.1 Plato and Parmenides

In support of the suggestion that it was Plato who gave in to the first argument, commentators sometimes appeal to the *Sophist*. The *Sophist* contains a response to Parmenides that, at least on the face of it, seems to match Aristotle's description at 187a1–2: 'some gave in... [by saying] that what is not is'. To solve the puzzles standing in the way of defining the sophist, the Eleatic Visitor says that it will be necessary 'to subject to examination the saying [*logos*] of father Parmenides,[6] and to force it through that what is not *is*, in a way, and again in turn that what is somehow *is not*' (241d5–7).[7] The ensuing refutation of Parmenides' *logos* is concluded at 258c–259b, where the Visitor sums up his achievement as follows: 'we not only proved that things that are not are, we have also shown what the Form of Not-Being actually is' (258d5–7).[8]

But although it is true that the Visitor responds to Parmenides by arguing that 'what is not is', it seems unlikely that this is what Aristotle is thinking of at 187a1–2. For one thing, the Visitor does not present his vindication of not-being as a response to Parmenides' argument for monism. Further, Aristotle's claim that the unnamed respondents 'gave in' to the Eleatic arguments implies that, in engaging with these arguments, the respondents were led to concede things that they should not have conceded. But when the Visitor says that he has shown that 'things that are not are', he seems to mean that he has shown that there *are* things that have the property of *not being* other things, as for example the Form Being has the property of *not*

accepted by some modern commentators, including Ross (1924, 1: xc), Wicksteed and Cornford (1957, 27 and 37), and Owen (1957–8, 207). Cf. also Sedley 2008, 308. For Xenocrates' theory of indivisible lines, see the texts collected by Isnardi Parente (1982, 100–11).

[6] The 'saying of Parmenides' refers specifically to B 7.1: 'For never shall this prevail, that things that are not are', quoted at 237a8 and again at 258d2.

[7] Τὸν τοῦ πατρὸς Παρμενίδου λόγον ἀναγκαῖον ἡμῖν ἀμυνομένοις ἔσται βασανίζειν, καὶ βιάζεσθαι τό τε μὴ ὂν ὡς ἔστι κατά τι καὶ τὸ ὂν αὖ πάλιν ὡς οὐκ ἔστι πῃ.

[8] Ἡμεῖς δέ γε οὐ μόνον τὰ μὴ ὄντα ὡς ἔστιν ἀπεδείξαμεν, ἀλλὰ καὶ τὸ εἶδος ὃ τυγχάνει ὂν τοῦ μὴ ὄντος ἀπεφηνάμεθα. Cf. also *Pol.* 284b7–8.

being the Form Change.[9] Aristotle clearly agrees that there are 'things that are not' in this sense, and so it is hard to imagine that he would consider the *Sophist*'s response to Parmenides a case of 'giving in' to Parmenides.

If Aristotle is not thinking of the *Sophist*, might he instead be thinking of a different Platonist response to Parmenides? Consider the following passage from *Metaphysics N* 2, on the origins of the Platonists' dualistic theory of principles:[10]

Now, there are many reasons for their [*sc.* the Platonists'] being led away towards these causes [*sc.* their two principles]. But especially the fact that they were puzzled in an old-fashioned way. For it seemed to them that all things will be one, Being itself [*auto to on*], unless someone meets with and refutes the saying of Parmenides: 'For never shall this prevail, that things that are not are'. But it is necessary, they thought, to show that what is not is; for in this way, from Being and from something else, will the things that are be, if they are many.[11]   (1088b35–1089a6)

This passage has been thought to confirm that Aristotle sees the Platonists as engaging with Parmenides' argument for monism, and as claiming that 'what is not is' in an attempt to resist that argument. The passage has thus been taken to support the idea that the anonymous respondents at the end of *Physics* 1.3 are the Platonists.

I doubt, however, that the *Metaphysics N* 2 passage is a good parallel for our passage at the end of *Physics* 1.3. Contrary to what is sometimes suggested,[12] Aristotle does not actually say in *N* 2 that the Platonists were responding to Parmenides' argument for monism.

---

[9] Cf. *Soph.* 257a1–6.

[10] I take it that this passage describes a Platonist response to Parmenides which is distinct from that offered in the *Sophist*, pace Ross (1924, 2: 475). At any rate, there is no explicit reference in the *Sophist* to the monistic puzzle that Aristotle mentions in *Metaphysics N* 2.

[11] πολλὰ μὲν οὖν τὰ αἴτια τῆς ἐπὶ ταύτας τὰς αἰτίας ἐκτροπῆς, μάλιστα δὲ τὸ ἀπορῆσαι ἀρχαϊκῶς. ἔδοξε γὰρ αὐτοῖς πάντ᾽ ἔσεσθαι ἓν τὰ ὄντα, αὐτὸ τὸ ὄν, εἰ μή τις λύσει καὶ ὁμόσε βαδιεῖται τῷ Παρμενίδου λόγῳ "οὐ γὰρ μήποτε τοῦτο δαμῇ, εἶναι μὴ ἐόντα," ἀλλ᾽ ἀνάγκη εἶναι τὸ μὴ ὂν δεῖξαι ὅτι ἔστιν· οὕτω γάρ, ἐκ τοῦ ὄντος καὶ ἄλλου τινός, τὰ ὄντα ἔσεσθαι, εἰ πολλά ἐστιν.

[12] See e.g. Annas 1976, 201–2.

His claim is that they were trying to avoid a certain kind of monism, and they thought that to do this they needed to take issue with Parmenides' saying, 'For never shall this prevail, that things that are not are'. This does not imply that the Platonists were responding to Parmenides' own argument for monism, but just that they were responding to his rejection of what is not.

What the Platonists are puzzled by, according to *Metaphysics N* 2, is an argument that seems to show that reality consists of just one thing, the Form, Being itself ('it seemed to them that all things will be one, Being itself'). But Parmenides' own argument for monism, as understood by Aristotle, is not meant to establish this conclusion. I suggested in Chapter 5 that Aristotle takes Parmenides to be arguing that reality consists of a continuous, uniform plenum. This is very different from the conclusion that reality consists of a single Platonic Form.[13] So the argument to which the Platonists are described as responding in *Metaphysics N* 2 must be distinguished from the Parmenidean argument under discussion in *Physics* 1.3—even though both are monistic arguments that rely on the claim that 'never shall this prevail, that things that are not are'. The most we can say is that the argument to which the Platonists are responding is *neo*-Parmenidean, or Parmenidean in inspiration, relying as it does on an authentically Parmenidean premise, and establishing a comparably austere (but nonetheless distinct) monistic ontology.[14]

---

[13] This is obscured somewhat by the fact that Aristotle sometimes uses the same Greek expression, αὐτὸ τὸ ὄν, to refer to these two different entities.

[14] Cf. *Metaph.* B 4, 1001a29–b1, another passage describing the monistic puzzle facing the Platonists: 'But if there is to be a Being itself and a One itself [i.e. a Form of Being and a Form of One], there is a great puzzle as to how there will be anything different, besides these—I mean, in other words, how the beings will be more than one. For what is different from Being is not, so that, according to the saying of Parmenides [sc. 'never shall this prevail, that things that are not are'], it necessarily follows that all beings are one, and this is Being' (ἀλλὰ μὴν εἴ γ' ἔσται τι αὐτὸ ὂν καὶ αὐτὸ ἕν, πολλὴ ἀπορία πῶς ἔσται τι παρὰ ταῦτα ἕτερον, λέγω δὲ πῶς ἔσται πλείω ἑνὸς τὰ ὄντα. τὸ γὰρ ἕτερον τοῦ ὄντος οὐκ ἔστιν, ὥστε κατὰ τὸν Παρμενίδου συμβαίνειν ἀνάγκη λόγον ἓν ἅπαντα εἶναι τὰ ὄντα καὶ τοῦτο εἶναι τὸ ὄν). Next, at 1001b4–6, Aristotle describes an analogous puzzle regarding the hypothesis of a One itself: 'For from what will there be some *other* one besides the One itself? For it is necessary that it not be one; yet all beings are either one or many, each of which is one' (ἐκ τίνος γὰρ

The anonymous respondents of *Physics* 1.3 are presented as responding to Parmenides' own argument for monism—the argument which Aristotle has been discussing since 186a23. They are not presented as responding to an argument that is merely Parmenidean in inspiration. It follows that the *Metaphysics N* 2 passage is not a parallel for *Physics* 1.3, 187a1–3. I conclude that the *N* 2 passage does not support the view that the anonymous respondents are the Platonists.

7.2.2 Parmenides' Argument and the Atomists' Introduction of Void

My proposal in Chapter 5 was that Aristotle takes Parmenides' principal argument for monism to be the argument of B 8.22–5. This is the first argument mentioned at 187a1–3, 'the argument that all things will be one, if being signifies one thing'. I suggested that Aristotle takes this argument to depend on two key assumptions about being: (1B), that a thing exists only if it is a being, and (2B), that being is said in a single way, or signifies one thing. The first assumption leads Parmenides to the pervasiveness thesis, the claim that the universe is fully pervaded by being, with no regions of non-being. The second assumption explains why he neglects to consider the possibility that void is itself something that exists, which in turn explains why he moves from the pervasiveness thesis to the claims that the universe is continuous and of a uniform consistency, and thus all alike.

We are told that the anonymous respondents, whoever they are, 'gave in' to Parmenides' argument by asserting that 'what is not is'. We know from other passages that the atomists affirmed the existence

---

παρὰ τὸ ἓν ἔσται αὐτὸ ἄλλο ἔν; ἀνάγκη γὰρ μὴ ἓν εἶναι· ἅπαντα δὲ τὰ ὄντα ἢ ἓν ἢ πολλὰ ὧν ἓν ἕκαστον). A crucial thing to notice about this B 4 passage is that it describes a monistic puzzle which arises from a specifically Platonist assumption: that there is a Form of Being (a 'Being itself') or a Form of One (a 'One itself'). The Parmenidean argument under discussion in *Physics* 1.3 rests on no such assumption.

of void by affirming the existence of 'what is not'.[15] The advantage of taking the anonymous respondents of 187a1–3 to be the atomists is that the atomistic introduction of void makes excellent philosophical sense as a response to Parmenides' argument at B 8.22–5. As interpreted by Aristotle, that argument works by equating regions of void to regions of non-being; it is this that explains why Parmenides moves from the pervasiveness thesis to his monistic conclusions. So a natural way of resisting the argument is to say exactly what the atomists say: *void exists no less than body does.* If void is itself something that exists, then the pervasiveness thesis is consistent with a world consisting of regions of body broken up by regions of void, and is therefore consistent with the existence of a non-continuous, non-uniform universe.

It is important to note that on this understanding of the atomists' response, they are not simply ignoring Parmenides' argument for monism by assuming a basic plurality of bodies.[16] The dialectical situation is rather this: Parmenides' argument depends on an implicit assumption that there is just one way of being—corporeal being. The atomists propose that we can rescue plurality by abandoning this implicit assumption and saying that void exists in addition to body. This is not to ignore Parmenides' argument, but rather to challenge it directly by denying one of its key assumptions.

In my view, then, we have strong grounds for thinking that the anonymous respondents of 187a1–3 are the atomists. While Plato and others in the Academy may have argued, *contra* Parmenides, that 'what is not is', we have no reason to think that this was put forward specifically as a response to the Parmenidean argument under discussion in *Physics* 1.3. The atomists' introduction of void, by contrast, makes perfect sense as a response to this argument.

---

[15] It is plausible that the atomists wanted to distinguish two different ways of being: corporeal being and a way of being shared by bodies and void alike. So the apparent paradox in their assertion that 'what is not is' can be resolved as follows: while void lacks the former way of being, and so 'is not', it nonetheless has the latter way of being, and so 'is'. Cf. Burnet 1930, 337; Hussey 2004, 251–2.

[16] For this worry, see Curd 1991, 241; 1998, 3–4; Osborne 2006b, 224.

Additional support for the idea that Aristotle takes the atomists to have been responding to the argument of Parmenides B 8.22–5 comes from *De Generatione et Corruptione* 1.8. There, as we have seen, Aristotle describes several Eleatic arguments that led to the formulation of atomism. As I noted in section 5.7, the second of these Eleatic arguments (at 325a5–6) looks to be a formulation of Parmenides' argument for continuity. Another relevant passage is *Physics* 4.6, 213a33–b1, where Aristotle characterizes void as an interval 'which divides the whole body *so that it is not continuous,* just as Democritus and Leucippus say, and many other natural philosophers'.[17] By the 'whole body' Aristotle here means 'the body of the universe'.[18] His remark therefore suggests that the intended function of the void was to break up the continuity of the universe, which again fits well with the idea that the atomists introduced void in order to resist Parmenides' argument at B 8.22–5.

7.3 The Dichotomy

The second argument Aristotle mentions at 187a1–3 is 'the argument from the dichotomy'. If it is true that he is referring in these lines to the atomists, then this is the argument that prompted the atomists to introduce atoms ('atomic magnitudes'). A 'dichotomy' is literally a cutting or a dividing in two: a bisection. So far we have not heard anything about this argument.[19] Aristotle's reference to it comes seemingly out of the blue.

---

[17] ὃ διαλαμβάνει τὸ πᾶν σῶμα ὥστε εἶναι μὴ συνεχές, καθάπερ λέγουσιν Δημόκριτος καὶ Λεύκιππος καὶ ἕτεροι πολλοὶ τῶν φυσιολόγων. Cf. also *Cael.* 1.7, 275b29–31.

[18] Cf. Ross 1936, 582.

[19] It is fairly clear, I think, that 'the argument from the dichotomy', whatever it is, cannot be the argument that Aristotle has just been giving at 186b14–35 (in my terminology, 'the argument from definitional divisibility'). There is a sense in which the latter argument might be said to rely on the dichotomous division of an essence into its two constituent parts: the genus and the differentia. But this is one of Aristotle's own anti-monistic arguments, and so it cannot be the argument to which the earlier pluralists were 'giving in'.

Two possible candidates for this argument are (i) Zeno's paradox of the racetrack or the runner, and (ii) the 'large' half of Zeno's small–large antinomy.[20] The former argument is one of the famous paradoxes of motion. As Aristotle describes it, this is the argument that motion is impossible 'because what is moving must arrive at the halfway point before the end' (*Phys.* 6.9, 239b12–13).[21] Imagine a runner, trying to run from one end of a racetrack to the other. In order to complete the distance, she first needs to get to the halfway point: call this halfway point 'h_1'. But then, in order to complete the remaining distance, from h_1 to the finish line, she needs to get to a second halfway point, h_2. And in order to get from that halfway point to the finish line, she needs to get to a third halfway point, h_3. And so on ad infinitum. The runner has to reach an infinite number of halfway points—or run an infinite number of distances—before she reaches her destination. And this, Zeno claims, cannot be done.

The second candidate argument is preserved by Simplicius, who quotes the following lines in the course of his own discussion of the argument from the dichotomy:

If it is, each thing must have some magnitude and thickness, and one part of it must be away from the other part. And the same argument holds with regard to the part out in front. For that too will have magnitude, and some part of it will be out in front. Now it is the same to say this once and to be saying it always. For no such part of it will be the final part, nor will one part not be related to another.[22]

(Simplicius, *In Phys.* 141.2–6 = part of Zeno B 1)

This argument rests on two main ideas:

---

[20] See Sedley 2008, 306–8 for the suggestion that the argument from the dichotomy is one or other of these Zenonian arguments.

[21] διὰ τὸ πρότερον εἰς τὸ ἥμισυ δεῖν ἀφικέσθαι τὸ φερόμενον ἢ πρὸς τὸ τέλος. Cf. also *Phys.* 6.2, 233a21–3; 8.8, 263a4–6.

[22] εἰ δὲ ἔστιν, ἀνάγκη ἕκαστον μέγεθός τι ἔχειν καὶ πάχος καὶ ἀπέχειν αὐτοῦ τὸ ἕτερον ἀπὸ τοῦ ἑτέρου. καὶ περὶ τοῦ προύχοντος ὁ αὐτὸς λόγος. καὶ γὰρ ἐκεῖνο ἕξει μέγεθος καὶ προέξει αὐτοῦ τι. ὅμοιον δὴ τοῦτο ἅπαξ τε εἰπεῖν καὶ ἀεὶ λέγειν· οὐδὲν γὰρ αὐτοῦ τοιοῦτον ἔσχατον ἔσται οὔτε ἕτερον πρὸς ἕτερον οὐκ ἔσται.

(A) Anything that exists has 'some magnitude and thickness'.

(B) Anything that has some magnitude and thickness is divisible, at least in thought, into distinct parts: the front half and the back half, say.

It follows from (A) and (B) that anything that exists is divisible into infinitely many parts. Take some arbitrary object, X. If X exists, then, by (A), it has some magnitude and thickness. And thus, by (B), it has a front half that is distinct from its back half. But this front half, assuming that it too is something that exists,[23] also has some magnitude and thickness, again by (A). And so, again by (B), it too has a front half and a back half. And so on ad infinitum. We can conclude from this that X contains an infinite number of parts. And so it follows, supposedly, that X is so large as to be unlimited.[24]

Each of these Zenonian arguments—the paradox of the runner and the 'large' half of the small–large antinomy—clearly involves a process of dichotomous division. In the runner paradox, what gets divided is the distance left to run; in the 'large' argument, what gets divided is the arbitrary existing object. So it would seem that both arguments could appropriately be described as arguments 'from the dichotomy'. And in *Physics* 6 Aristotle even *calls* the runner paradox 'the dichotomy', adding some support to the idea that he is referring to this paradox in *Physics* 1.3.[25]

The problem, however, is that it is not at all clear why either of these arguments should have been thought to call for the introduction of atoms. Suppose that the universe consists of atomic bodies. On this hypothesis it is still the case that, in order to get from one end of a racetrack to the other,

---

[23] If the front and back halves of X did not exist, then it is hard to see how X could have any thickness.

[24] This last step of the argument is typically thought to depend on the false assumption that if an object has an infinite number of parts, each of which has some size, then the object itself will be infinite in size. However, for a defence of an interesting alternative interpretation, see Hasper 2006, 68–78. On Hasper's reading, Zeno's point is that objects cannot have 'final' (ἔσχατα) parts, and so cannot have limits, and so must be unlimited in size. Cf. also Fränkel 1942.

[25] See *Phys.* 6.9, 239b18–22. Owen (1957–8, 207) and Charlton (1992, 63) both think that 'the argument from the dichotomy' of *Physics* 1.3 is the runner paradox.

a runner must traverse an infinite number of distances. Positing atomic bodies does nothing to explain how this is possible. Again, any extended body, even an atom, can be regarded as having a front half and a back half. And so it would seem that Zeno's 'large' argument can be given whether the universe consists of atoms or not.

One response to this problem would be to conclude that Aristotle is not referring to the atomists at 187a1–3 after all. But in fact these two arguments are not our only options; there is a third candidate that we also need to consider. As Stephen Makin has suggested,[26] the dichotomy argument may be a different Eleatic argument, one described by Porphyry in his lost commentary on the *Physics*, in a passage preserved by Simplicius:

> For indeed, since it [sc. what is] is everywhere alike, if it is divisible,[27] it will be divisible everywhere alike, and not divisible here but not there. So let it have been divided everywhere. Then it is again clear that nothing will remain, but it will have vanished, and if indeed it is composed, it will again be composed of nothing. For if something remains, it will not yet have been divided everywhere. So from these considerations, too, he [sc. Parmenides] says, it is obvious that what is will be indivisible, partless, and one.[28]
>
> (Simplicius, *In Phys.* 140.1–6)

This is one of two Eleatic arguments that Porphyry gives in the context of explaining Aristotle's reference to the argument from the dichotomy. For ease of reference I shall call it the 'indivisibility argument'.[29] It can be set out like this:

---

[26]   Makin 1993, 52. Cf. also Hasper 1999, 5 n. 7.

[27]   In this sentence 'divisible' (not 'divided') is the correct translation of διαιρετόν. If the word meant 'divided' then the next sentence would be superfluous.

[28]   καὶ γὰρ δὴ ἐπεὶ πάντῃ ὅμοιόν ἐστιν, εἴπερ διαιρετὸν ὑπάρχει, πάντῃ ὁμοίως ἔσται διαιρετόν, ἀλλ' οὐ τῇ μέν, τῇ δὲ οὔ. διῃρήσθω δὴ πάντῃ· δῆλον οὖν πάλιν ὡς οὐδὲν ὑπομενεῖ, ἀλλ' ἔσται φροῦδον, καὶ εἴπερ συστήσεται, πάλιν ἐκ τοῦ μηδενὸς συστήσεται. εἰ γὰρ ὑπομενεῖ τι, οὐδέ πω γενήσεται πάντῃ διῃρημένον. ὥστε καὶ ἐκ τούτων φανερόν φησιν, ὡς ἀδιαίρετόν τε καὶ ἀμερὲς καὶ ἓν ἔσται τὸ ὄν.

[29]   Both of the arguments given by Porphyry aim to establish indivisibility, but since I shall only be discussing the argument just quoted, this label should not cause any confusion. Porphyry's account of the other argument is quoted by Simplicius in the preceding lines, at 139.27–32: 'For if, he [sc. Parmenides] says, it is divisible, let it have been divided in two, and then let each of the parts be divided in two, and, with this

(1) What is is everywhere alike. (Compare Parmenides B 8.22.)

(2) So, if what is is divisible, it must be divisible everywhere, rather than being divisible at some points but not at others. (Since it is entirely uniform, there is no reason why it should be divisible at some points but not at others.)

(3) So, suppose that what is has actually been divided everywhere. (That is, suppose that all of its formerly continuous parts have been physically separated from one another.)

(4) On this supposition, nothing will be left. ('For if something remains, [what is] will not yet have been divided everywhere.')

(5) It follows that what is is composed of nothing, which is impossible.

(6) So, what is is not divisible everywhere.

(7) So, what is is indivisible.

It is important to note, as a caveat, that we know nothing about Porphyry's source for this argument. The words appear to be Porphyry's own; while he writes as though he is telling us what Parmenides 'says', there is no evidence that he is quoting from or even paraphrasing an earlier presentation of the indivisibility argument.[30] It is possible that he is simply conjecturing as to what the 'argument from the dichotomy' might have been.

having happened forever, it is clear, he says, that either there will remain some final minimal atomic magnitudes, infinite in multitude, and the whole will be composed of an infinite multitude of minima, or it will have vanished and dissolved into nothing, and will be composed of nothing. Both of which options are absurd. Therefore it will not be divided, but will remain one' (εἰ γὰρ εἴη, φησί, διαιρετόν, τετμήσθω δίχα, κἄπειτα τῶν μερῶν ἑκάτερον δίχα, καὶ τούτου ἀεὶ γενομένου δῆλόν φησιν, ὡς ἤτοι ὑπομενεῖ τινὰ ἔσχατα μεγέθη ἐλάχιστα καὶ ἄτομα, πλήθει δὲ ἄπειρα, καὶ τὸ ὅλον ἐξ ἐλαχίστων, πλήθει δὲ ἀπείρων συστήσεται· ἢ φροῦδον ἔσται καὶ εἰς οὐθὲν ἔτι διαλυθήσεται καὶ ἐκ τοῦ μηδενὸς συστήσεται· ἅπερ ἄτοπα. οὐκ ἄρα διαιρεθήσεται, ἀλλὰ μενεῖ ἕν).

[30] The present argument should be distinguished from the Eleatic argument reported by Aristotle at GC 1.8, 325a6–13 and discussed in section 6.3. While both are concerned with 'division everywhere', the latter is an argument for a different conclusion (that the universe is continuous), and does not assume that if a thing is divisible everywhere then it is possible that it actually be divided everywhere. The closest parallel for Porphyry's argument is the Democritean argument presented at GC 1.2, 316a14–34. I shall say more about this parallel in a moment.

Even so, a good case can be made that Porphyry is on the right track. Perhaps he is wrong to attribute the indivisibility argument to Parmenides,[31] but there is reason nonetheless to suspect that this argument—or something very close to it—is the second Eleatic argument to which Aristotle is referring in *Physics* 1.3.

I start with what might seem to be the obvious difficulty for this proposal: in the Porphyrian version at Simplicius, *In Physica* 140.1–6, the indivisibility argument does not explicitly mention a process of dichotomous division, unlike the runner paradox and the 'large' half of the small–large antinomy. This does not seem to me to be a serious problem, however, because the indivisibility argument can easily be formulated in such a way that it does mention such a process. For example: 'If what is is divisible everywhere alike, then let it be divided in two, and let each of the resulting parts be divided in two, and so on and so on. Suppose that this whole process has been completely carried out. Then nothing will remain ... '.[32] Since the argument can easily be presented in this way, with explicit reference to dichotomous division, it seems clear that it could have been regarded as an argument 'from the dichotomy'.

Next, supposing the indivisibility argument to be an authentic Eleatic argument, we can understand why it might have led the atomists to posit atoms. A consequence of the atomists' introduction of void is that the first premise of the indivisibility argument is false. Reality consists of two fundamentally different kinds of thing, body and void, and so is not uniform or 'all alike'. Nevertheless, it is still the case that reality has *parts* that are all alike: the atomists hold that there are solid bodies (in other words, bodies which do not contain any void), and any such body will be uniform.[33] A question therefore

---

[31] The argument is generally thought to be Zenonian, although it cannot be identified with any of the arguments in the surviving fragments. Cf. Makin 1982.

[32] Compare the first argument that Porphyry describes, quoted in n. 29. It seems likely that Porphyry expects us to understand that, in the second argument, the division is once again to be carried out by means of the repeated bisection of parts, as in the first argument.

[33] In the atomists' view there is just a single kind of bodily stuff, which is configured in different ways. (See *Metaph. H* 2, 1042b11–15; *Phys.* 1.2, 184b20–2;

arises as to whether such bodies are (physically) divisible or indivisible. The indivisibility argument suggests that they would have to be indivisible. Supposing that a body is uniform, if it is divisible some-where, it would have to be divisible everywhere. (There is no reason why a uniform body should be divisible only at some points and not at others.) But it is impossible for a body to be divisible everywhere—or so the indivisibility argument seems to show. For suppose that the body actually has been divided everywhere. Then there will be noth-ing left. But in that case the body must have been composed of nothing, which is impossible. So a uniform body cannot be divisible anywhere. In other words, it must be an atom.[34]

In this way we can see how reflection on the Eleatic indivisibility argument could have led the atomists to posit atoms. What is more, this account of the motivation for atoms closely matches the account given by Aristotle in *De Generatione et Corruptione* 1.2. At 316a14–34 he describes the puzzle that led Democritus to think that there must be atomic magnitudes:[35]

For there is a puzzle if one is going to suppose that a body and a magnitude is divisible everywhere, and that this is possible. For what will there be that escapes the division? For if it is divisible everywhere, and this is possible, then this thing could also be, all at the same time, in a state of having been divided everywhere, even if it has not undergone the division all at the same time.

Cael. 1.7, 275b31–276a1.) It is therefore reasonable for them to think that any solid (ναστόν) or voidless parcel of this stuff will be uniform. The basic thought here is Milesian: qualitative differences are due to differences in the configuration of the single underlying stuff; so, if some parcel of the underlying stuff has the same consistency throughout its extent, it will also be qualitatively uniform throughout. Aristotle notes the similarities between the atomist and Milesian theories at *Metaph. A* 4, 985b10–19.

[34] This explanation of the atomists' reasoning is indebted to Makin 1993, 49–50.

[35] I assume that Aristotle here means to be giving us Democritus' own argument for positing atoms. This is suggested by the immediately preceding lines (316a13–14): 'But Democritus would appear to have been persuaded by appropriate, that is, physical, arguments. What we mean will become clear as we go on' (Δημόκριτος δ᾽ ἂν φανείη οἰκείοις καὶ φυσικοῖς λόγοις πεπεῖσθαι. δῆλον δ᾽ ἔσται ὃ λέγομεν προιοῦσιν). Cf. also Sedley 2004, 67. Note, however, that some scholars have questioned whether the argument at 316a14–34 derives in its entirety from Democritus: see e.g. Rosen and Malink 2012, 221–2.

And if this happened, there would be nothing impossible about it. So, in the same way both by halves but also in general, if it is by nature divisible everywhere, then, if it has been divided, nothing impossible will have happened, since not even if it has been divided into a hundred million pieces will there be anything impossible (although presumably no one could so divide it). Since, therefore, the body is like this everywhere, let it have been divided [everywhere]. Then what magnitude will remain? For it is not possible [for there to be one]. For then there will be something that has not been divided, yet it was divisible everywhere. But if there is no body or magnitude [left], but nonetheless a division has taken place, then either [the body] will be composed of points, and its components will be without magnitude, or there will be nothing at all, so that it would both come to be from and be composed of nothing, and in that case the whole thing would be nothing but an appearance. And similarly, even if it is composed of points, it will have no quantity. For when [the points] were touching and there was one magnitude and they were together, they did not make the whole any bigger. For when something has been divided into two or more parts, the whole is no smaller or bigger than it was before. So that even if all [the points] are put together, they will not produce any magnitude.[36]

According to this passage, the Democritean argument for atoms proceeds by way of a *reductio ad absurdum* of the assumption that there are bodies that are divisible everywhere. The supposed absurdity of this assumption is revealed by considering a body that has actually been divided everywhere. This, of course, fits very nicely with the idea that the atomists' introduction of atoms was prompted by the Eleatic

---

[36] ἔχει γὰρ ἀπορίαν, εἴ τις θήσει σῶμά τι εἶναι καὶ μέγεθος πάντῃ διαιρετόν, καὶ τοῦτο δυνατόν. τί γὰρ ἔσται ὅπερ τὴν διαίρεσιν διαφεύγει; εἰ γὰρ πάντῃ διαιρετόν, καὶ τοῦτο δυνατόν, κἂν ἅμα εἴη τοῦτο πάντῃ διῃρημένον, καὶ εἰ μὴ ἅμα διῄρηται· κἂν εἰ τοῦτο γένοιτο, οὐδὲν ἂν εἴη ἀδύνατον. οὐκοῦν καὶ κατὰ μέσον ὡσαύτως, καὶ ὅλως δέ, εἰ πάντῃ πέφυκε διαιρετόν, ἂν διαιρεθῇ, οὐδὲν ἔσται ἀδύνατον γεγονός, ἐπεὶ οὐδ᾽ ἂν εἰς μυρία μυριάκις διῃρημένα ᾖ, οὐδὲν ἀδύνατον· καίτοι ἴσως οὐδεὶς ἂν διέλοι. ἐπεὶ τοίνυν πάντῃ τοιοῦτόν ἐστι τὸ σῶμα, διῃρήσθω. τί οὖν ἔσται λοιπὸν μέγεθος; οὐ γὰρ οἷόν τε· ἔσται γάρ τι οὐ διῃρημένον, ἦν δὲ πάντῃ διαιρετόν. ἀλλὰ μὴν εἰ μηδὲν ἔσται σῶμα μηδὲ μέγεθος, διαίρεσις δ᾽ ἔσται, ἢ ἐκ στιγμῶν ἔσται, καὶ ἀμεγέθη ἐξ ὧν σύγκειται, ἢ οὐδὲν παντάπασιν, ὥστε κἂν γίνοιτο ἐκ μηδενὸς κἂν εἴη συγκείμενον, καὶ τὸ πᾶν δὴ οὐδὲν ἀλλ᾽ ἢ φαινόμενον. ὁμοίως δὲ κἂν ᾖ ἐκ στιγμῶν, οὐκ ἔσται ποσόν. ὁπότε γὰρ ἥπτοντο καὶ ἓν ἦν μέγεθος καὶ ἅμα ἦσαν, οὐδὲν ἐποίουν μεῖζον τὸ πᾶν. διαιρεθέντος γὰρ εἰς δύο καὶ πλείω, οὐδὲν ἔλαττον οὐδὲ μεῖζον τὸ πᾶν τοῦ πρότερον, ὥστε κἂν πᾶσαι συντεθῶσιν, οὐδὲν ποιήσουσι μέγεθος. The text is Rashed's, with three changes: at 316a22 I read εἰς μυρία μυριάκις; at a24 I put the question mark after μέγεθος (with Sedley 2008, 329 n. 27); and at a29 I read ἀλλ᾽ ἢ instead of ἀλλά.

indivisibility argument. The latter argument raises an almost identical problem for the assumption that an object (in this case, the universe as a whole) is divisible everywhere.[37] The present passage therefore supports the idea that 'the argument from the dichotomy'—the Eleatic argument to which the atomists were 'giving in' with their introduction of atoms—is the indivisibility argument. If this identification is correct, it means that Aristotle's brief comment about the introduction of atoms in *Physics* 1.3 harmonizes with his fuller account of the motivation for atoms in *De Generatione et Corruptione* 1.2.

7.4 Why the Atomists Concede Too Much

I have suggested that the two Eleatic arguments referred to at 187a1–3 are (i) Parmenides' argument for the continuity and uniformity of what is, and (ii) the indivisibility argument described by Porphyry *apud* Simplicius, *In Physica* 140.1–6. The anonymous respondents to these arguments are the atomists, Leucippus and Democritus. The atomists attempted to resist the first argument by claiming that void ('what is not') is something that exists. And they thought that the second argument demanded the introduction of atoms, or 'atomic magnitudes'.

Aristotle objects that in positing atoms and void the atomists were 'giving in' to the two Eleatic arguments. By this he does not mean that the atomists accepted the arguments' monistic conclusions; clearly they did not. Rather, he means that in their attempt to maintain pluralism in the face of these arguments, the atomists made philosophical concessions that they ought not to have made. In this way Aristotle casts doubt on a rival theory of principles to his own.

Aristotle does not explain why the introduction of atoms was a case of conceding too much to the Eleatics, but we can appreciate why he might think this. The Eleatic indivisibility argument contains a fallacy: it assumes that if a body is divisible everywhere, then it is

---

[37] I say 'almost identical', because the indivisibility argument, as presented by Porphyry, does not consider the possibility that the parts resulting from the complete division are points. Apart from that difference, the problems are the same.

possible for it to have been divided everywhere. But this assumption is mistaken. For a body to be 'divisible everywhere' is for it to be the case that, for every point within the body, it is possible that the body has been divided there. But this does not mean that it is possible that, at every point within the body, the body has been divided there.[38] For this reason, the indivisibility argument fails to show that it is impossible for a uniform body to be divisible everywhere. If the atomists had noticed this fallacy, they would have seen that the argument does not justify the introduction of atoms. Moreover, there are, in Aristotle's view, positive reasons to *reject* atoms.[39] Thus we can appreciate why he should think that by positing atoms the atomists were making a concession to the Eleatics that they ought not to have made.

How about the atomists' response to the first Eleatic argument, their introduction of void? Why does this concede too much to Parmenides' argument for monism? Here Aristotle gives us the following explanation:

But it is also obvious that it is not true that if being signifies one thing, and if it is impossible for the contradictory to hold at the same time, then there will be nothing that is not. For nothing prevents what is not from being—not from being, without qualification, but from being what is not *something*. But then it is absurd to claim that all things will be one, if there is nothing else besides what is itself. For who understands what is itself unless as what is essentially some kind of being [*to hoper on ti*]? But if this is so, then nevertheless nothing prevents the things that are from being many, as has been said.   (187a3–10)

As I suggest we read these lines, their message is that the atomists' introduction of 'what is not' is unnecessary; we do not need to claim that void exists in order to resist Parmenides' argument for monism.

Aristotle starts by pointing out that Parmenides' assumptions are consistent with its being the case that there is some X and some Y

---

[38] A helpful analogy to bring out the fallaciousness of the inference is a presidential election. For every candidate that stands, it is possible that that candidate will win. But it is not possible that every candidate will win.

[39] See *Cael.* 3.4, 303a20–4; *GC* 1.2, 316b16–18.

such that *X is not Y*. This seems to be the meaning of the sentence at 187a5–6: 'For nothing prevents what is not from being—not from being, without qualification, but from being what is not *something*'. In other words, while Parmenides may be correct that there is nothing that is not *without qualification*, nevertheless his assumptions do not rule out the existence of things that have the property of not being other things.[40] This is a point that Aristotle takes over from the *Sophist*.

The next part of the passage argues that, given that this is so, Parmenides does not have a good argument for monism, regardless of the existence or otherwise of void. It is absurd, Aristotle says, to claim that if there is nothing besides 'what is itself' (*auto to on*), then it follows that all things are one (187a6–8). Here I take the expression *auto to on* to refer to the Parmenidean One—the entity that Parmenides calls 'what is' (*to eon*)—and not to the property being (nor to the Form, Being itself).[41] Parmenides argues that the universe contains nothing else apart from what is: 'For nothing else <either> is or will be | besides what is, since Fate bound it | to be whole and unchanging' (B 8.36–8).[42] Aristotle's claim at 187a6–8 is that even if this were true, it would not follow that everything is one.

The argument for why this does not follow is given in the next two sentences: 'For who understands what is itself [*auto to on*] unless as what is essentially some kind of being [*to hoper on ti*]? But if this is so, then nevertheless nothing prevents the things that are from being many, as has been said' (187a8–10). Aristotle is returning here, I think, to the implications of the earlier argument from definitional divisibility (186b14–35). That argument purported to show that, for any property *F*, if *F* is an essential property of each of its bearers, then the definitional components of *F* are essential properties of each of their bearers too. Now, if the Parmenidean One *is*, there must be

---

[40] Cf. the distinction drawn at 186b9–10.

[41] Cf. the use of αὐτὸ τὸ ὄν at *Phys.* 1.8, 191a33.

[42] οὐδὲν γὰρ <ἢ> ἔστιν ἢ ἔσται | ἄλλο πάρεξ τοῦ ἐόντος, ἐπεὶ τό γε Μοῖρ᾽ ἐπέδησεν | οὖλον ἀκίνητόν τ᾽ ἔμεναι.

something *that* it is. To put it another way, there must be some kind of being such that the Parmenidean One is *essentially* that kind of being. If the essence of the One is divisible into parts, then the argument from definitional divisibility entails that the One has multiple essential properties. And in that case Parmenides is committed to pluralism, both entity pluralism and essence pluralism, even if he is right that the natural world is an illusion and the only inhabitant of (concrete) reality is his solid, undifferentiated sphere. Of course, Parmenides might insist that the essence of the One is indivisible, and thus deny that he is committed to the existence of multiple essential properties. But there is nothing in his argument to suggest that the essence of the One would have to be indivisible, and so there is nothing to prevent both forms of pluralism—entity pluralism and essence pluralism—from being true.

If Parmenides were able to rule out the possibility of one thing's not being another thing, *then* he would be in a position to claim that the essence of the One is indivisible. The essence of the One could not have a plurality of definitional components, because each of these components would have to have the property of *not being* the others. But Parmenides' starting assumptions only rule out the existence of what is not *without qualification*; they do not rule out the possibility that there is some X and some Y such that X is not Y. This is where the previous lines (187a3–6) become relevant: because Parmenides' assumptions only exclude the existence of things that 'are not *without qualification*', they are insufficient to establish that the essence of the One is indivisible.

The upshot is that the atomists' introduction of void is unnecessary, at least for the purposes of avoiding the Parmenidean conclusion that everything is one. The atomists posit void so as to resist Parmenides' argument for monism: their idea is that if void exists, then the world need not be the continuous, homogeneous whole that Parmenides claims it to be. Aristotle's reply to the atomists is that even if the world were like this—a continuous, homogeneous whole—it still would not follow that everything is one. There is nothing in Parmenides' argument to prevent his 'One' from having a plurality of essential properties which differ from one another in account. *Contra* the atomists, then, we do not need void in order to block Parmenides' argument for monism.

It is important to be clear on what Aristotle is *not* saying here. He is not saying (here) that the atomists are wrong to think that void is needed to explain how the world can be non-continuous and qualitatively differentiated. As a matter of fact, Aristotle does think that the atomists are wrong about this. (According to his own physical theory, the cosmos is a corporeal plenum which nonetheless consists of many non-continuous, heterogeneous bodies.) But this is not the message of the present passage. Aristotle's claim here is that there is a simple, non-atomistic way of resisting Parmenides' argument for monism. This way of resisting the argument does not require any innovations in physics; it only requires us to appreciate a point of ontology. Parmenides' premises fail to rule out the possibility that the One has multiple essential properties. This means that, regardless of whether or not he is successful in establishing that the universe is a continuous, uniform whole, he fails to make a sufficient case for his extreme monism.

7.5 The Birth of Atomism

Aristotle is our primary source of information about the original motivation of Presocratic atomism. It is clear that he thinks the atomist theory was developed in response to the Eleatics, but it is controversial precisely which Eleatic arguments he thinks the atomists were responding to. Some scholars have denied that Aristotle thinks that Parmenides' arguments were an important influence on the atomists.[43] The main basis for this denial is the idea that in *De Generatione et Corruptione* 1.8 Aristotle presents atomism primarily as a response to Melissus' version of the Eleatic theory. Against this,

---

[43] See e.g. Kirk et al. 1983, 408–9; Palmer 2009, 48–9.

I have suggested that at 325a2–17 Aristotle is thinking of Parmenides just as much as Melissus.[44]

The closing section of *Physics* 1.3 confirms that in Aristotle's view atomism arose (in part) out of a direct confrontation with Parmenides' argument for monism. Aristotle is telling us that the atomists affirmed the existence of void ('what is not') in order to block Parmenides' argument for continuity and uniformity. Aristotle also mentions a second Eleatic argument: the argument 'from the dichotomy', which led to the introduction of atoms. This is likely to be a second-generation Eleatic argument, possibly due to Zeno, which was designed to vindicate the original Parmenidean move from uniformity to indivisibility.

Aristotle gives reasons for rejecting atoms and void in other places. In the closing section of *Physics* 1.3 his aim is not to establish that atomism is false, but rather to cast doubt on its motivation. In the light of his preceding criticisms of Parmenides' argument for monism, we can see that the atomists' introduction of void is unnecessary for the purposes of defending pluralism. The atomists correctly spot a fatal flaw in Parmenides' argument; in effect, they dispute the key Parmenidean assumption that being is said in just a single way. But in Aristotle's eyes they are wrong to think that we must rely on the highly problematic concept of void in order to resist Parmenides' monistic conclusions.

---

[44] See section 5.7. Aristotle may be thinking of Zeno too: the second of the three Eleatic arguments mentioned at 325a2–17 has a Zenonian ring to it.

8

Did Aristotle Change His Mind about Parmenides?

8.1 Introduction

Aristotle's critique of the Eleatics in *Physics* 1.2–3 shows that he reads them as radical monists who deny the possibility of change. An immediate consequence of this theory is that the pluralistic, changing world of the senses—the world studied by natural philosophy—is just an illusion. This is why Aristotle says, in the preface to his critique, that they 'do not speak about nature' (185a18). They effectively deny that the world of nature exists.[1]

There is a sense, of course, in which Parmenides obviously did 'speak about nature'. In the second main part of the poem, the *Doxa*, he provided a theory of the natural world, covering topics from astronomy to human embryology. Aristotle does not mention the *Doxa* in *Physics* 1.2–3, but his criticisms of Parmenides strongly suggest a certain view of the *Doxa*'s intended status. Specifically, they suggest that Aristotle favours an 'anti-cosmological' interpretation of Parmenides' poem, on which the *Doxa* is meant to present a false theory of an illusory world. The theory of the *Doxa* is pluralistic, and so if Parmenides were to endorse it he would be a kind of pluralist.[2] But if Parmenides were a

---

[1] This is also why Aristotle contrasts Parmenides and Melissus with 'the natural philosophers' (οἱ φυσικοί): see 184b16–17, 186a20–1, and *Phys.* 1.4, 187a12.

[2] The theory is committed to the existence of many entities and of many kinds of entity. So, if Parmenides endorsed the theory, he would be both an entity pluralist and an essence pluralist.

pluralist—or even if he were merely open to pluralism as a possible view—then it would make no sense to try to argue against him by showing that he is committed to pluralism. And yet this is exactly what Aristotle tries to do.[3] We can infer that Aristotle does not regard Parmenides as a pluralist or as someone who is open to pluralism. Consequently, we can infer that Aristotle takes Parmenides to reject the pluralistic theory of the *Doxa*.

There are other passages, beyond *Physics* 1.2–3, which likewise suggest that Aristotle favours an anti-cosmological interpretation of Parmenides:

(i) When he returns to the Eleatics in *Physics* 1.8, to address their argument against the possibility of coming to be, he again presents them as radical monists who think that change is impossible.[4] Here he does not mention Parmenides by name,[5] but he alludes to Parmenides' ways or roads of enquiry at 191a24–7: 'the first people to proceed philosophically got turned off course in their enquiry after truth and the nature of things, driven as it were onto some other road by their inexperience'.[6]

(ii) In *De Caelo* 3.1, Aristotle says that the circle of Melissus and Parmenides completely abolish the possibility of generation and destruction, and claim that things only *seem* to come into and go out of existence (298b14–17). The *Doxa* is explicitly committed to the reality of generation and destruction (see B 10, 11, and 19), and so this passage from the *De Caelo* suggests that Aristotle does not take the *Doxa* to represent Parmenides' actual position.

---

[3] See *Phys.* 1.2, 185a20–32 and 185b9–11.

[4] For their rejection of change, see 191b31–3. For their monism, see 191a32–3: 'they deny that the many are, and say that only what is itself is' (οὐδ' εἶναι πολλά φασιν ἀλλὰ μόνον αὐτὸ τὸ ὄν). I take Aristotle to be referring here specifically to Eleatic monism, and not also to material monism. Unlike the Eleatics, the material monists do not deny that 'many things are': cf. *Phys.* 1.4, 187a12–16.

[5] Although see *Phys.* 1.9, 192a1.

[6] ζητοῦντες γὰρ οἱ κατὰ φιλοσοφίαν πρῶτοι τὴν ἀλήθειαν καὶ τὴν φύσιν τῶν ὄντων ἐξετράπησαν οἷον ὁδόν τινα ἄλλην ἀπωσθέντες ὑπὸ ἀπειρίας. See Clarke 2015, 130–1. On Aristotle's use of allusion, cf. McCabe 2015, 26.

(iii) In *De Generatione et Corruptione* 1.8, Aristotle once again portrays the Eleatics as holding that the universe is one and unchanging. They reject the testimony of the senses in favour of a worldview so paradoxical that it seems to border on madness, 'for no mad person is so out of their mind that they think that fire and ice are one' (325a19–21).[7] As in *Physics* 1.8, the individual Eleatics are not mentioned by name, but it is hard to doubt that Parmenides is one of the philosophers under discussion.

(iv) Finally, Sextus Empiricus (*Against the Physicists* 2.46) tells us that Aristotle referred to Parmenides and Melissus as '*stasiōtai* of nature' and 'unnaturalists' (*aphusikoi*). These labels must derive from one of Aristotle's lost works, possibly his *On Philosophy*. The first is an untranslatable pun, borrowed from Plato's *Theaetetus*.[8] As Richard Bett explains:

Stasis can mean a stationary position, or a position in an argument... The noun derived from it that occurs here, *stasiōtēs*, usually means a supporter of a particular position or faction; but in this case, since Parmenides and Melissus denied the reality of motion, there is also a pun on the other meaning of *stasis*.[9]

The point of calling Parmenides and Melissus '*stasiōtai* of nature' is that they are supporters of a position that brings nature to a complete stop. By doing away with motion and change, their theory does away with nature itself; hence the second label, 'unnaturalists'. The labels are further evidence that Aristotle regarded Parmenides as an

---

[7] οὐδένα γὰρ τῶν μαινομένων ἐξεστάναι τοσοῦτον ὥστε τὸ πῦρ ἓν εἶναι δοκεῖν καὶ τὸν κρύσταλλον. Aristotle's thought here is that, according to the Eleatic theory, 'fire' and 'ice' refer to one and the same thing. He may be thinking of Parmenides B 8.38–9: 'thus it [*sc.* what is] is named all [names] | which mortals have set down, trusting them to be true' (τῷ πάντ' ὀνόμασται | ὅσσα βροτοὶ κατέθεντο πεποιθότες εἶναι ἀληθῆ). For this text and construal see Burnyeat 1982, 19 n. 22. Cf. also *Phys.* 1.2, 185b19–25, where Aristotle argues that Eleatic essence monism entails that supposedly opposite properties (such as good and bad) are identical.

[8] At *Theaet.* 181a7–8 the Eleatics are referred to as 'the *stasiōtai* of the whole' (οἱ τοῦ ὅλου στασιῶται).

[9] Bett 2012, 90 n. 23.

opponent of natural philosophy, including—we may assume—the natural philosophy of his own *Doxa*.

So there is a lot of evidence that Aristotle adopted an anti-cosmological interpretation of Parmenides. But still we may ask: Did he *consistently* adopt this interpretation? Other texts have been thought to suggest otherwise. In particular, a passage in *Metaphysics A* 5 is widely believed to show that—here, at least—Aristotle favours a 'cosmological' interpretation of the poem, on which the *Doxa* presents Parmenides' own views about the (really existing) natural world.[10]

This passage from the *Metaphysics* has led some commentators to think that Aristotle substantially revised his view of Parmenides.[11] At first, these commentators suggest, Aristotle interpreted Parmenides as defending the same sort of theory as Melissus, and as entirely rejecting plurality and change. But later on, as a result of further reflection on the poem, Aristotle came to see Parmenides as a sort of pluralist. On Aristotle's revised interpretation, Parmenides offers the pluralistic *Doxa* not as a false theory of an illusory world, but as his own account of reality 'in its phenomenal aspect'.[12]

Is this developmentalist story true? Did Aristotle change his mind about Parmenides? My goal in this chapter is to argue that he did not. I want to argue that, contrary to what is often thought, *Metaphysics A* 5 provides no basis for attributing to Aristotle a cosmological interpretation of Parmenides.[13] Instead, there is good reason to think that Aristotle consistently maintains the radically monistic, anti-cosmological interpretation that he favours in *Physics* 1.2–3.

[10] The passage is 986b25–987a2. For this very common reading, see Ross 1924, 1: 133–4; Cherniss 1935, 220–1; McDiarmid 1953, 121; Chalmers 1960, 10; Tarán 1965, 284–91; Owens 1974, 379–80 and 393–5; Miller 1977, 254; Nehamas 1981, 107 and 111 n. 32; Mansfeld 1986, 5 and 15; Wardy 1988, 127; Curd 1998, 98 n. 2; Finkelberg 1999, 248; Palmer 2008, 542–3; 2009, 35–42, 222–3, and 321; Cordero 2010, 244; Brémond 2017, 36–7.

[11] See Mansfeld 1986, 5 and 15; Palmer 2008, 542–3.

[12] According to Palmer (2009, 35–42), Aristotle came to see the two main parts of the poem as providing two complementary accounts of reality, 'first in its intelligible and then in its phenomenal aspects'.

[13] On this point I agree with Wedin 2014, 247–8.

8.2 The Eleatics in *Metaphysics A* 5

Aristotle's stated aim in *Metaphysics A* 3–7 is to examine his predecessors' views about causation, in order to confirm his own doctrine of the four causes (the doctrine that there are four, and just four, different types of cause: formal, material, efficient, and final).[14] After discussing the Presocratic natural philosophers in *A* 3–4, and the Pythagoreans in the first part of *A* 5, he comes in the second part of *A* 5 to the Eleatic monists:[15]

But there are some people [*sc.* the Eleatics] who spoke about the universe as though it were one nature. But they do not all speak in the same way— neither in terms of the excellence of what they say, nor in terms of its conformity to nature. Now, the discussion of them is in no way appropriate to our present investigation into causes. For—unlike some of the natural philosophers who, although they suppose what is to be one, nevertheless generate from the one as from matter—these people [*sc.* the Eleatics] speak in a different way. For those people [*sc.* the natural philosophers] add change— at any rate they generate the universe—but these others say that it is unchanging.[16]   (*Metaph. A* 5, 986b10–17)

Aristotle mentions the Eleatics so as to set them aside: they will not be of any use to the present investigation into causes. His rationale for setting them aside is not fully spelled out, but it seems plausible that his thought is that if their position were correct, then there would be no causes at all.[17]

---

[14] See *Metaph. A* 3, 983b1–6. For a full discussion of the aims, stated and otherwise, of *Metaphysics A*'s historical survey, see Frede 2004.

[15] The Eleatics already appeared briefly back in *A* 3, where Aristotle was explaining the limitations of material monism (see section 8.5).

[16] εἰσὶ δέ τινες οἳ περὶ τοῦ παντὸς ὡς ἂν μιᾶς οὔσης φύσεως ἀπεφήναντο, τρόπον δὲ οὐ τὸν αὐτὸν πάντες οὔτε τοῦ καλῶς οὔτε τοῦ κατὰ τὴν φύσιν. εἰς μὲν οὖν τὴν νῦν σκέψιν τῶν αἰτίων οὐδαμῶς συναρμόττει περὶ αὐτῶν ὁ λόγος (οὐ γὰρ ὥσπερ ἔνιοι τῶν φυσιολόγων ἓν ὑποθέμενοι τὸ ὂν ὅμως γεννῶσιν ὡς ἐξ ὕλης τοῦ ἑνός, ἀλλ' ἕτερον τρόπον οὗτοι λέγουσιν· ἐκεῖνοι μὲν γὰρ προστιθέασι κίνησιν, γεννῶντές γε τὸ πᾶν, οὗτοι δὲ ἀκίνητον εἶναί φασιν).

[17] *Pace* Palmer (2008, 542), I doubt that Aristotle's exclusion of the Eleatics here is due to the fact that their position 'belongs to a higher science [*sc.* than physics]'—in other words, to metaphysics. The scope of the historical survey in *Metaphysics A* 3–7 is not restricted to physical theories (consider e.g. the discussion of the Platonic theory

Recall that in *Physics* 1.2 Aristotle argued that Eleatic monism is incompatible with the existence of principles: if reality is one, as the Eleatics claim, then there can be no principles, for a principle is a principle *of* some thing or things—and this requires that there be at least two entities (185a3–5, discussed in section 1.3). A similar argument can be used to show that on the Eleatic view (as Aristotle understands it) there can be no causes. A cause is a cause *of* some thing or things, and so for there to be causes there must be at least two entities, the cause and the thing of which it is the cause. The Eleatics' radical entity monism is therefore incompatible with the existence of causes, just as it is incompatible with the existence of principles. The Eleatics' position is to be distinguished from that of the material monists, who (*a*) accept the existence of change, and (*b*) generate a plurality from their original undifferentiated mass, and so (*c*) as entity pluralists are able to allow for the existence of principles and causes. The Eleatic One, by contrast, never becomes many, and so there is no room in the Eleatics' barren ontology for causes and principles.

Despite the fact that the Eleatics are to be excluded from *Metaphysics A*'s investigation into causes, Aristotle next proceeds to enter two qualifications. First, there is a difference in Parmenides' and Melissus' respective conceptions of their one being, a difference which in fact does have some significance from the point of view of the present enquiry:

However, this much, at least, is relevant to the present investigation: Parmenides seems to grasp the one in virtue of the account [*kata ton logon*], while Melissus seems to grasp the one in virtue of the matter [*kata tēn hulēn*]—this is why the former says that it is limited, the latter that it is unlimited. Xenophanes, the first of these monists (for Parmenides is said to have been his pupil),[18] made nothing clear, nor does he seem to have

of Forms in *A* 6), and so it would be odd for Aristotle to exclude the Eleatics on the grounds that their theory is metaphysical and not physical.

[18] Following Plato, *Soph.* 242d4–7, Aristotle here treats Xenophanes as a proto-Eleatic. Aristotle's comments suggest that he took Xenophanes to be a pantheist who identified the cosmos ('the whole heaven') with a single god (cf. Barnes 1982, 99). On this interpretation, Xenophanes is rightly thought of as a certain kind of monist.

apprehended the nature of either of these. Instead, looking towards the whole heaven, he says that the One is god.[19] (986b17–24)

Precisely what this difference between Parmenides and Melissus amounts to is not obvious. We should start by trying to understand what Aristotle means by 'one in virtue of the account'. In my view, this notion should be distinguished from the notion of 'one in account' that we find in *Physics* 1.2–3, despite the obvious terminological similarities. To say that reality is 'one in account' in the *Physics* 1.2–3 sense is to say that all of reality has the same essence—in other words, that it is uniform. As we have seen, Aristotle certainly attributes this view to Parmenides, but there is good evidence that he attributes it to Melissus too.[20] So it is unlikely that this is what he has in mind in *Metaphysics A 5* when he *contrasts* Parmenides and Melissus.

A better interpretation, I think, is the following. Aristotle is suggesting that the Parmenidean One can be viewed as a composite of matter and form. Like a bronze sphere, the Parmenidean One is made up of material stuff which collectively instantiates the form of sphericity.[21] As with other matter–form composites, this form is the source of the One's unity—the cause (as it were) of its being one object and not many.[22] Therefore we can say that the Parmenidean One is one *in virtue of its form* (*eidos*). Equivalently, given that Aristotle often uses 'account'

And his theory has further affinities with that of Parmenides and Melissus: like their unmoving One, Xenophanes' cosmic god 'always remains in the same place, not moving at all, | nor is it fitting for him to go to different places at different times' (αἰεὶ δ' ἐν ταὐτῷ μίμνει κινούμενος οὐδέν | οὐδὲ μετέρχεσθαί μιν ἐπιπρέπει ἄλλοτε ἄλλῃ) (B 26). Cf. Bryan 2012, 93–100.

[19] οὐ μὴν ἀλλὰ τοσοῦτόν γε οἰκεῖόν ἐστι τῇ νῦν σκέψει. Παρμενίδης μὲν γὰρ ἔοικε τοῦ κατὰ τὸν λόγον ἑνὸς ἅπτεσθαι, Μέλισσος δὲ τοῦ κατὰ τὴν ὕλην (διὸ καὶ ὁ μὲν πεπερασμένον ὁ δ' ἄπειρόν φησιν εἶναι αὐτό)· Ξενοφάνης δὲ πρῶτος τούτων ἑνίσας (ὁ γὰρ Παρμενίδης τούτου λέγεται μαθητής) οὐδὲν διεσαφήνισεν, οὐδὲ τῆς φύσεως τούτων οὐδετέρας ἔοικε θιγεῖν, ἀλλ' εἰς τὸν ὅλον οὐρανὸν ἀποβλέψας τὸ ἓν εἶναί φησι τὸν θεόν.

[20] See sections 2.2.2 and 4.7.

[21] Of course, Aristotle is well aware that Parmenides does not explicitly distinguish matter and form. But I take the suggestion here to be that, even so, the Parmenidean One can be viewed as having these two different aspects.

[22] At *Metaph. Δ* 6, 1016b11–17, Aristotle gives the example of a shoe: its material parts (sole, straps, and so on) collectively instantiate a single form, and it is this that makes the object a genuine unity.

(*logos*) as a synonym for 'form' (*eidos*), we can also say that it is one 'in virtue of the account'.

In contrast to the Parmenidean One, the Melissan One is unlimited in all directions and has no shape or structure. As a consequence, there is no single form that its matter collectively instantiates.[23] What makes the Melissan One one thing is simply that it is an unbroken, homogeneous plenum. We can put this by saying that the Melissan One is one thing merely *in virtue of its matter*. So the Parmenidean One and the Melissan One are each one thing, but the unity of this one thing is to be explained in a different way in each case.[24]

Why does Aristotle interpret Parmenides and Melissus as having these differing views about the source of the One's unity? The answer is that this provides him with a way of explaining their disagreement over whether the One has spatial limits. As he says, 'this is why the former [*sc.* Parmenides] says that it is limited, the latter [*sc.* Melissus] that it is unlimited' (986b20–1). Parmenides gives his One spatial limits. The effect of this is to give it a determinate form, which functions as the source of its unity. Melissus, by contrast, is content for his One to be one merely in virtue of its matter; accordingly he has no comparable motivation to give it spatial limits and (thereby) a determinate form.

This reading of Aristotle's contrast between Parmenides and Melissus explains why it is 'relevant to the present investigation' (986b18). The Eleatics' different views about the source of the One's unity suggest that they had a rudimentary appreciation of the causal significance of matter and—in Parmenides' case—of form. The importance of this, from the perspective of the project of *Metaphysics* A 3–7, is that matter and form are two of the four Aristotelian causes. Thus we can say that Eleatics had an inkling of these crucial causal

[23] This is so even though the Melissan One is uniform—one 'in account' or 'in form' in the *Physics* 1.2–3 sense.

[24] Notice that if this is what Aristotle means by contrasting 'one in virtue of the account' and 'one in virtue of the matter', there is no implication that Parmenides' One is not a material object, *pace* e.g. McDiarmid (1953, 117), Bicknell (1964, 111), Tarán (1965, 287–8), and Kirk et al. (1983, 171).

notions, even though they did not explicitly distinguish them, and even though there is no room within their radically monistic ontology for the existence of causes.[25] Having made this first qualification to his claim that a discussion of the Eleatics does not belong in the enquiry into causes, Aristotle then goes on to add a second. Unlike the 'unsophisticated' Melissus and Xenophanes, Parmenides deserves a place in the enquiry for a further reason. It is this next passage which has often been taken to show that Aristotle now favours a cosmological interpretation of Parmenides. (There are some issues about the text and the translation, to which I shall return.)

These people, then, as we said, must be left aside by our present enquiry; the two of them completely, since they are a little too unsophisticated, namely Xenophanes and Melissus. But Parmenides seems perhaps to speak with more insight than they do. For, holding that besides what is, what is not is nothing, he thinks that, of necessity, what is is one, and nothing else is—we have spoken about this more clearly in the *Physics*. But being compelled to follow the appearances, and holding that <what is>[26] is one in virtue of the account [or: according to reason], but more in virtue of perception [or: according to perception], he again sets down two causes or two principles, hot and cold, speaking, that is, of fire and earth. And of these he aligns the one with what is and the other with what is not.[27]   (986b25–987a2)

---

[25] For a similar interpretation, cf. Alexander, *In Metaph.* 44.4–6.

[26] For the time being I read τὸ <ὂν> ἕν at 986b32, with Barnes (1984) and Palmer (2009, 37 n. 95). However, we can make sense of the text without the supplement. I come back to this point below.

[27] οὗτοι μὲν οὖν, καθάπερ εἴπομεν, ἀφετέοι πρὸς τὴν νῦν ζήτησιν, οἱ μὲν δύο καὶ πάμπαν ὡς ὄντες μικρὸν ἀγροικότεροι, Ξενοφάνης καὶ Μέλισσος· Παρμενίδης δὲ μᾶλλον βλέπων ἔοικέ που λέγειν· παρὰ γὰρ τὸ ὂν τὸ μὴ ὂν οὐθὲν ἀξιῶν εἶναι, ἐξ ἀνάγκης ἓν οἴεται εἶναι τὸ ὄν, καὶ ἄλλο οὐθέν (περὶ οὗ σαφεστέρως ἐν τοῖς περὶ φύσεως εἰρήκαμεν), ἀναγκαζόμενος δ᾽ ἀκολουθεῖν τοῖς φαινομένοις, καὶ τὸ <ὂν> ἓν μὲν κατὰ τὸν λόγον πλείω δὲ κατὰ τὴν αἴσθησιν ὑπολαμβάνων εἶναι, δύο τὰς αἰτίας καὶ δύο τὰς ἀρχὰς πάλιν τίθησι, θερμὸν καὶ ψυχρόν, οἷον πῦρ καὶ γῆν λέγων· τούτων δὲ τὸ μὲν κατὰ τὸ ὂν [τὸ θερμὸν] τάττει θάτερον δὲ κατὰ τὸ μὴ ὄν. The final sentence here (the claim that Parmenides aligns one of his physical principles with what is and the other with what is not) has often puzzled interpreters. As Long (1963, 100–1) suggests, the remark seems to be based on a reading of B 8.53–4: 'For they [*sc.* the mortals] made up their minds to name two forms, | of which one it is not right to name—in this they have gone astray' (μορφὰς γὰρ κατέθεντο δύο γνώμας ὀνομάζειν, | τῶν μίαν οὐ χρεών ἐστιν— ἐν ᾧ πεπλανημένοι εἰσίν).

Why might this passage be thought to show that Aristotle favours a cosmological over an anti-cosmological interpretation of Parmenides? I think that we can identify three possible reasons.

First, Aristotle says that Parmenides was led to set down 'two causes or two principles' as a result of his being 'compelled to follow the appearances'. This mention of a dualistic theory of causes is a clear reference to the *Doxa*, where Parmenides makes use of two basic principles, light and night, which Aristotle interprets as Parmenides' versions of fire and earth.[28] The suggestion that Parmenides was 'compelled to follow the appearances' has been taken to mean that he found himself compelled to accept the testimony of the senses— which is why he developed the theory of the *Doxa*. If this is right, he does not reject the natural world as a mere illusion, contrary to the anti-cosmological interpretation.[29]

Second, Aristotle says (or supposedly says) that for Parmenides there is *one way* in which what is is one, but *another way* in which it is many. It is one 'in virtue of the account', but it is many 'in virtue of perception'. Palmer glosses this as the claim that, on Parmenides' view, what is 'may be differentiated with respect to its phenomenal qualities', even though it is not differentiated with respect to 'the account of its essence'.[30] The idea that Parmenides took what is to be differentiated with respect to its phenomenal qualities is in conflict with the anti-cosmological interpretation, according to which what is is entirely uniform.

Third, the main point of the passage is to praise Parmenides for his insight in developing the dualistic theory of the *Doxa*. This might be thought to suggest that Aristotle takes Parmenides to have accepted the theory of the *Doxa*, on the grounds that it would be strange to praise a philosopher for a theory they do not accept as true.

---

[28] Cf. B 8.56-9, where light is referred to as the 'aetherial fire of flame' (φλογὸς αἰθέριον πῦρ), and night as 'a dense and heavy body' (πυκινὸν δέμας ἐμβριθές τε).

[29] See e.g. Cherniss 1935, 220-1; Wardy 1988, 127 and 141.

[30] Palmer 2009, 37. To clarify, by 'phenomenal qualities' Palmer means to refer to qualities that what is really does have, rather than qualities that it merely appears to have.

In the three sections that follow I want to consider each of these reasons in turn. I shall argue that none of them stands up to scrutiny.

8.3 Being Compelled to Follow the Appearances

The claim that Parmenides follows the appearances or the phenomena implies that he is somehow guided by the way things appear to be. One might easily infer from this—indeed, commentators often have inferred from this—that Aristotle is saying that Parmenides takes the appearances to be a guide to the facts.

We might compare Aristotle's claim here to his reference in *De Anima* 1.2 to the people who 'follow names' when investigating the nature of the soul (405b26–9). 'Following names' is a matter of treating the etymologies of words as a guide to the real natures of their referents.[31] It might seem that, in a similar way, 'following the appearances' will be a matter of treating the way things appear as a guide to the way things really are. If this is the right understanding of 'following the appearances', then it suggests that Aristotle thinks Parmenides accepts the testimony of the senses, which in turn suggests a cosmological and not an anti-cosmological reading of the poem.

Yet there is reason to be sceptical of this interpretation of 'following the appearances'. Even if Parmenides is firmly convinced that the universe is completely different from how it appears to be—that it is radically monistic, entirely changeless, and so on—it would still be appropriate to describe him, in developing the theory of the *Doxa*, as 'following the appearances'. The theory of the *Doxa* was intended to be a comprehensive theory of the natural world, the pluralistic, changing world that appears to perception. It is clear that in developing this theory Parmenides was guided by the appearances—by the way the world appears (perceptually) to be. But this tells us nothing of his

---

[31] Aristotle has in mind people such as those who defend their identification of the soul with the hot by appealing to the supposed etymological connection between the verbs ζῆν ('to live') and ζεῖν ('to boil').

stance on the *truth* of these appearances, or on the truth of the theory itself. The more general point here is that it is possible to 'follow' or be guided by some set of data in the construction of a theory without believing one's data to be an accurate guide to how things are.

Thus the claim that Parmenides follows the appearances reveals nothing about how Aristotle conceives of the intended status of the *Doxa*. The claim is silent on the question of whether or not Parmenides took the appearances to correspond to the way the world really is.

Of course, Aristotle not only tells us that Parmenides *followed* the appearances, he also tells us that he was *compelled* to do so. But it is hard to see that this changes things. The language of compulsion is perfectly compatible with the anti-cosmological interpretation. Aristotle can be taken to mean that even though Parmenides took the natural world to be an illusion—holding that reality is one and unchanging—he still could not bring himself to abandon the project of natural philosophy. That is, he still found himself compelled to 'follow the appearances' and to develop his own physical theory. This does not imply that Parmenides was compelled to take the appearances to be accurate or the theory to be true.[32]

8.4 One in One Way, Many in Another?

Let us turn then to the second reason for thinking that Aristotle favours a cosmological reading of the poem: that he takes Parmenides to hold

---

[32] The language of compulsion at 986b31 is reminiscent of other passages in which Aristotle explains the philosophical advances of his predecessors by the fact that they were compelled—by 'the truth itself' or 'the facts themselves'—to investigate a certain topic, or develop a certain theory. See *Metaph. A* 3, 984a18–19 and 984b8–11; *Phys.* 1.5, 188b27–30; *PA* 1.1, 642a18–28. (For discussion see Barney 2012, 96–8; Betegh 2012, 107–12.) The difference between the present passage and these others is that Aristotle does not here identify the *agent* of the compulsion. So what was it, in Aristotle's view, that compelled Parmenides to follow the appearances? My own speculative suggestion is this. Parmenides had misled himself into thinking that reason shows the natural world to be an illusion. But even this was not enough to temper his (natural) desire to engage in natural philosophy. So Parmenides was compelled, by the same natural force that drives all human enquiry into nature, to follow the appearances and develop a theory of the natural world, despite its being a world that he had convinced himself was unreal.

that what is is one in one way but many in another. Palmer reads
Aristotle as saying that what is is one 'with respect to the account of its
essence', but differentiated 'with respect to its phenomenal qualities'. As
I mentioned above, this is incompatible with the anti-cosmological
interpretation, on which reality is supposed to be entirely uniform.
Again, however, this argument seems unpersuasive. Aristotle's
remark at 986b31–3 admits of another reading, one consistent with
the anti-cosmological interpretation. The question is how to understand the phrases *kata ton logon* and *kata tēn aisthēsin*. These phrases
might be taken, as Palmer takes them, as telling us that there is a way in
which what is is one and another way in which it is many: it is one 'in
virtue of the account', but many 'in virtue of perception'. I shall call this
the 'ontological' reading of the phrases, since on this reading the point is
that for Parmenides what is is *in fact* both one and many in these
different ways. But the phrases might alternatively be construed as
meaning 'according to reason' and 'according to perception', and as
specifying the different psychic faculties, reason and perception, *according to which* what is is one and many respectively. (Note that Aristotle's
word for 'account', *logos*, is also his word for 'reason'.) I shall call the
latter reading the 'psychological' reading of the phrases.

If the phrases are understood in the latter way—psychologically—
then Aristotle's remark provides no evidence that he takes Parmenides to hold that there is a way in which what is is (in fact) many. To
see this, imagine that you are looking at a straight stick, half sub-
merged in water. According to perception, the stick is crooked. But
you can clearly agree that the stick 'is crooked according to perception'
even though you believe it to be (in fact) straight. Similarly, Parmenides can hold that the world 'is many according to perception' even
though he believes it to be (in fact) one. Read in this way, Aristotle's
point is simply that Parmenides takes reason to judge the world to be
one, and perception to judge it to be many. There is no implication that
Parmenides thinks of perception as correct in its judgement.[33]

---

[33] Aristotle's claim, thus construed, would still be *consistent* with its being his view
that Parmenides takes what is to be (in fact) many. For instance, he might think that

So what is the right way to understand the phrases *kata ton logon* and *kata tēn aisthēsin*? Should we prefer the ontological or the psychological reading? One *prima facie* consideration in favour of the former is that Aristotle has already used the phrase *hen kata ton logon* in *A* 5. As we saw above, at 986b19, thirteen lines earlier, he claimed that Parmenides 'seems to grasp the one in virtue of the account' (*tou kata ton logon henos*), whereas Melissus 'seems to grasp the one in virtue of the matter'. This is clearly an 'ontological' distinction, a distinction between two ways of being (in fact) one. This may be thought to suggest that when the words *hen...kata ton logon* repeat at 986b32, an ontological reading is again preferable.

Yet despite this consideration in favour of the ontological reading of the phrases at 986b31–3, the psychological reading still seems more likely. The fact that Aristotle contrasts *logos* with *aisthēsis* makes it hard not to read him as referring to the psychic faculties of reason and perception. Not only is the contrast between reason (*logos*) and perception (*aisthēsis*) a very common Aristotelian contrast, but Parmenides himself emphatically distinguishes between reason (*logos*) and perception in the poem:

> nor let habit, born of much experience, force you down this way,
> by making you use an aimless eye or an echoing ear
> and tongue; but judge by reason the strife-encompassed refutation
> spoken by me.[34]   (B 7.3–6)

Here the goddess instructs the youth to judge her radical claims by reason. We must not dismiss her 'strife-encompassed refutation' simply on the grounds that it conflicts with the reports of the senses (our eyes, ears, and tongue). The lines are a vivid statement of

Parmenides' view is not only that the world appears many to perception, but also that perception is correct in its judgement. My point is simply that if κατὰ τὸν λόγον and κατὰ τὴν αἴσθησιν are understood as meaning 'according to reason' and 'according to perception', then Aristotle's comment does not provide any positive evidence that he favoured a cosmological as opposed to an anti-cosmological reading of the poem.

[34] μηδέ σ' ἔθος πολύπειρον ὁδὸν κατὰ τήνδε βιάσθω, | νωμᾶν ἄσκοπον ὄμμα καὶ ἠχήεσσαν ἀκουήν | καὶ γλῶσσαν, κρῖναι δὲ λόγῳ πολύδηριν ἔλεγχον | ἐξ ἐμέθεν ῥηθέντα. The translation is adapted from that of Kirk et al. (1983, 248).

Parmenides' rationalism, his demand that we be guided in our beliefs about the world by reason rather than by perception.

Given these lines, it would be entirely appropriate for Aristotle to describe Parmenides' monism (or any other position defended in the *Alētheia*) as a view about how the world is *kata ton logon*, according to reason, and the pluralism presupposed in the *Doxa*, where the goddess returns to the mortal opinions she disparaged in B 6–7, as a view about how the world is *kata tēn aisthēsin*, according to perception.

There is, moreover, a passage in *De Generatione et Corruptione* 1.8 in which Aristotle appeals to precisely this contrast, reason (*logos*) versus perception (*aisthēsis*), in order to explain the Eleatics' methodological stance:

> So, on the basis of these arguments, passing over perception and disregarding it on the ground that one ought to follow reason, they [*sc.* the Eleatics] say that the universe is one and unchanging, and—some say—unlimited (for the limit would be a limit against the void). So some people declared themselves in this way and for these reasons about the truth.[35]   (325a13–17)

The contrast between *logos* and *aisthēsis* here is clearly a contrast between reason and perception. If reason and perception are in conflict, the Eleatics demand that we follow reason—and we must do so even if this means rejecting the apparently obvious truths that things are many and subject to change.[36] This makes it likely that when in *Metaphysics* A 5 Aristotle describes Parmenides' position in terms of a contrast between *logos* and *aisthēsis*, he again intends a contrast between reason and perception.

There is also an important textual point to consider. The argument I mentioned in favour of the ontological reading was that Aristotle

---

[35] For the Greek see section 5.7, n. 49.

[36] Notice that here we have more talk of 'following' (ἀκολουθεῖν). There is no conflict between this claim that the Eleatics think we ought to 'follow reason' and the claim in *Metaphysics* A 5 that Parmenides 'was compelled to follow the appearances'. The fact that Parmenides is guided by the appearances in constructing the theory of the *Doxa* is consistent with its being his view that in theorizing about reality (as opposed to appearance) we must be guided by reason and not perception.

had earlier (at 986b19) used the phrase *hen kata ton logon* to mean 'one in virtue of the account'. Because the same phrase is apparently used again at 986b32, it seems natural to understand it in the same way on both occasions. However, this argument assumes a supplement to the text at 986b31–3:

holding that <what is> is one *kata ton logon*, but more *kata tēn aisthēsin*, he again sets down two causes or two principles.

The supplement is unnecessary; the manuscripts' text makes good sense as it stands. If we read the unemended text, we can take the expression *kata ton logon* to modify the sentence 'the One exists' (*to hen einai*), rather than the predicate 'one':[37]

holding that the One exists *kata ton logon*, but that more things exist *kata tēn aisthēsin*, he again sets down two causes or two principles.[38]

On this construal of the manuscripts' text, Aristotle does not repeat the phrase *hen kata ton logon*. This undermines the previously mentioned consideration in favour of the ontological reading.

I conclude that the psychological reading of the phrases at 986b31–3 rests on stronger ground than the alternative, ontological reading. As a result, Aristotle's remark does not provide evidence that he favoured a cosmological as opposed to an anti-cosmological interpretation of Parmenides' poem. The remark could only provide such

---

[37] For this construal cf. also Cornford 1939, 50; Schofield 2012, 158; Laks and Most 2016, 5: 103.

[38] The unemended text is printed by Primavesi (2012), whose apparatus confirms that ὄν has no manuscript support. Palmer (2009, 37 n. 95) defends the insertion of ὄν by appealing to Alexander's paraphrase of the lines at *In Metaph.* 45.2–4: 'He [*sc.* Aristotle] reports the twofold opinion of Parmenides, who, being compelled also to follow the appearances, said that *what is* is one according to reason and the truth, but more than one according to perception [ἓν μὲν κατὰ λόγον καὶ τὴν ἀλήθειαν ἔλεγε τὸ ὄν εἶναι, πλείω δὲ κατὰ τὴν αἴσθησιν].' But it is doubtful that this paraphrase of 986b31–3 can be regarded as evidence for the text. It is, after all, a paraphrase, and it would be an apt paraphrase of the transmitted text. One way of paraphrasing the claim that '*the One exists* according to reason' would be to say that '*what is* is one according to reason'.

evidence if the ontological reading were correct, but, as we have seen, the psychological reading is preferable.

8.5 Praise for Parmenides' Dualism

What of the third argument for thinking that Aristotle favours a cosmological interpretation? Aristotle ranks Parmenides above the 'unsophisticated' Xenophanes and Melissus (986b26–7), and the explanation for this is that Parmenides seems to speak with more insight than these others, in offering the dualistic causal theory of the *Doxa*. It would be odd—or so this argument goes—to praise somebody for a theory they reject as false; so this is evidence that Aristotle takes Parmenides to have accepted the theory of the *Doxa*.[39]

In response to this argument, it is indeed true that Aristotle praises Parmenides for the dualistic theory that he develops in the *Doxa*. But this does not mean that he takes Parmenides to have accepted that theory. Aristotle has already indicated what he takes to be the special significance of the *Doxa*, back in *Metaphysics A* 3. In the *Doxa*, as Aristotle understands it, Parmenides made an important theoretical advance: he identified *two* basic causes or principles (light and night, or, as Aristotle describes them, hot and cold, or fire and earth). This set him apart from material monists such as Thales, Anaximenes, and so on, in that it enabled him to give an explanation of change. The main limitation of Milesian-style material monism, Aristotle suggests, was that there was no room in the theory for the efficient cause: 'Why does this happen and what is the cause? For the underlying thing itself, at any rate, does not make itself change...but rather something else is the cause of the change' (984a21–5).[40] Aristotle thinks that material *dualism*—the view according to which there are two

---

[39] I am not aware of any commentators who explicitly offer this argument, although Palmer (1998, 4; 2009, 222–3) suggests that the reason why Aristotle thinks more highly of Parmenides than of Melissus is that Aristotle sees Parmenides as a sort of pluralist, and Melissus as an extreme monist.

[40] διὰ τί τοῦτο συμβαίνει καὶ τί τὸ αἴτιον; οὐ γὰρ δὴ τό γε ὑποκείμενον αὐτὸ ποιεῖ μεταβάλλειν ἑαυτό...ἀλλ' ἕτερόν τι τῆς μεταβολῆς αἴτιον.

fundamental material principles—was a way (if not ultimately the best way) of meeting this need for an efficient cause:

> But indeed for those who posit more [than one element], it is more possible to speak of it [*sc.* the efficient cause]; for example, for those who posit hot and cold or fire and earth. For they treat fire as having a nature which allows it to bring about change, and water and earth and such things they treat in the contrary way.[41]   (984b5–8)

As a dualistic theory, therefore, the theory of the *Doxa* allows for the existence of an efficient cause. And thus Parmenides, uniquely among the early Greek monists (both the material monists and the Eleatics), can in some sense be credited with having comprehended this type of cause:

> So it turned out that of those who said that the universe is only one, no one comprehended this sort of cause, except perhaps Parmenides, and he only to the extent that he sets it down that there is not only one but also in a way two causes.[42]   (984b1–4)

This explains why, in A 5, Aristotle commends Parmenides for his perceptiveness in developing the theory of the *Doxa*. Unlike his fellow Eleatics, Parmenides offered a system of the physical world which made an important advance over its material monistic antecedents. But he can be credited with this important advance regardless of whether he actually endorsed the theory.[43] The fact that Aristotle praises Parmenides' perceptiveness in developing the theory of the *Doxa* implies that he takes it to be *Parmenides'* theory—a theory of

---

[41] τοῖς δὲ δὴ πλείω ποιοῦσι μᾶλλον ἐνδέχεται λέγειν, οἷον τοῖς θερμὸν καὶ ψυχρὸν ἢ πῦρ καὶ γῆν· χρῶνται γὰρ ὡς κινητικὴν ἔχοντι τῷ πυρὶ τὴν φύσιν, ὕδατι δὲ καὶ γῆ καὶ τοῖς τοιούτοις τοὐναντίον.

[42] τῶν μὲν οὖν ἓν μόνον φασκόντων εἶναι τὸ πᾶν οὐθενὶ συνέβη τὴν τοιαύτην συνιδεῖν αἰτίαν πλὴν εἰ ἄρα Παρμενίδῃ, καὶ τούτῳ κατὰ τοσοῦτον ὅσον οὐ μόνον ἓν ἀλλὰ καὶ δύο πως τίθησιν αἰτίας εἶναι.

[43] It is plausible that Aristotle's note of hesitation in the *Metaphysics* A 3 passage ('except *perhaps* Parmenides') is to be explained by the fact that he does not think Parmenides actually endorsed the theory. In the *Doxa* Parmenides posits two causal principles, light and night, of which the former may be regarded as playing the role of the efficient cause. But if Parmenides does not actually subscribe to this theory, this complicates the question of whether he is a genuine exception to the general claim that none of the monists comprehended the efficient cause. Hence the note of hesitation.

Parmenides' own invention.[44] But authoring a theory is not the same as endorsing it, and so Aristotle's praise cannot be taken to imply that he favours a cosmological reading of Parmenides.

8.6 Other References to the *Doxa*

Aristotle thinks of the theory of the *Doxa* as an important early physical theory. He refers to it in several other places:

Now, everyone makes the contraries principles, both those who say that the universe is one and does not change—for even Parmenides makes hot and cold principles, and calls these fire and earth—and those [who speak of] the rare and the dense.[45] (*Phys.* 1.5, 188a19–22)

For it makes a difference what the changing thing changes into. For example, perhaps the path towards fire is simple generation, but the destruction *of something* (for example, of earth); while the generation of earth is a kind of generation and not generation *simpliciter*, but is destruction *simpliciter* (for example, of fire), just as Parmenides speaks of two things, saying that what is and what is not are fire and earth respectively.[46] (*GC* 1.3, 318b2–7)

But those who make [the elements] two from the beginning, as does Parmenides with fire and earth, make the ones in between (such as air and water) mixtures of these.[47] (*GC* 2.3, 330b13–15)

For instance, Parmenides and certain others say that women are hotter than men, on the grounds that menstruation occurs because of heat and an abundance of blood, whereas Empedocles says the contrary.[48]
(*PA* 2.2, 648a28–31)

---

[44] Contrast e.g. the view that the *Doxa* is 'a sketch of contemporary Pythagorean cosmology' (Burnet 1930, 185).

[45] Πάντες δὴ τἀναντία ἀρχὰς ποιοῦσιν οἵ τε λέγοντες ὅτι ἓν τὸ πᾶν καὶ μὴ κινούμενον (καὶ γὰρ Παρμενίδης θερμὸν καὶ ψυχρὸν ἀρχὰς ποιεῖ, ταῦτα δὲ προσαγορεύει πῦρ καὶ γῆν) καὶ οἱ μανὸν καὶ πυκνόν.

[46] διαφέρει γὰρ εἰς ὃ μεταβάλλει τὸ μεταβάλλον, οἷον ἴσως ἡ μὲν εἰς πῦρ ὁδὸς γένεσις μὲν ἁπλῆ, φθορὰ δέ τινος, οἷον γῆς, ἡ δὲ γῆς γένεσις τὶς γένεσις, γένεσις δ' οὐχ ἁπλῶς, φθορὰ δ' ἁπλῶς, οἷον πυρός, ὥσπερ Παρμενίδης λέγει δύο, τὸ ὂν καὶ τὸ μὴ ὂν εἶναι φάσκων πῦρ καὶ γῆν.

[47] οἱ δ εὐθὺς δύο ποιοῦντες, ὥσπερ Παρμενίδης πῦρ καὶ γῆν, τὰ μεταξὺ μίγματα ποιοῦσι τούτων, οἷον ἀέρα καὶ ὕδωρ.

[48] οἷον Παρμενίδης τὰς γυναῖκας τῶν ἀνδρῶν θερμοτέρας εἶναί φησι καὶ ἕτεροί τινες, ὡς διὰ τὴν θερμότητα καὶ πολυαιμούσαις γινομένων τῶν γυναικείων, Ἐμπεδοκλῆς δὲ τοὐναντίον. Cf. *GA* 4.1, 765b17–28.

But one might suspect that Hesiod was the first to seek this sort of thing [sc. the efficient cause], or someone else who put love or desire in beings as a principle, as for example Parmenides also did. For he, in constructing the genesis of the universe, says that first 'of all the gods she devised Love'.[49]

(Metaph. A 4, 984b23–7)

And in general, because they suppose perception to be thought [phronēsis], and this [sc. perception] to be an alteration, they say that what appears in perception must be true. For it is for these reasons that Empedocles and Democritus and practically all the others have come to be subject to such opinions. For Empedocles says that when people change their state they change their thought... And Parmenides too expresses himself in the same way.[50]

(Metaph. Γ 5, 1009b12–21)

In these passages Aristotle attributes the physical doctrines of the Doxa to Parmenides. But, to repeat the point of the previous section, this does not show that he takes Parmenides to have accepted the theory of the Doxa. Aristotle attributes the theory to Parmenides because Parmenides was its author—something quite different.

It is only the last of the quoted passages, from Metaphysics Γ 5, that might be read as implying that Parmenides actually accepts some claim he makes in the Doxa. Here Aristotle might be read as including Parmenides among those thinkers who suppose that perception is thought (phronēsis) and a kind of alteration; the verb 'suppose' (hupolambanein) connotes acceptance. But I doubt that very much weight can be placed on this passage. Aristotle refers to Parmenides because he is trying to convey the prevalence of the doctrine in question. Given that the doctrine appears in the Doxa, it seems

---

[49] Ὑποπτεύσειε δ' ἄν τις Ἡσίοδον πρῶτον ζητῆσαι τὸ τοιοῦτον, κἂν εἴ τις ἄλλος ἔρωτα ἢ ἐπιθυμίαν ἐν τοῖς οὖσιν ἔθηκεν ὡς ἀρχήν, οἷον καὶ Παρμενίδης· καὶ γὰρ οὗτος κατασκευάζων τὴν τοῦ παντὸς γένεσιν πρῶτον μέν φησιν "ἔρωτα θεῶν μητίσατο πάντων".

[50] ὅλως δὲ διὰ τὸ ὑπολαμβάνειν φρόνησιν μὲν τὴν αἴσθησιν, ταύτην δ' εἶναι ἀλλοίωσιν, τὸ φαινόμενον κατὰ τὴν αἴσθησιν ἐξ ἀνάγκης ἀληθὲς εἶναί φασιν· ἐκ τούτων γὰρ καὶ Ἐμπεδοκλῆς καὶ Δημόκριτος καὶ τῶν ἄλλων ὡς ἔπος εἰπεῖν ἕκαστος τοιαύταις δόξαις γεγένηνται ἔνοχοι. καὶ γὰρ Ἐμπεδοκλῆς μεταβάλλοντας τὴν ἕξιν μεταβάλλειν φησὶ τὴν φρόνησιν... καὶ Παρμενίδης δὲ ἀποφαίνεται τὸν αὐτὸν τρόπον. The quotation that follows is Parmenides B 16.

legitimate for Aristotle to cite Parmenides as someone who expresses himself in this way, even if Parmenides does not actually endorse it.

8.7 Aristotle's Interpretation of the Two Parts of the Poem

I have been arguing that, contrary to widespread opinion, there is no evidence in *Metaphysics A* 5—or anywhere else, for that matter—that Aristotle favours a cosmological reading of Parmenides. Everything Aristotle says about the *Doxa* is consistent with his favouring the anti-cosmological interpretation, on which the natural world is an illusion and the *Doxa* a 'way of falsity'.[51]

Accordingly, there is no evidence that Aristotle changes his mind about the *Doxa*, and comes to favour a cosmological reading of the poem over the anti-cosmological reading that he favours in *Physics* 1.2–3 and elsewhere. It is much more plausible, in fact, to think that he consistently maintains the view that Parmenides is a radical monist and an opponent of change.

For one thing, this nicely explains the cross-reference to *Physics* 1.2–3 at *Metaphysics A* 5, 986b28–31:

For, holding that besides what is, what is not is nothing, he [*sc.* Parmenides] thinks that, of necessity, what is is one, and nothing else is—we have spoken about this more clearly in the *Physics.*

The cross-reference makes sense precisely because Aristotle's view of Parmenides has not changed: he continues to think of Parmenides' position as being the radical monism ('what is is one, and nothing else is') that he criticized in *Physics* 1.2–3.

This also explains why Aristotle says in *Metaphysics A* 5 that a discussion of Parmenides and Melissus 'is in no way appropriate to our present investigation into causes' (986b12–14). On the anti-cosmological interpretation, Parmenides' official position is, like Melissus', simply incompatible with the existence of causes (see

[51] The expression is Barnes's (1982, 156).

section 8.2). But if Aristotle instead favoured the cosmological interpretation, it is hard to see what his basis could be for excluding
Parmenides from the investigation.[52]

Thus there is good reason to think that Aristotle consistently
maintains the interpretation of Parmenides' poem that is implied by
his extensive critique of Eleatic monism in *Physics* 1.2–3. On this
interpretation, the *Alētheia* presents Parmenides' official view of how
the world is: radically monistic and unchanging. The *Doxa* presents a
theory of a pluralistic, changing world, but it is a world of mere
appearance.

[52] Of course, we have seen that Aristotle proceeds to enter two qualifications to his
initial claim that the Eleatics are to be excluded from the present investigation. But we
still need to explain why he makes that initial claim, and my suggestion is that we can
explain this only if he continues to favour an anti-cosmological view of Parmenides.

Conclusion

In the preceding chapters I have offered a comprehensive account of how Aristotle understands Parmenides' and Melissus' monism, how he tries to refute their position, how he interprets their arguments for monism, and where he thinks these arguments go wrong.

I have argued that Aristotle reads Parmenides and Melissus as defending two kinds of monism: entity monism, the view that reality consists of just a single entity, and essence monism, the view that reality is all of the same essence.[1] On Aristotle's reading, the Parmenidean universe is constituted by a single object, which is solid, continuous, and entirely uniform. Aristotle consistently regards Parmenides' official theory of reality as being the monistic theory of the *Alētheia*; the pluralistic *Doxa* is intended as a way of falsity.

The main difference between Parmenides' and Melissus' positions, in Aristotle's view, lies not in the nature of their monism, but in the spatial properties that each attributes to the One. While Parmenides' One has determinate spatial boundaries, Melissus' One extends

---

[1] In section 2.4, I noted one passage where Aristotle seems to ascribe to the Eleatics a more moderate position. At *Metaph. Z* 1, 1028b2–7, he seems to imply that when the Eleatics claim that 'what is is one', what they really mean is that there is just one substance. However, I do not think that there is any serious inconsistency between this passage and *Physics* 1.2–3. Aristotle's thought in *Z* 1 is that if the Eleatics had been aware of the distinction between substance and attribute, they would have stated their position by saying that there is just one substance. But in fact the Eleatics were not aware of this distinction. Their ignorance of the distinction explains why they actually claimed, not that there is just one substance, but (more radically) that *what is* is one.

infinitely in all directions.[2] Aristotle has a higher opinion of Parmenides than of Melissus, but this is not because he regards Parmenides' monism as more moderate and thus closer to the truth. Rather, his more positive assessment of Parmenides is due to the fact that Parmenides has a better argument for his view.[3] Aristotle also approves of Parmenides for not letting his official monism prevent him from putting forward an innovative physical theory—even if by Parmenides' own lights this was a theory of an unreal world.[4]

It is sometimes claimed that Aristotle uncritically assimilates Parmenides' position to Melissus'.[5] It is true that Aristotle sees Parmenides and Melissus as defenders of versions of the same theory, and in this he is following a preexisting exegetical tradition.[6] But while Aristotle's own interpretation of Parmenides may to some extent be informed by this tradition, it is very hard to believe that he was carelessly conflating the views of the two philosophers. Aristotle clearly thinks of Parmenides as the most sophisticated representative of Eleaticism, and this assessment gives every impression of being based on a close engagement with the arguments he finds in the Eleatic texts.

Aristotle does not spell out how he takes Parmenides' monistic argument to work, but we can recover his interpretation by examining his criticisms. Aristotle's interpretation has been thought to have only a tenuous textual basis. I have suggested that this is unfair: he

---

[2] See *Phys* 1.2, 185b17–18; 3.6, 207a15–17; *GC* 1.8, 325a13–16; *Metaph.* A 5, 986b18–21.

[3] See especially *Phys* 1.2, 185a10–12.   [4] See *Metaph.* A 5, 986b25–987a2.

[5] This suggestion tends to be made by modern interpreters who want to draw a sharp distinction between the theories of Parmenides and Melissus, and who therefore need to find an explanation of why ancient interpreters apparently treat them as proponents of a single view. See e.g. Barnes 1979, 21 n. 77; Mourelatos 2008, 130; Palmer 2008, 541–3. Cf. also Kirk et al. 1983, 395: 'when Plato and Aristotle represent monism as the principal thesis of the Eleatics...they must be reading Parmenides through Melissan spectacles'.

[6] See Plato, *Theaet.* 180d7–e4 and 183c8–e5; Isocrates, *Antidosis* 268. Palmer (2009, 35) suggests that Parmenides and Melissus were grouped together in a doxographical preface to Gorgias' *On What Is Not, or On Nature*. They may also have been associated in other discussions of Eleatic monism, such as Protagoras' *On What Is* (for which see Eusebius, *Praeparatio Evangelica* 10.3.25).

takes Parmenides' primary monistic argument to be the argument at B 8.22–5 for the continuity and uniformity of what is.[7] Aristotle interprets this argument as depending on an overly narrow, corporealistic conception of being. This allows us to explain how Parmenides moves in these lines from the claim that what is is 'all full of being' to his conclusions that it is continuous and all alike.

I suggested that, in Aristotle's view, Parmenides' narrow conception of being leads him to overlook the possibility that void or empty space might be something that exists. This causes him to equate regions of void with regions of what is not. Parmenides argues that such regions cannot be, and so it seems to follow that the universe consists of a solid, corporeal plenum. From this he draws his monistic conclusions. When the atomists later respond to the Eleatics by introducing void—by claiming that 'what is not *is*'—they are challenging Parmenides' argument by rejecting the restrictive conception of being on which it rests.

The Eleatics' restrictive conception of being is the central focus of *Physics* 1.2–3. Not only does this explain why Parmenides was led to his monism in the first place, it also explains why he and Melissus failed to see that their theory is untenable. They did not see that they were committed to the existence of further entities besides their 'One'—specifically, its multiple properties and spatial parts. These commitments mean that their theory is impossible.[8] In addition, the fact that Parmenides fails to recognize the existence of properties explains why he overlooks various problems for his attempt to show that reality is all of the same essence.[9]

We have seen that in criticizing Eleatic monism Aristotle is thinking ahead to the second half of *Physics* 1, where he articulates his own theory of principles.[10] On that theory, natural beings—animals and plants and so on—are constituted by an underlying substratum

---

[7] These lines may also be read as containing an argument for indivisibility, the other way of being one distinguished at *Phys.* 1.2, 185b5–9.

[8] This is the main lesson of the arguments of *Phys.* 1.2, 185a20–b25.

[9] See *Phys* 1.3, 186a28–b35.   [10] See especially sections 2.4 and 6.9.

and a form, and come to be when the substratum goes from having the privation to having the form. To be in a position to formulate this theory, we need to move beyond the restrictive ontology of the Eleatics, and recognize the existence of entities of different ontological kinds. Specifically, the theory requires us to broaden our ontological horizons and recognize properties as entities distinct from their bearers.

Aristotle's critique of Eleatic monism in *Physics* 1.2–3 thus serves a number of important functions within the broader project of *Physics* 1. First, it serves to defend a fundamental presupposition of the enquiry into principles—that there *are* principles—against the Eleatics' monistic attack. Second, by showing that we can resist Eleatic monism without recourse to atomism, the critique casts doubt on the motivation of a rival theory to Aristotle's own. Third, the critique serves as an opportunity for Aristotle to highlight the Eleatics' metaphysical naivety, and to introduce the more expansive ontological framework that is needed for his own theory of principles.

I have tried in this book to emphasize the appeal of Aristotle's way of thinking about Eleatic monism. If we attribute to the Eleatics a restrictive conception of being, then we can explain how they could have claimed that reality is 'one' and 'all alike' while also conceiving it as spatially extended and as possessing multiple properties. Moreover, Aristotle's diagnosis suggests a plausible account of the origins of Parmenides' monism, making sense of the argument of a difficult but centrally important section of his poem. That said, my aim has not been to try to settle the question of whether Aristotle's interpretation of Eleatic monism is the right one. Whether it is or is not I leave to the reader to decide.

Appendix
Text and Translation of *Physics* 1.2–3

Physics 1.2

[184b15] There must either be one principle or more than one. If there is one, it must either be unchanging, as Parmenides and Melissus say, or changing, as the natural philosophers say, some saying that the first principle is air, others that it is water. And if there is more than one, there must either be a limited or an unlimited number. If a limited number greater than one, there must either be two or three or [b20] four or some other number. And if there are an unlimited number, then either, as Democritus says, the genus is one and they are distinguished by shape or by species, or they are also contraries. And those who enquire into how many beings there are are also enquiring in a similar way. For they enquire primarily into the things *from which* the beings are, asking whether these things are one or many, and if they are many, whether there are a limited or unlimited number, so that [b25] they are enquiring into whether the principles and the elements are one or many.

[184b25] Now, to investigate whether what is is one and unchanging is not [185a1] to investigate into nature. For, just as for the geometer too there is no longer any argument to give against an opponent who destroys the principles, but this is instead something either for another science or for one common to all, so too for the person [investigating] principles. For there is no longer any principle if it is only one, and one in this way; for a principle is a principle *of* some thing or [a5] things. So, to investigate whether it is one in this way is like arguing dialectically against any other thesis put forward for the sake of argument (like the Heraclitean thesis, or if someone should say that what is is one human being), or like solving an eristical argument, which is just what both arguments contain, both Melissus' and Parmenides'. For

Ἀνάγκη δ' ἤτοι μίαν εἶναι τὴν ἀρχὴν ἢ πλείους, καὶ εἰ   184b15
μίαν, ἤτοι ἀκίνητον, ὥς φησι Παρμενίδης καὶ Μέλισσος, ἢ κι-
νουμένην, ὥσπερ οἱ φυσικοί, οἱ μὲν ἀέρα φάσκοντες εἶναι οἱ δ'
ὕδωρ τὴν πρώτην ἀρχήν· εἰ δὲ πλείους, ἢ πεπερασμένας ἢ ἀπείρους, καὶ εἰ πεπερασμένας πλείους δὲ μιᾶς, ἢ δύο ἢ τρεῖς ἢ τέτ-
ταρας ἢ ἄλλον τινὰ ἀριθμόν, καὶ εἰ ἀπείρους, ἢ οὕτως ὥσπερ   20
Δημόκριτος, τὸ γένος ἕν, σχήματι δὲ ἢ εἴδει
διαφερούσας,¹ ἢ καὶ ἐναντίας. ὁμοίως δὲ ζητοῦσι καὶ οἱ τὰ ὄντα
ζητοῦντες πόσα· ἐξ ὧν γὰρ τὰ ὄντα ἐστί, ζητοῦσι πρῶτον² ταῦτα
πότερον ἓν ἢ πολλά, καὶ εἰ πολλά, πεπερασμένα ἢ ἄπειρα, ὥστε
τὴν ἀρχὴν καὶ τὸ στοιχεῖον ζητοῦσι πότερον ἓν ἢ πολλά.   25
                                                          τὸ μὲν   25
οὖν εἰ ἓν καὶ ἀκίνητον τὸ ὂν σκοπεῖν οὐ περὶ φύσεώς ἐστι σκο-
πεῖν· ὥσπερ γὰρ καὶ τῷ γεωμέτρῃ οὐκέτι λόγος ἔστι πρὸς   185a
τὸν ἀνελόντα τὰς ἀρχάς, ἀλλ' ἤτοι ἑτέρας ἐπιστήμης ἢ πασῶν κοινῆς, οὕτως οὐδὲ τῷ περὶ ἀρχῶν· οὐ γὰρ ἔτι ἀρχὴ
ἔστιν, εἰ ἓν μόνον καὶ οὕτως ἕν ἐστιν. ἡ γὰρ ἀρχὴ τινὸς ἢ τι-
νῶν. ὅμοιον δὴ τὸ σκοπεῖν εἰ οὕτως ἓν καὶ πρὸς ἄλλην θέσιν   5
ὁποιανοῦν διαλέγεσθαι τῶν λόγου ἕνεκα λεγομένων (οἷον τὴν
Ἡρακλείτειον, ἢ εἴ τις φαίη ἄνθρωπον ἕνα τὸ ὂν εἶναι), ἢ

---

¹ I read σχήματι δὲ ἢ εἴδει διαφερούσας with E, I, Simplicius, and Themistius. Ross
prints σχήματι δὲ <διαφερούσας>, ἢ εἴδει διαφερούσας.
² Ross prints Bonitz's emendation: πρώτων, ζητοῦσι. Manuscripts F, I, and J have
ζητοῦσι πρῶτον. E has πρῶτον ζητοῦσι.

[a10] they assume falsehoods, and are not deductive. Or rather, the argument of Melissus is crude and contains no difficulty—grant him one absurdity and the others follow: this is not very hard. But, for our part, let it be assumed that natural things, either all or some of them, undergo change. This is clear from induction. And at the same time nor does it belong [to us] to solve everything, but [a15] only those things which someone falsely proves from the principles, but not others, just as it is the task of the geometer to solve the quadrature by way of segments, but not the quadrature of Antiphon. However, although [the Eleatics] do not speak about nature, they nonetheless happen to state physical difficulties. So it is presumably a good idea to have a little [a20] dialectical discussion about them. For the investigation does contain some philosophy.

[185a20] Since being is said in many ways, the most appropriate starting point of all is to ask in what way those who say that 'all things are one' speak [of being]—whether all things are substance, or quantities, or qualities, and again whether all things are one substance, like one human being, or one horse, or [a25] one soul, or whether all things are quality, and this is one, like white or hot or one of the other things of this sort. For all these differ a great deal, and all are impossible to maintain. For if, on the one hand, there is substance and quality and quantity, then whether these things are detached from one another or not, the things that are will be many. But if, on the other hand, all things are quality or quantity, then whether substance is [a30] or is not, this is absurd, if one should call the impossible absurd. For none of the others is separate apart from substance. For all [the others] are said of substance as a subject. And Melissus says that what is is unlimited. Therefore what is is a quantity. For the unlimited is in the [category of] quantity, and [b1] it is not possible for a substance or a quality or an affection to be unlimited, except accidentally, if they are at the same time also certain quantities. For the account of the unlimited employs quantity, but not substance or quality. If, therefore, it is both a substance and a quantity, what is is two and not one. But if it is substance alone, [b5] then it is not unlimited, nor even will it have any magnitude at all. For then it will be a quantity.

[185b5] Further, since one itself is also said in many ways, just as being is, it is necessary to investigate in what way they say that the universe is *one*. And we call one either the continuous, or the indivisible, or those things of which the account of their essence is one and the same, such as

λύειν λόγον ἐριστικόν, ὅπερ ἀμφότεροι μὲν ἔχουσιν οἱ λόγοι,
καὶ ὁ Μελίσσου καὶ ὁ Παρμενίδου· καὶ γὰρ ψευδῆ λαμβάνουσι καὶ ἀσυλλόγιστοί εἰσιν· μᾶλλον δ᾽ ὁ Μελίσσου φορ-   10
τικὸς καὶ οὐκ ἔχων ἀπορίαν, ἀλλ᾽ ἑνὸς ἀτόπου δοθέντος τὰ
ἄλλα συμβαίνει· τοῦτο δὲ οὐδὲν χαλεπόν. ἡμῖν δ᾽ ὑποκεί-
σθω τὰ φύσει ἢ πάντα ἢ ἔνια κινούμενα εἶναι· δῆλον δ᾽ ἐκ
τῆς ἐπαγωγῆς. ἅμα δ᾽ οὐδὲ λύειν ἅπαντα προσήκει, ἀλλ᾽
ἢ ὅσα ἐκ τῶν ἀρχῶν τις ἐπιδεικνὺς ψεύδεται, ὅσα δὲ μή,   15
οὔ, οἷον τὸν τετραγωνισμὸν τὸν μὲν διὰ τῶν τμημάτων γεω-
μετρικοῦ διαλῦσαι, τὸν δὲ Ἀντιφῶντος οὐ γεωμετρικοῦ· οὐ
μὴν ἀλλ᾽ ἐπειδὴ περὶ φύσεως μὲν οὔ, φυσικὰς δὲ ἀπορίας
συμβαίνει λέγειν αὐτοῖς, ἴσως ἔχει καλῶς ἐπὶ μικρὸν δια-
λεχθῆναι περὶ αὐτῶν· ἔχει γὰρ φιλοσοφίαν ἡ σκέψις.   20

ἀρχὴ   20
δὲ οἰκειοτάτη πασῶν, ἐπειδὴ πολλαχῶς λέγεται τὸ ὄν,
πῶς λέγουσιν οἱ λέγοντες εἶναι ἓν τὰ πάντα, πότερον
οὐσίαν τὰ πάντα ἢ ποσὰ ἢ ποιά, καὶ πάλιν πότερον οὐσίαν
μίαν τὰ πάντα, οἷον ἄνθρωπον ἕνα ἢ ἵππον ἕνα ἢ ψυχὴν
μίαν, ἢ ποιὸν ἓν δὲ τοῦτο, οἷον λευκὸν ἢ θερμὸν ἢ τῶν ἄλλων   25
τι τῶν τοιούτων. ταῦτα γὰρ πάντα διαφέρει τε πολὺ καὶ
ἀδύνατα λέγειν. εἰ μὲν γὰρ ἔσται καὶ οὐσία καὶ ποιὸν καὶ
ποσόν, καὶ ταῦτα εἴτ᾽ ἀπολελυμένα ἀπ᾽ ἀλλήλων εἴτε μή,
πολλὰ τὰ ὄντα· εἰ δὲ πάντα ποιὸν ἢ ποσόν, εἴτ᾽ οὔσης οὐσίας
εἴτε μὴ οὔσης, ἄτοπον, εἰ δεῖ ἄτοπον λέγειν τὸ ἀδύνατον.   30
οὐθὲν γὰρ τῶν ἄλλων χωριστόν ἐστι παρὰ τὴν οὐσίαν· πάντα
γὰρ καθ᾽ ὑποκειμένου λέγεται τῆς οὐσίας. Μέλισσος δὲ τὸ
ὂν ἄπειρον εἶναί φησιν. ποσὸν ἄρα τι τὸ ὄν· τὸ γὰρ ἄπειρον ἐν τῷ ποσῷ, οὐσίαν δὲ ἄπειρον εἶναι ἢ ποιότητα ἢ πά-
θος οὐκ ἐνδέχεται εἰ μὴ κατὰ συμβεβηκός, εἰ ἅμα καὶ πο-   185b
σὰ ἄττα εἶεν· ὁ γὰρ τοῦ ἀπείρου λόγος τῷ ποσῷ προσ-
χρῆται, ἀλλ᾽ οὐκ οὐσίᾳ οὐδὲ τῷ ποιῷ. εἰ μὲν τοίνυν καὶ οὐσία ἐστὶ καὶ ποσόν, δύο καὶ οὐχ ἓν τὸ ὄν· εἰ δ᾽ οὐσία μόνον,
οὐκ ἄπειρον, οὐδὲ μέγεθος ἕξει οὐδέν· ποσὸν γάρ τι ἔσται.   5

ἔτι   5
ἐπεὶ καὶ αὐτὸ τὸ ἓν πολλαχῶς λέγεται ὥσπερ καὶ τὸ ὄν,
σκεπτέον τίνα τρόπον λέγουσιν εἶναι ἓν τὸ πᾶν. λέγεται δ᾽

methu and *oinos*. Now, if it is [b10] continuous, the One is many. For the continuous is divisible to infinity. (And there is a difficulty with regard to the part and the whole, although presumably it is not [a difficulty] for the argument, but [a difficulty] in its own right. That is, whether the part and the whole are one or more than one, and how they are one or more than one, and if they are more, how they are more. This also applies with regard to non-continuous parts. [b15] And if each [part] is one with the whole by being indivisible [with respect to the whole], then [there is the difficulty] that they [*sc.* the parts] also bear this relation to one another.) But if it is one by being indivisible, then nothing will be a quantity or a quality, nor then will what is be unlimited, as Melissus says, nor limited, as Parmenides says. For the limit is indivisible, but not the limited thing. But if [b20] all beings are one in account, as are mantle and cloak, then it follows that they are affirming the account of Heraclitus. For to be good and bad will be the same, and to be good and not-good, so that the same thing will be good and not-good, and a human and a horse, and their account will not be about the fact that the beings are one, but about the fact that they are [b25] nothing. And to be this quality and this quantity will be the same.

[185b25] And the more recent of the early thinkers were also troubled lest the same thing should turn out for them to be at the same time both one and many. This is why some took away the 'is', like Lycophron, while others refashioned their speech, saying not that the human 'is white', but that he 'has whitened', and not that [b30] he 'is walking', but that he 'walks', so that they would never make the one be many by adding the 'is', supposing that one or being is said in only one way. But the things that are are many, either in account (for example, to be white and to be musical are different, yet the same thing is both; therefore the one is many), or by division (as with the whole and the parts). [186a1] But here [*sc.* with regard to the whole and the parts] they were already in difficulty, and they conceded that the one is many, as though it were not possible for the same thing to be both one and many—although not the opposites. For the one is both potentially and actually.

ἓν ἢ τὸ συνεχὲς ἢ τὸ ἀδιαίρετον ἢ ὧν ὁ λόγος ὁ αὐτὸς καὶ
εἷς ὁ τοῦ τί ἦν εἶναι, ὥσπερ μέθυ καὶ οἶνος. εἰ μὲν τοίνυν
συνεχές, πολλὰ τὸ ἕν· εἰς ἄπειρον γὰρ διαιρετὸν τὸ συνε-   10
χές. (ἔχει δ' ἀπορίαν περὶ τοῦ μέρους καὶ τοῦ ὅλου, ἴσως δὲ
οὐ πρὸς τὸν λόγον ἀλλ' αὐτὴν καθ' αὑτήν, πότερον ἓν ἢ
πλείω τὸ μέρος καὶ τὸ ὅλον, καὶ πῶς ἓν ἢ πλείω, καὶ εἰ
πλείω, πῶς πλείω, καὶ περὶ τῶν μερῶν τῶν μὴ συνεχῶν·
καὶ εἰ τῷ ὅλῳ ἓν ἑκάτερον ὡς ἀδιαίρετον, ὅτι καὶ αὐτὰ αὑ-   15
τοῖς.) ἀλλὰ μὴν εἰ ὡς ἀδιαίρετον, οὐθὲν ἔσται ποσὸν οὐδὲ
ποιόν, οὐδὲ δὴ ἄπειρον τὸ ὄν, ὥσπερ Μέλισσός φησιν, οὐδὲ
πεπερασμένον, ὥσπερ Παρμενίδης· τὸ γὰρ πέρας ἀδιαίρετον, οὐ τὸ πεπερασμένον. ἀλλὰ μὴν εἰ τῷ λόγῳ ἓν τὰ
ὄντα πάντα ὡς λώπιον καὶ ἱμάτιον, τὸν Ἡρακλείτου λόγον   20
συμβαίνει λέγειν αὐτοῖς· ταὐτὸν γὰρ ἔσται ἀγαθῷ καὶ κακῷ
εἶναι, καὶ ἀγαθῷ καὶ μὴ ἀγαθῷ εἶναι,³ ὥστε ταὐτὸν ἔσται ἀγα-
θὸν καὶ οὐκ ἀγαθόν, καὶ ἄνθρωπος καὶ ἵππος, καὶ οὐ περὶ
τοῦ ἓν εἶναι τὰ ὄντα ὁ λόγος ἔσται ἀλλὰ περὶ τοῦ
μηδέν.⁴ καὶ τὸ τοιῳδὶ εἶναι καὶ τοσῳδὶ ταὐτόν.   25
                                            ἐθορυ-   25
βοῦντο δὲ καὶ οἱ ὕστεροι τῶν ἀρχαίων ὅπως μὴ ἅμα γένη-
ται αὐτοῖς τὸ αὐτὸ ἓν καὶ πολλά. διὸ οἱ μὲν τὸ ἐστιν ἀφεῖ-
λον, ὥσπερ Λυκόφρων, οἱ δὲ τὴν λέξιν μετερρύθμιζον, ὅτι
ὁ ἄνθρωπος οὐ λευκός ἐστιν ἀλλὰ λελεύκωται, οὐδὲ βαδί-
ζων ἐστὶν ἀλλὰ βαδίζει, ἵνα μή ποτε τὸ ἐστὶ προσάπτοντες   30
πολλὰ εἶναι ποιῶσι τὸ ἕν, ὡς μοναχῶς λεγομένου τοῦ ἑνὸς
ἢ τοῦ ὄντος. πολλὰ δὲ τὰ ὄντα ἢ λόγῳ (οἷον ἄλλο τὸ
λευκῷ εἶναι καὶ μουσικῷ, τὸ δ' αὐτὸ ἄμφω· πολλὰ ἄρα
τὸ ἕν) ἢ διαιρέσει, ὥσπερ τὸ ὅλον καὶ τὰ μέρη. ἐνταῦθα
δὲ ἤδη ἠπόρουν, καὶ ὡμολόγουν τὸ ἓν πολλὰ εἶναι—ὥσπερ   186a
οὐκ ἐνδεχόμενον ταὐτὸν ἕν τε καὶ πολλὰ εἶναι, μὴ τἀντικεί-
μενα δέ· ἔστι γὰρ τὸ ἓν καὶ δυνάμει καὶ ἐντελεχείᾳ.

---

³ I remove Ross's dash after εἶναι, and replace it with a comma.
⁴ Removing the dash after μηδέν, and replacing it with a full stop.

Physics 1.3

[186a4] So, if we approach the matter in this way, it appears impossible [a5] for the things that are to be one. And the arguments which they use to prove this claim are not hard to solve. For both reason eristically, both Melissus and Parmenides.

[186a10] That Melissus argues fallaciously is clear. For, in assuming that everything which has come to be has a beginning, he thinks he has also assumed that that which has *not* come to be *does not* have a beginning. Next, this is also absurd, that there is a beginning of everything—of the thing and not [only] of the time, and not [only] [a15] of simple coming to be but also of alteration, as though no change takes place all at once. Next, why is it unmoving, if it is one? For just as even the part, being one—for example, this water—moves within itself, why not the universe too? Next, why could there not be alteration? But nor indeed is it possible for it to be one in form, except with regard to what it is from. [a20] And even some of the natural philosophers say that it is one in this way, although not in that way. For human is different from horse in form, and the contraries [are different in form] from one another.

[186a22] And the same sorts of arguments apply to Parmenides too, even if certain other arguments are specific [to him]. The solution [to Parmenides' argument] is partly that it is false, and partly that it does not establish its conclusion. It is false because [a25] it assumes that being is said in a single way, when in fact it is said in many ways. And it is inconclusive because if the white things were assumed to be the only things, and if the white signifies one thing, nevertheless the white things will be many and not one. For the white will not be one by continuity, nor in account. For to be white and to be the thing that has received [it]

Τόν τε δὴ τρόπον τοῦτον ἐπιοῦσιν ἀδύνατον φαίνεται   186a4
τὰ ὄντα ἓν εἶναι, καὶ ἐξ ὧν ἐπιδεικνύουσι, λύειν οὐ χα-   5
λεπόν. ἀμφότεροι γὰρ ἐριστικῶς συλλογίζονται, καὶ Μέλισσος καὶ Παρμενίδης [καὶ γὰρ ψευδῆ λαμβάνουσι καὶ
ἀσυλλόγιστοί εἰσιν αὐτῶν οἱ λόγοι· μᾶλλον δ' ὁ Μελίσσου
φορτικὸς καὶ οὐκ ἔχων ἀπορίαν, ἀλλ' ἑνὸς ἀτόπου δοθέντος
τἆλλα συμβαίνει· τοῦτο δ' οὐθὲν χαλεπόν].⁵   10
                        ὅτι μὲν οὖν πα-   10
ραλογίζεται Μέλισσος, δῆλον· οἴεται γὰρ εἰληφέναι, εἰ
τὸ γενόμενον ἔχει ἀρχὴν ἅπαν, ὅτι καὶ τὸ μὴ γενόμενον
οὐκ ἔχει. εἶτα καὶ τοῦτο ἄτοπον, τὸ παντὸς εἶναι ἀρχήν—
τοῦ πράγματος καὶ μὴ τοῦ χρόνου, καὶ γενέσεως μὴ τῆς
ἁπλῆς ἀλλὰ καὶ ἀλλοιώσεως, ὥσπερ οὐκ ἀθρόας γιγνο-   15
μένης μεταβολῆς. ἔπειτα διὰ τί ἀκίνητον, εἰ ἕν; ὥσπερ
γὰρ καὶ τὸ μέρος ἓν ὄν, τοδὶ τὸ ὕδωρ, κινεῖται ἐν ἑαυτῷ,
διὰ τί οὐ καὶ τὸ πᾶν; ἔπειτα ἀλλοίωσις διὰ τί οὐκ ἂν εἴη;
ἀλλὰ μὴν οὐδὲ τῷ εἴδει οἷόν τε ἓν εἶναι, πλὴν τῷ ἐξ οὗ.
οὕτως δὲ ἓν καὶ τῶν φυσικῶν τινες λέγουσιν, ἐκείνως δ'   20
οὔ·⁶ ἄνθρωπος γὰρ ἵππου ἕτερον τῷ εἴδει καὶ τἀναντία ἀλλήλων.   22
        καὶ πρὸς Παρμενίδην δὲ ὁ αὐτὸς τρόπος τῶν λό-   22
γων, καὶ εἴ τινες ἄλλοι εἰσὶν ἴδιοι· καὶ ἡ λύσις τῇ μὲν ὅτι
ψευδὴς τῇ δὲ ὅτι οὐ συμπεραίνεται, ψευδὴς μὲν ᾗ ἁπλῶς
λαμβάνει τὸ ὂν λέγεσθαι, λεγομένου πολλαχῶς, ἀσυμ-   25
πέραντος δὲ ὅτι, εἰ μόνα τὰ λευκὰ ληφθείη, σημαίνοντος
ἓν τοῦ λευκοῦ, οὐθὲν ἧττον πολλὰ τὰ λευκὰ καὶ οὐχ ἕν·
οὔτε γὰρ τῇ συνεχείᾳ ἓν ἔσται τὸ λευκὸν οὔτε τῷ λόγῳ. ἄλλο

---

⁵ 186a7–10 is an almost verbatim repetition of 185a9–12. For the case for excising
the repeated lines, see Ross 1936, 462.
⁶ Ross places οὕτως ... οὔ in parentheses, which I remove.

will be different—and there will not be [a30] anything separate beyond the white; for it is not by being separate but in being that the white and that to which it belongs are different. But Parmenides did not yet see this. It is necessary, then, [for him] to assume not only that being signifies one thing of whatever it is predicated of, but also that [it signifies] *essentially being* and *essentially one*. For the accident [a35] is said of an underlying subject in such a way that the thing to which being is accidental will not be; for it is different [b1] from being. So, there will be a non-being. Now, what essentially is will not be something that belongs to something different. For it will be impossible for it to be a being, unless being signifies many things in such a way that each *is* something. But being is assumed to signify one thing. So, if what essentially is [b5] is accidental to nothing, but <the other things> are accidental to that, then why does what essentially is signify what is rather than what is not? For if what essentially is is also white, and to be white is not essentially a being—for nor can being be accidental to it, for nothing is a being which is not essentially a being—then the white will be a non-being. And [it will be a non-being] not insofar as it is not *something*, but insofar as it [b10] is not *at all*. So, what essentially is is a non-being. For it is true to say that it is white, and this signified a non-being. So, the white too signifies what essentially is. But then being signifies more than one thing. Therefore, nor even will what is have magnitude, if indeed what is is what essentially is. For the being of each of the two parts will be different. But [b15] it is obvious that what essentially is is divided into essentially some other kind of being, also in respect of the account. For example, if human is essentially some kind of being, then animal must be essentially some kind of being, and biped too. For if they are not essentially some kind of being, they will be accidents. So [they will be accidents] either of human or of some other underlying subject. But this is impossible. For, first, the accident is said to be this: either what is able to belong and not [b20] to belong, or that in whose account the thing to which it is accidental belongs. For example, being seated [is an accident] insofar as it is separate, while the account of nose (to which we say the snub is accidental) belongs in the snub. Further, [b25] the account of the whole does not belong in the account of those things that are in the definitional account, or from which it is composed. For example, the account of human [does not belong] in biped, and the account of white

γὰρ ἔσται τὸ εἶναι λευκῷ καὶ τῷ δεδεγμένῳ. καὶ οὐκ ἔσται
παρὰ τὸ λευκὸν οὐθὲν χωριστόν· οὐ γὰρ ᾗ χωριστὸν ἀλλὰ   30
τῷ εἶναι ἕτερον τὸ λευκὸν καὶ ᾧ ὑπάρχει. ἀλλὰ τοῦτο
Παρμενίδης οὔπω συνεώρα. ἀνάγκη δὴ λαβεῖν μὴ μόνον ἓν
σημαίνειν τὸ ὄν, καθ' οὗ ἂν κατηγορηθῇ, ἀλλὰ καὶ ὅπερ
ὂν καὶ ὅπερ ἕν. τὸ γὰρ συμβεβηκὸς καθ' ὑποκειμένου τινὸς
λέγεται, ὥστε ᾧ συμβέβηκε τὸ ὄν, οὐκ ἔσται (ἕτερον γὰρ   35
τοῦ ὄντος)· ἔσται τι ἄρα οὐκ ὄν. οὐ δὴ ἔσται ἄλλῳ ὑπάρ-   186b
χον τὸ ὅπερ ὄν. οὐ γὰρ ἔσται ὄν τι αὐτὸ εἶναι, εἰ μὴ
πολλὰ τὸ ὂν σημαίνει οὕτως ὥστε εἶναί τι ἕκαστον. ἀλλ'
ὑπόκειται τὸ ὂν σημαίνειν ἕν. εἰ οὖν τὸ ὅπερ ὂν μηδενὶ συμβέβηκεν ἀλλὰ <τὰ ἄλλα> ἐκείνῳ, τί μᾶλλον τὸ ὅπερ ὂν σημαίνει   5
τὸ ὂν ἢ μὴ ὄν; εἰ γὰρ ἔσται τὸ ὅπερ ὂν [ταὐτὸ] καὶ λευκόν,
τὸ λευκῷ δ' εἶναι μὴ ἔστιν ὅπερ ὄν (οὐδὲ γὰρ συμβεβηκέναι αὐτῷ οἷόν τε τὸ ὄν· οὐδὲν γὰρ ὂν ὃ οὐχ ὅπερ ὄν), οὐκ ἄρα
ὂν τὸ λευκόν· οὐχ οὕτω δὲ ὥσπερ τι μὴ ὄν, ἀλλ' ὅλως μὴ
ὄν. τὸ ἄρα ὅπερ ὂν οὐκ ὄν· ἀληθὲς γὰρ εἰπεῖν ὅτι λευκόν,   10
τοῦτο δὲ οὐκ ὂν ἐσήμαινεν. ὥστε καὶ τὸ λευκὸν σημαίνει
ὅπερ ὄν· πλείω ἄρα σημαίνει τὸ ὄν. οὐ τοίνυν οὐδὲ μέγεθος
ἕξει τὸ ὄν, εἴπερ ὅπερ ὂν τὸ ὄν· ἑκατέρῳ γὰρ ἕτερον τὸ εἶναι τῶν μορίων. ὅτι δὲ διαιρεῖται τὸ ὅπερ ὂν εἰς ὅπερ ὄν τι
ἄλλο⁷ καὶ τῷ λόγῳ φανερόν.⁸ οἷον ὁ ἄνθρωπος εἰ ἔστιν ὅπερ   15
ὄν τι, ἀνάγκη καὶ τὸ ζῷον ὅπερ ὄν τι εἶναι καὶ τὸ δίπουν.
εἰ γὰρ μὴ ὅπερ ὄν τι, συμβεβηκότα ἔσται. ἢ οὖν τῷ ἀνθρώπῳ ἢ ἄλλῳ τινὶ ὑποκειμένῳ. ἀλλ' ἀδύνατον· συμβεβηκός
τε γὰρ λέγεται τοῦτο, ὃ ἐνδέχεται ὑπάρχειν καὶ μὴ ὑπάρχειν, ἢ οὗ ἐν τῷ λόγῳ ὑπάρχει τὸ ᾧ συμβέβηκεν [ἢ ἐν ᾧ   20
ὁ λόγος ὑπάρχει ᾧ συμβέβηκεν] (οἷον τὸ μὲν καθῆσθαι ὡς
χωριζόμενον, ἐν δὲ τῷ σιμῷ ὑπάρχει ὁ λόγος ὁ τῆς ῥινὸς
ᾗ φαμὲν συμβεβηκέναι τὸ σιμόν)· ἔτι ὅσα ἐν τῷ ὁριστικῷ
λόγῳ ἔνεστιν ἢ ἐξ ὧν ἐστιν, ἐν τῷ λόγῳ τῷ τούτων οὐκ ἐνυ-
πάρχει ὁ λόγος ὁ τοῦ ὅλου, οἷον ἐν τῷ δίποδι ὁ τοῦ ἀνθρώ-   25

---

⁷ Deleting the comma after ἄλλο.
⁸ Replacing the comma with a colon.

human [does not belong] in white. Therefore, if these things are so, and biped is accidental to human, either it is necessary for it to be separable, so that the human might not be a biped, or [b30] the account of human is in the account of biped. But this is impossible. For that is in the account of that. But if biped and animal are accidental to something else, and each is not essentially something, then human would also be among the accidents of something else. But let that which is essentially something be accidental to nothing, and [b35] let the thing that is composed of both [of two things] also be said of the thing of which both [of these two things] are said. Then is the universe composed of indivisibles?

[187a1] But some people gave in to both arguments: to the argument that all things will be one, if being signifies one thing, [by saying] that what is not is; and to the argument from the dichotomy, by positing atomic magnitudes. But it is also obvious that it is not true that if being signifies one thing, and if it is impossible for [a5] the contradictory to hold at the same time, then there will be nothing that is not. For nothing prevents what is not from being—not from being, without qualification, but from being what is not *something*. But then it is absurd to claim that all things will be one, if there is nothing else besides what is itself. For who understands what is itself unless as what is essentially some kind of being? But if this is so, then nevertheless nothing prevents the [a10] things that are from being many, as has been said. So, it is clear that it is impossible for what is to be one in this way.

που ἢ ἐν τῷ λευκῷ ὁ τοῦ λευκοῦ ἀνθρώπου. εἰ τοίνυν ταῦτα
τοῦτον ἔχει τὸν τρόπον καὶ τῷ ἀνθρώπῳ συμβέβηκε τὸ δίπουν, ἀνάγκη χωριστὸν εἶναι αὐτό, ὥστε ἐνδέχοιτο ἂν μὴ
δίπουν εἶναι τὸν ἄνθρωπον, ἢ ἐν τῷ λόγῳ τῷ τοῦ δίποδος
ἐνέσται ὁ τοῦ ἀνθρώπου λόγος. ἀλλ᾽ ἀδύνατον· ἐκεῖνο γὰρ ἐν   30
τῷ ἐκείνου λόγῳ ἔνεστιν. εἰ δ᾽ ἄλλῳ συμβέβηκε τὸ δίπουν
καὶ τὸ ζῷον, καὶ μὴ ἔστιν ἑκάτερον ὅπερ τι,⁹ καὶ ὁ ἄνθρωπος ἂν εἴη τῶν συμβεβηκότων ἑτέρῳ. ἀλλὰ τὸ ὅπερ τι¹⁰
ἔστω μηδενὶ συμβεβηκός, καὶ καθ᾽ οὗ ἄμφω [καὶ ἑκατέ-
ρον] καὶ τὸ ἐκ τούτων λεγέσθω· ἐξ ἀδιαιρέτων ἄρα τὸ πᾶν;   35
ἔνιοι δ᾽ ἐνέδοσαν τοῖς λόγοις ἀμφοτέροις, τῷ μὲν ὅτι πάντα   187a
ἕν, εἰ τὸ ὂν ἓν σημαίνει, ὅτι ἔστι τὸ μὴ ὄν, τῷ δὲ ἐκ τῆς
διχοτομίας, ἄτομα ποιήσαντες μεγέθη. φανερὸν δὲ καὶ ὅτι
οὐκ ἀληθὲς ὡς, εἰ ἓν σημαίνει τὸ ὂν καὶ μὴ οἷόν τε ἅμα
τὴν ἀντίφασιν, οὐκ ἔσται οὐθὲν μὴ ὄν· οὐθὲν γὰρ κωλύει, μὴ   5
ἁπλῶς εἶναι, ἀλλὰ μὴ ὄν τι εἶναι τὸ μὴ ὄν. τὸ δὲ δὴ φάναι, παρ᾽ αὐτὸ τὸ ὂν εἰ μή τι ἔσται ἄλλο, ἓν πάντα ἔσεσθαι, ἄτοπον. τίς γὰρ μανθάνει αὐτὸ τὸ ὂν εἰ μὴ τὸ ὅπερ
ὄν τι εἶναι; εἰ δὲ τοῦτο, οὐδὲν ὅμως κωλύει πολλὰ εἶναι τὰ
ὄντα, ὥσπερ εἴρηται. ὅτι μὲν οὖν οὕτως ἓν εἶναι τὸ ὂν ἀδύνα-   10
τον, δῆλον.

---

⁹ Reading ὅπερ τι with E and J. Ross prints ὅπερ ὄν τι, the reading of F, I, and
Philoponus.
¹⁰ Reading ὅπερ τι with E¹ and F. Ross prints ὅπερ ὄν, the reading of I, J²,
Philoponus, and Simplicius.

Bibliography

Angioni, L. (2009) *Aristóteles: Física I–II*, Campinas.

Annas, J. (1976) *Aristotle's Metaphysics Books M and N*, Oxford.

Barnes, J. (1979) 'Parmenides and the Eleatic One', *Archiv für Geschichte der Philosophie*, 61, 1–21; repr. in Barnes 2011, 262–87.

Barnes, J. (1982) *The Presocratic Philosophers*, rev. edn, London.

Barnes, J. (ed.) (1984) *The Complete Works of Aristotle*, 2 vols, Princeton.

Barnes, J. (1995) 'Metaphysics', in J. Barnes (ed.), *The Cambridge Companion to Aristotle*, Cambridge, 66–108.

Barnes, J. (2011) *Method and Metaphysics*, vol. 1 of *Essays in Ancient Philosophy*, ed. M. Bonelli, Oxford.

Barney, R. (2009) 'Simplicius: Commentary, Harmony, and Authority', *Antiquorum Philosophia*, 3, 101–19.

Barney, R. (2012) 'History and Dialectic in *Metaphysics* A 3', in Steel 2012, 69–104.

Berti, E. (1969) 'Physique et métaphysique selon Aristote: *Phys.* I 2, 184b25–185a5', in I. Düring (ed.), *Naturphilosophie bei Aristoteles und Theophrast*, Heidelberg, 18–31.

Betegh, G. (2006) 'Epicurus' Argument for Atomism', *Oxford Studies in Ancient Philosophy*, 30, 261–84.

Betegh, G. (2012) '"The Next Principle" (*Metaphysics* A 3–4, 984b8–985b22)', in Steel 2012, 105–40.

Bett, R. (2012) *Sextus Empiricus: Against the Physicists*, Cambridge.

Bicknell, P. J. (1964) 'Aristotle's Comments on the Parmenidean One', *Acta Classica*, 7, 109–12.

Bicknell, P. J. (1967) 'Parmenides' Refutation of Motion and an Implication', *Phronesis*, 12, 1–5.

Bolton, R. (1991) 'Aristotle's Method in Natural Science', in L. Judson (ed.), *Aristotle's Physics: A Collection of Essays*, Oxford, 1–29.

Bostock, D. (1994) *Aristotle: Metaphysics Books Z and H*, Oxford.

Bostock, D. (2006) 'Aristotle on the Eleatics in *Physics* I. 2–3', in D. Bostock, *Space, Time, Matter, and Form: Essays on Aristotle's Physics*, Oxford, 103–15.

Brémond, M. (2017) *Lectures de Mélissos: Édition, traduction et interprétation des témoignages sur Mélissos de Samos*, Berlin.

Brown, L. (1986) 'Being in the *Sophist*: A Syntactical Enquiry', *Oxford Studies in Ancient Philosophy*, 4, 49–70.

Brown, L. (2008) 'The *Sophist* on Statements, Predication, and Falsehood', in G. Fine (ed.), *The Oxford Handbook of Plato*, Oxford, 437–62.

Bryan, J. (2012) *Likeness and Likelihood in the Presocratics and Plato*, Cambridge.

Burnet, J. (1930) *Early Greek Philosophy*, 4th edn, London.

Burnyeat, M. F. (1982) 'Idealism and Greek Philosophy: What Descartes Saw and Berkeley Missed', *Philosophical Review*, 91, 3–40.

Castelli, L. (2010) *Problems and Paradigms of Unity: Aristotle's Accounts of the One*, Sankt Augustin.

Castelli, L. (2018a) *Aristotle: Metaphysics Book Iota*, Oxford.

Castelli, L. (2018b) '*Physics* I.3', in Quarantotto 2018, 82–105.

Cerami, C. (2018) '*Physics* I.4', in Quarantotto 2018, 106–29.

Chalmers, W. R. (1960) 'Parmenides and the Beliefs of Mortals', *Phronesis*, 5, 5–22.

Charles, D. (2000) *Aristotle on Meaning and Essence*, Oxford.

Charlton, W. (1992) *Aristotle: Physics Books I and II*, rev. edn, Oxford.

Cherniss, H. F. (1935) *Aristotle's Criticism of Presocratic Philosophy*, Baltimore.

Clarke, T. (2015) 'Aristotle and the Ancient Puzzle about Coming to Be', *Oxford Studies in Ancient Philosophy*, 49, 129–50.

Code, A. (1976) 'Aristotle's Response to Quine's Objections to Modal Logic', *Journal of Philosophical Logic*, 5, 159–86.

Code, A. (1986) 'Aristotle: Essence and Accident', in R. E. Grandy and R. Warner (eds), *Philosophical Grounds of Rationality: Intentions, Categories, Ends*, Oxford, 411–39.

Cordero, N.-L. (2010) 'The "*Doxa* of Parmenides" Dismantled', *Ancient Philosophy*, 30, 231–46.

Corkum, P. (2008) 'Aristotle on Ontological Dependence', *Phronesis*, 53, 65–92.

Cornford, F. M. (1939) *Plato and Parmenides: Parmenides' Way of Truth and Plato's Parmenides*, London.

Coxon, A. H. (2009) *The Fragments of Parmenides: A Critical Text with Introduction and Translation, the Ancient Testimonia and a Commentary*, rev. edn, Las Vegas.

Crivelli, P. (2012) *Plato's Account of Falsehood: A Study of the Sophist*, Cambridge.

Crubellier, M. (forthcoming) '*Physics* I 2', in Ierodiakonou et al., forthcoming.

Curd, P. (1991) 'Parmenidean Monism', *Phronesis*, 36, 241–64.

Curd, P. (1998) *The Legacy of Parmenides: Eleatic Monism and Later Presocratic Thought*, Princeton.

Curd, P. and Graham, D. W. (eds) (2008) *The Oxford Handbook of Presocratic Philosophy*, Oxford.

de Haas, F. and Mansfeld, J. (eds) (2004) *Aristotle's On Generation and Corruption I*, Oxford.

Diels, H. and Kranz, W. (1951–2) *Die Fragmente der Vorsokratiker*, 6th edn, 3 vols, Berlin.

Falcon, A. (2005) *Aristotle and the Science of Nature: Unity without Uniformity*, Cambridge.

Fine, G. (1984) 'Separation', *Oxford Studies in Ancient Philosophy*, 2, 31–87.

Fine, K. (1994) 'Essence and Modality', *Philosophical Perspectives*, 8, 1–16.

Finkelberg, A. (1999) 'Being, Truth and Opinion in Parmenides', *Archiv für Geschichte der Philosophie*, 81, 233–48.

Fränkel, H. (1942) 'Zeno of Elea's Attacks on Plurality', part 2, *American Journal of Philology*, 63, 193–206.

Frede, M. (1987) 'The Unity of General and Special Metaphysics: Aristotle's Conception of Metaphysics', in M. Frede, *Essays in Ancient Philosophy*, Minneapolis, 81–95.

Frede, M. (2004) 'Aristotle's Account of the Origins of Philosophy', *Rhizai*, 1, 9–44.

Furley, D. J. (1967) *Two Studies in the Greek Atomists*, Princeton.

Furth, M. (1968) 'Elements of Eleatic Ontology', *Journal of the History of Philosophy*, 6, 111–32.

Gershenson, D. E. and Greenberg, D. A. (1961) 'Melissus of Samos in a New Light: Aristotle's *Physics* 186a10–16', *Phronesis*, 6, 1–9.

Gershenson, D. E. and Greenberg, D. A. (1962) 'Aristotle Confronts the Eleatics: Two Arguments on "The One"', *Phronesis*, 7, 137–51.

Gill, M. L. (1989) *Aristotle on Substance: The Paradox of Unity*, Princeton.

Graham, D. W. (1999) 'Empedocles and Anaxagoras: Responses to Parmenides', in Long 1999, 159–80.

Graham, D. W. (2006) *Explaining the Cosmos: The Ionian Tradition of Scientific Philosophy*, Princeton.

Guthrie, W. K. C. (1969) *A History of Greek Philosophy*, vol. 2, Cambridge.

Hankinson, R. J. (2002) 'Parmenides and the Metaphysics of Changelessness', in V. Caston and D. W. Graham (eds), *Presocratic Philosophy: Essays in Honour of Alexander Mourelatos*, Aldershot, 65–80.

Harriman, B. (2015) 'The Beginning of Melissus' *On Nature or On What-Is*: A Reconstruction', *Journal of Hellenic Studies*, 135, 19–34.

Harriman, B. (forthcoming) *Melissus and Eleatic Monism*, Cambridge.

Harte, V. (2002) *Plato on Parts and Wholes: The Metaphysics of Structure*, Oxford.

Hasper, P. S. (1999) 'The Foundations of Presocratic Atomism', *Oxford Studies in Ancient Philosophy*, 17, 1–14.

Hasper, P. S. (2006) 'Zeno Unlimited', *Oxford Studies in Ancient Philosophy*, 30, 49–85.

Horstschäfer, T. M. (1998) '*Über Prinzipien*': *Eine Untersuchung zur methodischen und inhaltlichen Geschlossenheit des ersten Buches der Physik des Aristoteles*, Berlin.

Hussey, E. (2004) '*On Generation and Corruption* I. 8', in de Haas and Mansfeld 2004, 243–65.

Hussey, E. (2012) 'Aristotle on Earlier Natural Science', in C. Shields (ed.), *The Oxford Handbook of Aristotle*, Oxford, 17–45.

Ierodiakonou, K., Kalligas, P., and Karasmanis, V. (eds) (forthcoming) *Aristotle's Physics I*, Oxford.

Irwin, T. H. (1988) *Aristotle's First Principles*, Oxford.

Isnardi Parente, M. (1982) *Senocrate, Ermodoro: Frammenti*, Naples.

Johansen, T. K. (2016) 'Parmenides' Likely Story', *Oxford Studies in Ancient Philosophy*, 50, 1–29.

Judson, L. (forthcoming) 'Aristotle and Crossing the Boundaries between the Sciences', *Archiv für Geschichte der Philosophie*.

Kahn, C. H. (1966) 'The Greek Verb "to Be" and the Concept of Being', *Foundations of Language*, 2, 245–65; repr. in Kahn 2009, 16–40.

Kahn, C. H. (2004) 'A Return to the Theory of the Verb *Be* and the Concept of Being', *Ancient Philosophy*, 24, 381–405; repr. in Kahn 2009, 109–42.

Kahn, C. H. (2009) *Essays on Being*, Oxford.

Kechagia, E. (2011) *Plutarch Against Colotes: A Lesson in History of Philosophy*, Oxford.

Kerferd, G. B. (1991) 'Aristotle's Treatment of the Doctrine of Parmenides', *Oxford Studies in Ancient Philosophy*, suppl. vol., 1–7.

Kirk, G. S., Raven, J. E., and Schofield, M. (1983) *The Presocratic Philosophers: A Critical History with a Selection of Texts*, 2nd edn, Cambridge.

Kirk, G. S. and Stokes, M. C. (1960) 'Parmenides' Refutation of Motion', *Phronesis*, 5, 1–4.

Koslicki, K. (2008) *The Structure of Objects*, Oxford.

Kung, J. (1977) 'Aristotle on Essence and Explanation', *Philosophical Studies*, 31, 361–83.

Laks, A. and Most, G. W. (2016) *Early Greek Philosophy*, 9 vols, Cambridge, MA.

Lloyd, G. E. R. (1987) 'The Alleged Fallacy of Hippocrates of Chios', *Apeiron*, 20, 103–28.

Long, A. A. (1963) 'The Principles of Parmenides' Cosmogony', *Phronesis*, 8, 90–107.

Long, A. A. (1996) 'Parmenides on Thinking Being', *Proceedings of the Boston Area Colloquium in Ancient Philosophy*, 12, 125–51.

Long, A. A. (ed.) (1999) *The Cambridge Companion to Early Greek Philosophy*, Cambridge.

Mackenzie, M. M. (1982) 'Parmenides' Dilemma', *Phronesis*, 27, 1–12; repr. in McCabe 2015, 73–82.

Maier, H. (1900) *Die Syllogistik des Aristoteles*, vol. 2, part 2, Tübingen.

Makin, S. (1982) 'Zeno on Plurality', *Phronesis*, 27, 223–38.

Makin, S. (1993) *Indifference Arguments*, Oxford.

Makin, S. (2005) 'Melissus and His Opponents: The Argument of DK 30 B 8', *Phronesis*, 50, 263–88.

Malink, M. (2013) *Aristotle's Modal Syllogistic*, Cambridge, MA.

Mann, W.-R. (2011) 'Elements, Causes, and Principles: A Context for *Metaphysics Z* 17', *Oxford Studies in Ancient Philosophy*, 40, 29–61.

Mansfeld, J. (1986) 'Aristotle, Plato, and the Preplatonic Doxography and Chronology', in G. Cambiano (ed.), *Storiografia e dossografia nella filosofia antica*, Turin, 1–59; repr. in Mansfeld 1990, 22–83.

Mansfeld, J. (1990) *Studies in the Historiography of Greek Philosophy*, Assen.

Mansion, A. (1946) *Introduction à la physique aristotélicienne*, 2nd edn, Louvain.

Mansion, S. (1953) 'Aristote, critique des Eléates', *Revue philosophique de Louvain*, 51, 165–86.

Matthews, G. B. (1972) 'Senses and Kinds', *Journal of Philosophy*, 69, 149–57.

McCabe, M. M. (2015) *Platonic Conversations*, Oxford.

McDaniel, K. (2017) *The Fragmentation of Being*, Oxford.

McDiarmid, J. B. (1953) 'Theophrastus on the Presocratic Causes', *Harvard Studies in Classical Philology*, 61, 85–156.

McKirahan, R. D. (2008) 'Signs and Arguments in Parmenides B8', in Curd and Graham 2008, 189–229.

Miller, F. D. (1977) 'Parmenides on Mortal Belief', *Journal of the History of Philosophy*, 15, 253–65.

Morison, B. (2002) *On Location: Aristotle's Concept of Place*, Oxford.

Morison, B. (forthcoming) '*Physics* I 7, Part 1: The Complexity of the Subject in a Change', in Ierodiakonou et al., forthcoming.

Mourelatos, A. P. D. (2008) *The Route of Parmenides*, rev. edn, Las Vegas.

Mueller, I. (1982) 'Aristotle and the Quadrature of the Circle', in N. Kretzmann (ed.), *Infinity and Continuity in Ancient and Medieval Thought*, Ithaca, NY, 146–64.

Natorp, P. (1890) 'Aristoteles und die Eleaten', *Philosophische Monatshefte*, 26, 1–16 and 147–69.

Nehamas, A. (1981) 'On Parmenides' Three Ways of Inquiry', *Deucalion*, 33/34, 97–111; repr. in Nehamas 1999, 125–37.

Nehamas, A. (1999) *Virtues of Authenticity: Essays on Plato and Socrates*, Princeton.

Osborne, C. (2006a) *Philoponus: On Aristotle's Physics 1.1–3*, London.

Osborne, C. (2006b) 'Was There an Eleatic Revolution in Philosophy?', in S. Goldhill and R. Osborne (eds), *Rethinking Revolutions through Ancient Greece*, Cambridge, 218–45.

Owen, G. E. L. (1957–8) 'Zeno and the Mathematicians', *Proceedings of the Aristotelian Society*, 58, 199–222; repr. in Owen 1986, 45–61.

Owen, G. E. L. (1960) 'Eleatic Questions', in *Classical Quarterly*, 10, 84–102; repr. in Owen 1986, 3–26.

Owen, G. E. L. (1961) '*Τιθέναι τὰ φαινόμενα*', in S. Mansion (ed.), *Aristote et les problèmes de méthode*, Louvain, 83–103; repr. in Owen 1986, 239–51.

Owen, G. E. L. (1986) *Logic, Science and Dialectic: Collected Papers in Greek Philosophy*, ed. M. Nussbaum, Ithaca, NY.

Owens, J. (1974) 'The Physical World of Parmenides', in J. R. O'Donnell (ed.), *Essays in Honour of Anton Charles Pegis*, Toronto, 378–95.

Palmer, J. (1998) 'Xenophanes' Ouranian God in the Fourth Century', *Oxford Studies in Ancient Philosophy*, 16, 1–34.

Palmer, J. (2003) 'On the Alleged Incorporeality of What Is in Melissus', *Ancient Philosophy*, 23, 1–10.

Palmer, J. (2004) 'Melissus and Parmenides', *Oxford Studies in Ancient Philosophy*, 26, 19–54.

Palmer, J. (2008) 'Classical Representations and Uses of the Presocratics', in Curd and Graham 2008, 530–54.

Palmer, J. (2009) *Parmenides and Presocratic Philosophy*, Oxford.

Pellegrin, P. (1994) 'Aristote et la physique éléate', in M. Porte (ed.), *Passion des formes: Dynamique qualitative, sémiophysique et intelligibilité*, Fontenay/ St Cloud, 121–37.

Peramatzis, M. (2011) *Priority in Aristotle's Metaphysics*, Oxford.

Pfeiffer, C. (2018) *Aristotle's Theory of Bodies*, Oxford.

Popper, K. R. (1958–9) 'Back to the Pre-Socratics', *Proceedings of the Aristotelian Society*, 59, 1–24.

Primavesi, O. (2012) 'Text of *Metaphysics A* (and of the Corresponding Parts of *M* 4–5)', in Steel 2012, 465–516.

Quarantotto, D. (ed.) (2018) *Aristotle's Physics Book I: A Systematic Exploration*, Cambridge.

Quarantotto, D. (forthcoming) '*Physics* I 3', in Ierodiakonou et al., forthcoming.

Rapp, C. (2006) 'Zeno and the Eleatic Anti-Pluralism', in M. M. Sassi (ed.), *La costruzione del discorso filosofico nell'età dei Presocratici*, Pisa, 161–82.

Rashed, M. (2005) *Aristote: De la génération et la corruption*, Paris.

Reale, G. (1970) *Melisso: Testimonianze e frammenti*, Florence.

Rosen, J. and Malink, M. (2012) 'A Method of Modal Proof in Aristotle', *Oxford Studies in Ancient Philosophy*, 42, 179–261.

Ross, W. D. (1924) *Aristotle's Metaphysics: A Revised Text with Introduction and Commentary*, 2 vols, Oxford.

Ross, W. D. (ed.) (1930) *The Works of Aristotle*, vol. 2, Oxford.

Ross, W. D. (1936) *Aristotle's Physics: A Revised Text with Introduction and Commentary*, Oxford.

Rossi, G. (2017) 'Going through *aporiai*: The Critical Use of Aristotle's Dialectic', *Oxford Studies in Ancient Philosophy*, 52, 209–56.

Schaffer, J. (2007) 'From Nihilism to Monism', *Australasian Journal of Philosophy*, 85, 175–91.

Schofield, M. (2012) 'Pythagoreanism: Emerging from the Presocratic Fog (*Metaphysics A* 5)', in Steel 2012, 141–66.

Sedley, D. (1999) 'Parmenides and Melissus', in Long 1999, 113–33.

Sedley, D. (2004) '*On Generation and Corruption* I. 2', in de Haas and Mansfeld 2004, 65–89.

Sedley, D. (2008) 'Atomism's Eleatic Roots', in Curd and Graham 2008, 305–32.

Sedley, D. (2017) 'Zenonian Strategies', *Oxford Studies in Ancient Philosophy*, 53, 1–32.

Sharma, R. (2005) 'What Is Aristotle's "Third Man" Argument against the Forms?', *Oxford Studies in Ancient Philosophy*, 28, 123–60.

Simons, P. (2004) 'Extended Simples: A Third Way Between Atoms and Gunk', *The Monist*, 87, 371–84.

Spangler, G. A. (1979) 'Aristotle's Criticism of Parmenides in *Physics* I', *Apeiron*, 13, 92–103.

Steel, C. (ed.) (2012) *Aristotle's Metaphysics Alpha*, Oxford.

Stokes, M. C. (1971) *One and Many in Presocratic Philosophy*, Washington, DC.

Tarán, L. (1965) *Parmenides: A Text with Translation, Commentary, and Critical Essays*, Princeton.

Taylor, C. C. W. (1999) *The Atomists: Leucippus and Democritus*, Toronto.

Tierney, R. (2001) 'On the Senses of "*Symbebēkos*" in Aristotle', *Oxford Studies in Ancient Philosophy*, 21, 61–82.

Tor, S. (2017) *Mortal and Divine in Early Greek Epistemology*, Cambridge.

Wardy, R. B. B. (1988) 'Eleatic Pluralism', *Archiv für Geschichte der Philosophie*, 70, 125–46.

Wedin, M. V. (2014) *Parmenides' Grand Deduction: A Logical Reconstruction of the Way of Truth*, Oxford.

Wicksteed, P. H. and Cornford, F. M. (1957) *Aristotle: The Physics, Books I–IV*, rev. edn, Cambridge, MA.

Zeller, E. (1892) *Die Philosophie der Griechen in ihrer geschichtlichen Entwicklung*, 5th edn, vol. 1, part 1, Leipzig.

Index Locorum

General Index